Praise for *Life Without Lack*

"*Life Without Lack* rescues the 23rd Psalm from its status as wall-plaque material, and restores it to its intended purpose as a description of reality and guide to life. If you want to know how to live in abundant satisfaction, or how to actually love somebody, or how to spend a day with Jesus, or what work consists of, or how to die to your self so that your self might come alive—I can think of no better gift than this glorious unpacking of these grand old words."

—JOHN ORTBERG, senior pastor of Menlo Church; author
of *I'd Like You More If You Were More Like Me*

"Everything Dallas Willard has written is a treasure. But to have this new book now is an extraordinary and quite unexpected blessing."

—ERIC METAXAS, nationally syndicated radio host; #1 *New York Times* bestselling author of *Bonhoeffer* and *Martin Luther*

"Dallas Willard helps us to understand that the Twenty-Third Psalm is not meant as a nice sentiment or for kitschy decor, it is for the very thick of our lives, the very moment of crisis. Imagine what our personal lives, families, communities, and politics would look like if we rejected the frantic striving of our day, and instead embraced the life without lack offered to us in Jesus Christ. No one has helped me to imagine and enter into that life more than Dallas Willard. I recommend this book with great joy and hopeful expectation."

—MICHAEL WEAR, author of *Reclaiming Hope: Lessons Learned in the Obama White House About the Future of Faith in America*

"The clear voice of Dallas Willard in his most accessible work yet shows us that an abundant life of God's companionship, protection, and empowerment really is possible. *Life Without Lack* reveals how to embrace it."

—JAN JOHNSON, coauthor of *Renovation of the Heart in Daily Practice*; president, Dallas Willard Ministries

"Dallas Willard was a philosophical, theological, and spiritual shepherd. So when he humbly and nurturingly expounds Psalm 23, we understand its profundity: he so dwelt in the shepherding love and care of God that he could in turn shepherd us to do likewise."

—MARK LABBERTON, president, Fuller Theological Seminary

"Dallas Willard leads us into life without lack, through green pastures, beside still waters as he illuminates Psalm 23. Since childhood I have known this psalm by heart, using it in times of worry and stress. Here Dr. Willard offers fresh insights; he links the psalm to other powerful Bible passages. This book is full of wisdom and joy. In the valley of the shadow of death we need not fear, the Lord is always with us."

—EMILIE GRIFFIN, author of *Doors Into Prayer*, coauthor of *Spiritual Classics* with Richard J. Foster

"When I read Dallas Willard I am moved to praise, to awe, to wonder, and to faith. No one can define, explain, and expound on life in the Kingdom of the heavens like Dallas. I am so glad we have this book, shaped by Dallas's daily interaction with the 23rd Psalm. He tells us in the first chapter that the most important thing about us is our mind, and the most important thing about our mind is what it is fixed upon. His insights here are not speculative, they are real and practical and reliable."

—JAMES BRYAN SMITH, author of *The Good and Beautiful God*

"I had the privilege of getting to know Dallas Willard well during the latter years of his life. Two years before he died, he spoke at a meeting for major Christian leaders that I organized. Let me emphatically say that everything Dallas has shared needs to be read by those who want to understand kingdom purpose. The message delivered in *Life Without Lack* will inspire readers to lean on the all-sufficient Shepherd and enjoy a life 'abundant in rest, provision, and blessing.'"

—JAMES ROBISON, founder and president, LIFE Outreach International, founder and publisher, The Stream (stream.org)

"In the best books, living proceeds writing. This is true in spades for Dallas Willard. Several times I heard Dallas say that before his feet hit the floor in the morning he would remind himself that 'the Lord is my shepherd, I don't have to live in the state of want.' I observed the effect on him and his interactions with others. Now, through *Life Without Lack*, I know the full background, vision, and process for living such a life."

—TODD HUNTER, founding Bishop, Churches for the Sake of Others

life without lack

LIVING IN THE FULLNESS
OF **PSALM 23**

DALLAS WILLARD

NELSON
BOOKS

An Imprint of Thomas Nelson

Published in Nashville, Tennessee, by Nelson Books, an imprint of Thomas Nelson. Nelson Books and Thomas Nelson are registered trademarks of HarperCollins Christian Publishing, Inc.

Thomas Nelson titles may be purchased in bulk for educational, business, fund-raising, or sales promotional use. For information, please e-mail SpecialMarkets@ThomasNelson.com.

Any Internet addresses, phone numbers, or company or product information printed in this book are offered as a resource and are not intended in any way to be or to imply an endorsement by Thomas Nelson, nor does Thomas Nelson vouch for the existence, content, or services of these sites, phone numbers, companies, or products beyond the life of this book.

Unless otherwise noted, Scripture quotations are taken from the New King James Version®. © 1982 by Thomas Nelson. Used by permission. All rights reserved.

Scripture quotations marked ASV are from the American Standard Version, public domain.

Scripture quotations marked KJV are from the King James Version, public domain.

Scripture quotations marked THE MESSAGE are from The Message. Copyright © by Eugene H. Peterson 1993, 1994, 1995, 1996, 2000, 2001, 2002. Used by permission of NavPress. All rights reserved. Represented by Tyndale House Publishers, Inc.

Scripture quotations marked NASB are from the New American Standard Bible®, Copyright © 1960, 1962, 1963, 1968, 1971, 1972, 1973, 1975, 1977, 1995 by The Lockman Foundation. Used by permission. (www.Lockman.org)

Scripture quotations marked NIV are from the Holy Bible, New International Version®, NIV®. Copyright © 1973, 1978, 1984, 2011 by Biblica, Inc.™ Used by permission of Zondervan. All rights reserved worldwide. www.zondervan.com. The "NIV" and "New International Version" are trademarks registered in the United States Patent and Trademark Office by Biblica, Inc.™

Scripture quotations marked NLT are from the *Holy Bible*, New Living Translation. © 1996, 2004, 2007, 2013 by Tyndale House Foundation. Used by permission of Tyndale House Publishers, Inc., Carol Stream, Illinois 60188. All rights reserved.

Scripture quotations marked NRSV are from New Revised Standard Version Bible. Copyright © 1989 National Council of the Churches of Christ in the United States of America. Used by permission. All rights reserved.

Scripture quotations marked THE VOICE are from *The Voice*™. © 2008 by Ecclesia Bible Society. Used by permission. All rights reserved.

Scripture quotations marked PAR are paraphrased by Dallas Willard.

All italics in Scripture quotations are added by the author for emphasis.

ISBN 978-0-7180-9185-9 (eBook)
ISBN 978-0-7180-9184-2 (HC)

Library of Congress Cataloging-in-Publication Data

Names: Willard, Dallas, 1935-2013, author.
Title: Life without lack : living in the fullness of Psalm 23 / Dallas
  Willard.
Description: Nashville : Thomas Nelson, 2018.
Identifiers: LCCN 2017021619 | ISBN 9780718091842
Subjects: LCSH: Bible. Psalm, XXIII--Criticism, interpretation, etc.
Classification: LCC BS1450 23d .W55 2018 | DDC 223/.206--dc23 LC record available at https://lccn.loc.gov/2017021619

Printed in the United States of America

18 19 20 21 22 LSC 10 9 8 7 6 5 4 3

Dedication by Larry Burtoft

To my three sons, Matthew ("gift of Yahweh"), Kristopher ("Christ-bearer") and Jedidiah ("beloved of Yahweh"). May you each come to know the promise of your name, and of His.

And to the one who has been graciously patient, continually encouraging and quietly self-sacrificial throughout the long life of this project. She is my lovely lady, my wife, Lotus Jean Sipma Burtoft. This is her book.

Contents

Preface

God is able to make all grace abound toward you,
that you, always having all sufficiency in all things,
may have an abundance for every good work.

—2 CORINTHIANS 9:8

The world is a perfectly good and safe place to be.

—DALLAS WILLARD

Twenty-six years ago I was introduced to the possibility of a life in which I was never in need. Of anything. At any time. From anyone. A life that knows no fear or fluster. No anxiety or angst. No perturbation of any sort. It was, in short, the offer of a life without lack.

This offer was delivered by a messenger who knew well of what he spoke. Not because he had heard about such a life from someone else, although he certainly had. Rather, it appeared that he knew it by personal experience. Here was one who exuded peace, patience, and the freedom from self-absorption that is the hallmark of the truly unworried, the unconcerned, the carefree. Carefree, but not without care for others. Indeed, his freedom from any sense of personal threat was the other side of his freedom to show the compassion, openness, and kindness that anyone who knew him received.

The messenger, as you have probably guessed, was Dallas Willard. He had discovered the secret to gaining what many people have sacrificed so much in time, money, and relationships trying to possess. In a word, *contentment*. Here was a man, his face exuding serenity, who could say, in the words of one of his favorite authors, "I have learned, in whatsoever state I am, therewith to be content."* It was a lesson he had come to share with a small group of ordinary people who had found their way into a life connected, in various ways, to that of Jesus.

What you are about to read are the words this lackless brother shared with a little flock of ragtag Christians who gathered together in an upper room in Van Nuys, California, for eight weeks in the early months of 1991. Most of these folks were members of a small congregation, Valley Vista Christian Community, which I served as pastor. Dallas and his lovely wife, Jane, were a part of the congregation at that time, and they had been with us since I took over the shepherding responsibilities in 1985.

It was an intimate affair; there were usually about thirty of us gathered together to sit under Dallas's teaching and then interact with him in a free-flowing question-and-answer time after each presentation. He knew most of us by name. The gatherings would usually last about an hour and a half and were informal and relaxed. I am tempted to draw parallels to other Upper Room experiences I have read about, and I am certain that the same Spirit who visited those previous rooms was present when we came together as Dallas opened up the Word of God and fed us with the Bread of Life.

This book now exists because, after Dallas had finished the series, I recommended that he turn the talks into a book. He responded by saying that he did not have time and that I should use the recordings to write it instead. Although I started the project many times, I never managed to complete it as I originally imagined it, and eventually I gave up. Yet in May 2013, upon Dallas's death (I use the word figuratively, given Jesus' promise in John 11:26, "whoever lives and believes in Me shall never die," a promise Dallas fully believed and surely experienced), I decided to revisit the project.

---

* The author is Saint Paul, in his letter to the Christians in Philippi. The quotation is from Philippians 4:11, the King James Version, great swaths of which Dallas had memorized.

This teaching series was very meaningful to me, and I am convinced that others will benefit from the opportunity to read Dallas's own words—words that flowed from both his deep immersion in the Bible and his many years of following tirelessly in the Way of Christ. His experience with Jesus had convinced him that the Twenty-Third Psalm was not merely a pretty poem with charming sentiments but an accurate description of the kind of life that is available to anyone who will allow God to be their Shepherd.

So this book is my attempt to keep a semblance of an implicit promise I made to Dallas so many years ago when he offered me the gift of bringing the insights he shared with our little group to a much wider audience. It is my way of honoring my brother, mentor, and fellow pilgrim on the road that is marked by God's great sufficiency for all—*all!*—our needs. My heavenward request is that you, too, might experience the life that Dallas knew, that I and countless others are coming to know, and that is available to anyone and everyone.

You will encounter here the life-giving truths that Dallas shared with us during those rich evenings together. Those who attended the talks were truly blessed—given a priceless gift—by being in Dallas's presence, of seeing his facial expressions, of hearing his intonations, and of laughing with him as he reflected on some of the foolish ways we try to cope with life apart from the sufficiency of the Shepherd. It is my hope that we have been able to translate Dallas's spoken words into written form adequately, and to give you an opportunity to gain a sense of what it was like to be there. I have tried to bring out some of this by visually emphasizing some words and phrases, or with some of my editor's notes found in the footnotes.

In many ways, Dallas was a genius of theological jazz, often breaking out with insightful, free-associating "riffs" that are not easily or directly transferrable to the printed page. On occasion he expressed regret at not having time to further discuss some topics during the sessions. We have made only the minimal changes necessary to accommodate this while adapting his spoken words into an understandable and easy-to-follow format.

While writing, I have had the encouraging pleasure and decided privilege of keen and sensitive editorial assistance from Dallas's daughter, Rebecca Willard Heatley. Drawing upon her intimate acquaintance with her father's heart and vast knowledge of his seemingly endless trove of articles and talks, she has given invaluable suggestions that have clarified and enlarged the teachings Dallas presented during this series of talks. So, in places when Dallas said, "I wish we had more time," or did not develop a point sufficiently, we have supplemented his original presentations with material taken from other published and unpublished sources.

Finally, it will come as no surprise to those familiar with Dallas's teachings that he placed particular emphasis upon our choices and habits and practices, on how we live our daily lives, and above all, on what we do with our minds. Next to the reality of God, which is the substance and source of a life without lack, there is nothing more important to the *experience* of that life than keeping our minds on God as much as possible. Dallas believed it was possible to keep our minds constantly on God and that this was the heart and soul of spiritual formation in the kingdom of God. This is a book about why this is so, and about how it can be so for us.

Larry Burtoft

OPENING PRAYER

Lord Jesus Christ,
We are so thankful to you that you have said,
"Fear not, little flock,
for it is your Father's good pleasure
to give you the kingdom."
We are thankful for the ease with which you walked upon this earth,
the generosity and kindness you showed to people,
the devotion with which you cared for those
who were out of the way and in trouble,
the extent to which you even loved your enemies
and laid down your life for them.
We are so thankful to believe that this is a life for us,
a life without lack, a life of sufficiency.
It's so clear in you, the sufficiency of your Father
and the fullness of life that was poured through you,
and we're so thankful that you have promised that same love,
that same life, that same joy, that same power for us.
Lord, slip up on us today.
Get past our defenses, our worries, our concerns.
Gently open our souls, and speak your Word into them.
We believe you want to do it,
and we wait for you to do it now.
In your name, amen.

—DALLAS WILLARD

Introduction

We have all things and abound; not because
I have a good store of money in the bank, not
because I have skill and wit with which to win my
bread, but because the Lord is my shepherd.

—Charles Haddon Spurgeon

The LORD is my shepherd;
I shall not want. . . .
I will fear no evil;
For You are with me.

—Psalm 23:1, 4

I am glad you are reading this book. Read it as if we were having
a personal conversation—just you and me talking together, with
the Lord between us. I hope you will find in these pages a warm
invitation into the incomparably rich and fulfilling life that Jesus
makes possible.

One of our greatest needs today is for people to *really* see and
really believe the things they already profess to see and believe.
Knowing about things—knowing what they are, being able to identify them and say them—does not mean we actually believe them.
When we truly believe what we profess, we are set to act as if it were
true. Acting as if things are true means, in turn, that we live as if
they were so.

The words of the Twenty-Third Psalm are among those things
that people profess to believe. Many can recite the Twenty-Third

Psalm from memory, including people who don't believe much of anything about God. Some have learned the psalm purely as poetic literature. But far too few have experienced in their own lives the vivid reality described by the psalmist. Unfortunately, "The Lord is my Shepherd" is a sentiment carved on tombstones more often than a reality written in lives.[1]

The title of this book—*Life Without Lack*—reflects the very first verse of the psalm: "The LORD is my shepherd; I shall not want." It describes the life we all desire—a life in which we want for nothing, or better yet, lack nothing. The psalmist is portraying a life we were meant to enjoy, one that is imminently available to us. But do you believe this verse is actually true? Few people act as if it were.

This book is a series of in-depth meditations on the Twenty-Third Psalm intended to help you *really* see it, *really* believe it, and to live as if it were true. To gain the most from your reading, I encourage you to meditatively read Psalm 23 for ten minutes or so before you read each chapter. This will help renew your mind by giving the Holy Spirit opportunities to teach you about what it means for the Lord to be your Shepherd.

Meditate on It Day and Night

Memorization is an essential element of a life without lack. It is a primary way we fill our minds with the Word of God and have our thoughts formed by God's thoughts. Memorizing Scripture is even more important than a daily quiet time, for as we fill our minds with great passages and have them readily available for our meditation, "quiet time" takes over the entirety of our lives. Memorization enables us to keep God and his truth constantly before our minds, allowing his Word and wisdom to help us.

Memorizing this beautiful psalm will strengthen your concentration on the Good Shepherd by eliminating the distraction of trying to remember the words as you meditate. So, if you have not already done so, please make sure you have the Twenty-Third Psalm memorized.[2]

The Nature of Our Shepherd

I hope you will learn to see God in a new way in the pages that follow. We will begin by focusing on the glorious, eternal, all-sufficient, omnipotent Creator of the universe whose greatness surpasses anything we could imagine. Unlimited in resources, just as he is unlimited in love, he is the Good Shepherd who generously provides for our every need.

We will look at why he created humankind, why he desires to be in relationship with us, and how Satan attempts to interfere with God's good plan for human history. Then we will examine three conditions that must be present in our own lives if we are to experience the fullness of the wisdom, power, and love of God: faith, death to self, and agape love.

The final chapter of the book provides an exercise in how to live one day with Jesus so that every day can be a grace-infused masterpiece. This is where we put into practice the words from Psalm 23 that we believe are true:

The Lord is my shepherd.
> In other words, I'm in the care of someone else. I'm not the one in charge. I've taken my kingdom and surrendered it to the kingdom of God. I am living the with-God life. The Lord is my shepherd. And what follows from that?

I shall not want.
> That's the natural result. I shall not lack anything. That's what Jesus teaches: "Seek first the kingdom of God and His righteousness," and everything else will be added (Matt. 6:33).

He makes me to lie down in green pastures.

What kind of a sheep lies down in a green pasture? A sheep that has eaten its fill. If a sheep is in a green pasture and she's not full, she'll be eating, not lying down.

He leads me beside the still waters.

A sheep that is being led beside still water is a sheep that is not thirsty. Jesus said to the woman at the well, "Whoever drinks of this water will thirst again, but whoever drinks of the water that I shall give him will never thirst. But the water that I shall give him will become in him a fountain of water springing up into everlasting life" (John 4:13–14).

He restores my soul.

The broken depths of my soul are healed and reintegrated in a life in union with God: the eternal kind of life.

He leads me in the paths of righteousness for His name's sake.

The effect of the restoration of my soul is that I walk in paths of righteousness on his behalf as a natural expression of my renewed inner nature. As I walk these paths, my trust in the Shepherd runs so deep that I can declare:

Yea, though I walk through the valley of the shadow of death, I will fear no evil.

A life without lack is one that carries no fear of evil. Our confidence in God soars far above wants and fears. Would you like to have a life without fear, a life of soaring faith?
It seems like Jesus was constantly saying to his friends, "Fear not! Fear not!" Imagine what that would be like. No fear of life, aging or death, disease or hunger, no fear of any person or creature, not even the loss of all your possessions. You can live without fear even in the midst of a world dominated by fear.

I could easily have chosen "fear no evil" as this book's theme, because we are talking about a life from which fear is eliminated. While the psalmist clearly knows about life's dangers, he can still say, "I will fear no evil." Why? Please read his answer out loud:

For You are with me.

The central truth of this book is that *the complete sufficiency of the life without lack is based upon the presence of God*, and he is most clearly and fully present to us in Jesus Christ, Immanuel, God with us.[3]

Your rod and Your staff, they comfort me.

I know from experience that the rod and staff represent the Shepherd's strength and protective care. In this safe place where I have no fear, I am at liberty to enjoy the overwhelming generosity of my Shepherd.

You prepare a table before me in the presence of my enemies.

Since I love my enemies,* I would not feast upon a delicious meal in their presence and let them stand there hungry. The abundance of God's provision and safety in my life is so great, I would invite them to enjoy what God has prepared for me.

You anoint my head with oil.

Here you might think in terms of hot showers and warm fluffy towels, things that make us feel clean, comfortable, and special, and how God makes that possible. He is not only interested in my having something wonderful to eat, but also in blessing me with a life that is full and free and powerful in him—including clothing, comfortable furnishings, joyful experiences, and

---

* Jesus instructs us to do this in Matthew 5:43–47.

deep relationships. So much so that the abundance of God's provision rings out from the psalmist's pen:

My cup is full!

Is that what it says? No. *"My cup runs over."* I have more than my cup will hold. So much that I can be as generous as my Shepherd without fear of ever running out. So much so that I am convinced:

Surely goodness and mercy shall follow me all the days of my life, and I will dwell in the house of the LORD forever.

This is a description of the eternal life available to us now in the kingdom of the heavens; the abundant with-God life that comes from following the Shepherd, where we dwell and abide with God in the fullness of his life—a life in which all the promises of Christ's gospel are realized. Because of this we have no reason to be anxious (Phil. 4:6–7); the world is a perfectly safe place for us to be.

The Abundance of Abundance

Many other passages in Scripture show this divine abundance and would be valuable to memorize,[*] including two beautiful passages from the Old Testament that I'd like you to read with me. The first was written by the prophet Habakkuk, a man who had just seen his country completely devastated by war. Imagine what that would be like for you as someone who trusts in God. How could God allow this to happen? Surveying the destruction, all you see is famine, disease, and death.

Nevertheless, a vision of God's restorative power and love overcomes your grief, and you exclaim:

---

* See Appendix A for a list of verses to supplement your growth in God's abundance.

When I heard, my body trembled;
My lips quivered at the voice;
Rottenness entered my bones;
And I trembled in myself,
That I might rest in the day of trouble.
When he comes up to the people,
He will invade them with his troops.

Though the fig tree may not blossom,
Nor fruit be on the vines;
Though the labor of the olive may fail,
And the fields yield no food;
Though the flock may be cut off from the fold,
And there be no herd in the stalls—
Yet I will rejoice in the LORD,
I will joy in the God of my salvation.

The LORD God is my strength;
He will make my feet like deer's feet,
And He will make me walk on my high hills.

(HAB. 3:16–19)

These are the words of someone who trusts in God's abounding goodness and power *in conditions of complete desolation!* I believe that one of the reasons we resist fully surrendering our lives to God is the fear that he might allow desolation in our lives. This book will help if you are struggling with doubts about the plentiful provisions of God in circumstances that are anything but abundant. A life without lack is a life in which one is completely satisfied and sustained, no matter what happens. *No matter what happens!* It's not merely a matter of gritting your teeth and hanging on. It is a matter of real provisions directly from God to you.

The second passage worth memorizing is found in Psalm 103, an exuberant celebration of God's sufficiency and abundant goodness:

> Bless the LORD, O my soul,
> And all that is within me, bless His holy name!
> Bless the LORD, O my soul,
> And forget not all His benefits:
> Who forgives all your iniquities,
> Who heals all your diseases,
> Who redeems your life from destruction,
> Who crowns you with lovingkindness and tender mercies,
> Who satisfies your mouth with good things,
> So that your youth is renewed like the eagle's.
>
> (Ps. 103:1–5)

The psalm continues with more of the extravagant mercies of God, and I encourage you to read it in its entirety. Such merciful provision for his people is simply an expression of God's unchanging goodness, as true today as it has ever been, and as available.

Preparing to Receive

Before we begin chapter 1, remember to recite the Twenty-Third Psalm, out loud if possible, and take your time. Relax in this moment alone with God, say a verse or two, and then pause to allow God to fill your thoughts. If you do this prayerfully as you work your way through the book, I am certain that you will move increasingly into the experience of a life without lack.

CHAPTER 1

God in Himself, Part 1

The Glorious, Self-Sustaining, Eternal Being of the Shepherd

The God of love my shepherd is,
And he that doth me feed;
While he is mine and I am his,
What can I want or need?

—GEORGE HERBERT

The experience of a life without lack depends first and foremost upon the presence of God in our lives, because the source of this life is God himself.

In his goodness, God has arranged things so we are able to use our minds to understand and enter his glorious and plentiful kingdom. I am going to rely on this truth as we wrestle with matters that require serious thought. I am not asking that you believe them just because I have written them; I want you to *think about them*, deeply and often, using your mind to seek God. *Belief will come as you experience the truth about God.*

We must come to an awareness in our own minds concerning the nature of God. That is, we must think about God in ways that match what God is like. Without harmony between our ideas about God

1

and his true character, we will never be able to make the kind of contact with God that will give us confidence, *grounded in our experience*, in the complete sufficiency of God to provide for our needs.

It is worth noting that the only definition of eternal life found in Scripture is John 17:3: "And this is eternal life, that they might *know* You, the only true God, and Jesus Christ whom You have sent." Jesus is the way to the knowledge of God for us, and through his teachings about God we can grow in our experience-based knowledge of him. So I hope you have your thinking cap on.

The Most Important Thing About You

It is crucial to our whole outlook about ourselves and our understanding of God that we think correctly about two fundamental things: minds and people. We will discuss the importance of people in chapter 3, but now we will focus on the most important thing about you: your mind.[1] Not your brain, but your mind. You are, more than anything else, a mind. That is what makes you precious in a special way. Categorizing people and treating them in specific ways just because of their bodily features violates the central worth of the person as a mind. The body is important, but the mind is all-important. And the most important thing about your mind is what it is fixed upon.

I'm using *mind* as a general term in this case, not distinguishing it from spirit or soul. *Heart* could also be used here, as is often found in the Old Testament in cases such as Proverbs 23:7, "For as he thinks in his heart, so is he," and 1 Chronicles 22:19 (NRSV), "Now set your mind and heart to seek the LORD your God." The mind, thought about in this way, is the most significant aspect of our lives because it is through our minds that we make effective contact with reality.*

---

* Editor's Note: Dallas explores the mind in greater detail in *Renovation of the Heart*, where he identifies the four main elements of the mind as ideas, images, information, and our ability to think.

The ultimate freedom we have as individuals is the power to select what we will allow or require our minds to dwell upon and think about. By *think* we mean all the ways in which we are aware of things, including our memories, perceptions, and beliefs. The focus of your thoughts significantly affects everything else that happens in your life and evokes the feelings that frame your world and motivate your actions.[*]

The Transforming Power of Ideas

Thoughts are where we make our first movements toward God and where the divine Spirit begins to direct our will to God and his way. We have the ability and responsibility to keep God present in our minds, and those who do so will make steady progress toward him, for he will respond by making himself known to us.

One of the most powerful elements within the realm of our minds is that of ideas. Our ideas form the belief system upon which we base our actions and decisions, and these in turn determine the trajectory of our lives. Living a life without lack involves recognizing the idea systems that govern the present age and its respective cultures—as well as those that constitute life away from God—and replacing them with the idea system that was embodied and taught by Jesus Christ.

The apostle Paul warned us that "our struggle is not against flesh and blood, but against the rulers, against the powers, against the world forces of this darkness, against the spiritual forces of wickedness in the heavenly places" (Eph. 6:12 NASB). These higher-level powers and forces are spiritual agencies that work with the idea systems of this world. These evil systems have been used to dominate humanity through fear and self-obsession, so that the uppermost

---

[*] Interestingly, we cannot evoke thoughts by feeling a certain way. But we can evoke—and to some degree—control our feelings by directing our thoughts.

thing filling our minds is likely to be our selves. That is why Jesus' teachings emphasize the importance of death to self, giving up your life and not seeking to save yourself.* What does Jesus say about your life? "If you seek to save your life, you will lose it."** But, of course, that is what nearly everyone does, especially everyone who lives according to the ordinary, fallen course of the world. They spend their whole earthly existence trying to save, enhance, and enrich their lives. And what happens? They lose the most important things in their life: an intimate relationship with God and with others.

The Poison of Self-Obsession

The truth of the matter is that people are obsessed with themselves. This is often caused by the wounds they have received. When you hit your thumb with a hammer, what happens in the following days? You are very mindful of your thumb. The same is true when we are hurt; we become conscious of ourselves to such an extent that we are imprisoned in that consciousness. Of course, we are all hurt in one way or another, with our families and our communities being primary sources of that hurt. Then we, in turn, become sources of the hurt and pain of others. Thus we have, literally, "a world of hurt." And it does no good to say, "Now, now, don't think about yourself." We are locked into it, and by being locked into it we end up turning away from the only one who can deliver us—God himself.

So we live in a world filled with people trying to be their own saviors. They can't do it, which, of course, makes them all the more desperate and obsessed with themselves. Then, finally, the resulting anger and desperation leads to the many ways we attack one another. I must confess, I am astonished at the subtle ways that I have attacked people: the calculating tones of voice, the careful selection of words I

---

* Matt. 10:37–39; Mark 8:34–37; Luke 17:33. This will be discussed in depth in chapter 6.
** Matt. 16:25; Mark 8:35; Luke 9:24.

come up with so easily in order to needle someone. Often someone I love. And sometimes I come after them with a hammer instead of a needle.

The Antidote to Bad Ideas About God

Anger and desperation run deep in ordinary human life, which is why people provoke one another the way they do. This fury and despair flow from the hopelessness of their situation. Yet *there is every reason for hope if they would just stop looking at themselves and look at God instead*. But how do we learn about God? Primarily through the message that came in and through Jesus Christ.

That is why the preaching of the gospel of Jesus is absolutely fundamental. We preach and teach his gospel to let people know the good news about God and to allow them to think rightly about God. The preaching of the gospel will bring the mind to dwell intelligently upon God as he is presented in his Word, which will have the effect of causing us to love God passionately—in a way that brings us to think of God steadily. Thus he will always be before our minds.

When we fill our minds with the gospel, it must be *in its fullness* as Jesus presented and embodies it.* If we limit the gospel to what Jesus did during a few days at the end of his earthly existence, we miss most of the picture. We shouldn't reduce the saving work of Christ to his death on the cross or we will miss the fullness of God as he is in himself and as he provides for us and all his creation.

The gospel that Jesus himself proclaimed, manifested, and taught

---

* Editor's Note: As Dallas stated in his book *The Divine Conspiracy*, at least four gospels are commonly preached: (1) The gospel of sin management where you say the words and go to heaven when you die. (2) The social justice gospel that directs you to fill in the gaps that Jesus left behind. (3) The gospel of "take care of your church and it will take care of you." (4) The availability of the kingdom of the heavens through trust in Jesus Christ. See *The Divine Conspiracy*, chapters 2 and 3, for a more in-depth explanation regarding the gospel of Jesus Christ.

was about more than his death for the forgiveness of our sins, as important as that is. It was about the kingdom of God—God's immediate availability, his "with-us-ness" that makes a life without lack possible. There is so much more to our relationship with God than just his dealing with our guilt and sin. Once we have been forgiven, we are meant to live in the fullness of the life that Jesus came to give us (John 10:10).

In his letter to the Ephesian Christians, Paul gives us a picture of the world apart from God. Please notice his emphasis on the effect that the world apart from God has on the mind:

> This I say, therefore, and testify in the Lord, that you should no longer walk as the rest of the Gentiles walk, *in the futility of their mind, having their understanding darkened, being alienated from the life of God, because of the ignorance that is in them, because of the blindness of their heart;* who, being past feeling, have given themselves over to lewdness, to work all uncleanness with greediness. (Eph. 4:17–19)

How does Paul describe the mind caught up in the world? Futile, full of things that do not matter, darkened, blind. Why? Because it is alienated from the life of God.

Taste and See That the Lord Is Good

When we have heard the gospel, if we are not prepared to use our power of choice to turn our minds to God, then we do not have contact with God. You may very well say, "Can't God just move in on us and touch us or do something to us?" Yes, he can do that, and he does that on many occasions. But when it comes to experiencing the sufficiency of God, we are not talking about *what God can do*; we are talking about *what we need to do*. And what we need to do is to *turn our minds to God*.

Saying this may sound like recommending that we turn our minds toward an oblong blur of some sort. This results from a failure within our churches and Christian organizations to make God knowable to us. We have allowed God to remain an impersonal, distant mystery. Our own minds are often darkened, blind to the truth. We have no graspable conception of God—no realistic idea of what God is actually like.

You may remember the case of Nicodemus. He was just tied in knots by Jesus' simple question, "Don't you know that you must be born from above? Don't you know you need a life in you that goes beyond the natural one in your body? Don't you know that this is a reality, Nicodemus?" Jesus chided him and said, "You, being a ruler in Israel, you don't know these things?" (John 3:1–16 PAR). He said this because the history of Israel was full of the reality of God, and yet Nicodemus was totally oblivious to this. It didn't mean anything to him because he had not personally experienced it.

It is a sad but true fact that many of our "rulers in Israel" today—those who have taken on the duties and responsibilities of teaching, preaching, and manifesting the Word of God—have a diminished concept of the nature of God. Their knowledge of God and his nature does not carry the weight of experience. Consequently, when they are faced with the need to help others live as those who "will reign in life through the One, Jesus Christ" (Rom. 5:17), they have no more experience of God and his kingdom than Nicodemus and simply have nothing helpful to offer. For all practical purposes, God might as well not exist.

Our Minds: The Key to Our Lives

I interact with all the sources of power in the universe through my mind. If I am an African bushman making bows and arrows to shoot birds, it is through my mind that I become knowledgeable about things like shafts of wood and points of stone, birds, strings and bows, and so forth. If I do not make the choice to use my mind to understand and interact with them, then all of this remains shut away from me. It is through my mind that I learn about electricity, and I can use my mind in conjunction with that knowledge to do any number of practical things, like turning on lights, starting my car, or picking up a phone and listening to someone speaking from the other side of the world.

We grow in our knowledge of God in the same way. We bring the reality of God into our lives by making contact with him through our minds, and our actions are based on the understanding that results from the fullness of that contact. There is nothing mysterious here. This is why *the mind, and what we turn our minds to, is the key to our lives.*

Of all reality, spirit is the most basic. We know this because "God is Spirit" (John 4:24). He made us to live and to work in the domain of the mind and the spirit. I am afraid, however, that often the concept of spirit seems like another oblong blur, escaping our understanding. This means that we need to take the necessary time to think carefully and diligently about these things. So I ask you to hold on, and may the Lord give you both patience and insight as we engage in a deeper analysis of what God is like.

The Knowledge of God as a Human Responsibility

Let's begin with a close look at the first chapter of Paul's letter to the Romans, where the full weight of our responsibility before God rests on the claim of our knowledge about God. This responsibility, and the whole human condition, is based on our failure to think about God as he is. Here is Paul's stunning and sobering claim:

> For the wrath of God is revealed from heaven against all ungod-
> liness and unrighteousness of men, who suppress the truth in

unrighteousness, because what may be known of God is manifest in them, for God has shown it to them. For since the creation of the world His invisible attributes are clearly seen, being understood by the things that are made, even His eternal power and Godhead, so that they are without excuse, because, although they knew God, they did not glorify Him as God, nor were thankful, but became futile in their thoughts, and their foolish hearts were darkened. (Rom. 1:18–21)

Consider that statement for a moment. What percentage of people in the United States would you say profess to believe in God? Religious polls are taken regularly, and while it vacillates from year to year and between age groups, recent polls indicate it is about 90 percent.* How many people do you suppose believe in God in the jungles of Africa? About 100 percent! If you go to countries where there is an ideology such as Marxism, you will find the percentage is less because people are taught not to believe in God. But the natural human response to the world which they see about them is to believe in God.

What kind of a god is it that they believe in? This god is always an invisible power, and with a few arguable exceptions, it is an *ultimate* invisible power. This invisible power is always, to one degree or another, *personal*. In some animist religions there is less of a personal emphasis, but in all these religions the god in question is treated as someone who interacts with individual human beings. That is what we call a personal being.

---

* Editor's Note: When Dallas gave this talk, he indicated he had not seen it lower than 93 to 94 percent. That has since changed. These 2016 figures are according to Gallup (Frank Newport, "Most Americans Still Believe in God," June 29, 2016, http://www.gallup.com/poll/193271/americans-believe-god.aspx) and the Pew Research Center (David Masci and Gregory A. Smith, "Is God Dead? No, But Belief Has Declined Slightly," April 7, 2016, http://www.pewresearch.org/fact-tank/2016/04/07/is-god-dead-no-but-belief-has-declined-slightly/).

A Really, Really Big God

Paul is telling us something that is still true today. We can know important truths about God—his eternal power and divine nature—by paying attention to the things he has made. God has shown these things to all of us. Now, considering the world around us, how big would you say the God is who created that world? Pretty big. Immense. In the ancient world, which lacked our contemporary scientific knowledge, they could not even begin to calculate the vastness of the universe. And still today, the God who is responsible for our universe is great beyond our comprehension.

As you continue to read, keep in mind two fundamentally important things we have covered so far:

- God is an invisible being who has great power and dominion over everything he created.*
- God is personal. He has personality. He thinks. He wills. He feels. He values.**

A joyous God fills the universe. *Joy* is the ultimate word describing God and his world. Creation was an act of joy, of delight in the goodness of what was done. It is precisely because God is like this, and because we can know that he is like this, that a life of full contentment is possible.

A God of Energy

One of the great discoveries of modern science is that what we call *matter* is really *energy*. We know about this through nuclear reactions. Imagine holding just one uranium atom, rolling it around in your hand like a marble. How much would it weigh? Very little.

---

* Gen. 1:1; John 1:1; Rom. 1:20; 1 Tim. 1:17.
** Jer. 8:21; 9:24; John 14:9; Eph. 1:4–5.

How much space would it occupy? Very little. But the power in that tiny, lightweight piece of matter is incredibly immense—thousands of times more than what it consists of merely as an atom. Energy is the basic reality.

What does this have to do with God and his ability to care for us? Just this: God is energy. Mind is energy. *Your* mind is energy. You have energy at your disposal, and in this respect, you are like God. *You* are *like* God. God has made you so you have energy at your disposal, and that energy comes in the form of your thoughts and your feelings. By these you are able to exercise your will.

God gave you a certain nature—the nature of self-sufficient energy, in some small measure. You have enough power to bake a cake or, in chorus with many others, to create a nuclear weapon. But you do not have enough energy to create even one uranium atom, because the amount of energy in that one little piece of matter is immensely greater than anything we have at our disposal.

But God's power is unlimited. Jesus demonstrated this when he was faced with the challenge of feeding thousands of hungry people, having only five loaves and two fishes (Mark 6:32–44). What did he do? He produced matter—enough loaves and fishes to feed them all and still have leftovers. Suppose he had not had those five loaves and two fishes to start with. Do you think he could have still produced a few of them out of thin air? Of course he could. But he wanted to give us an indication of God's exceedingly ample power to meet our needs even though we have very little. So he took the very little and he multiplied it.

Just before he began his public ministry, Jesus went into the wilderness, where his faith was tested. At the end of forty days of fasting, he was famished. Satan suggested that he turn some stones into bread. Jesus replied, "One does not live by bread alone, but by every word that comes from the mouth of God" (Matt. 4:4 NRSV). What is the difference between the bread and the word that comes from the mouth of God? Simply put, one of them is matter and the other is energy. We must understand this: *God is energy in a form that is so incomprehensible to us because it is so great!* But here is a clue to help our comprehension: every time we look at a piece of matter, what we see is stuff that is *not* self-sufficient. Every piece of matter you can put your hand on, or that you can even think about, came from something else, and it is eventually going to become something else. That is what matter is.

This is why Paul says that when you think clearly and carefully about the things that are created, you are led directly to God, a glorious, self-sustaining, eternal being. Everything else in this universe is created and is perishing. It is dependent on something greater than itself for its existence. This points to a being who is both the source of everything else that exists and is *totally self-sufficient.** This being is so grand that it is easier for him to exist than not to exist. He is one who, out of his mere nature, pours forth life in infinite quantities that are incomprehensible, everlasting, unceasing, and will never be exhausted. That being is God!

God's Nature Shown in Fire and Cloud

We discover another clue to God's nature as energy in the many biblical references that speak of God revealing himself to human beings in the form of fire. As the author of Hebrews puts it, "Our God is a consuming fire" (Heb. 12:29).** Fire is energy released through combustion of matter. It is a primary manifestation of God, who exists as unbounded, unfounded, everlasting energy, needing nothing to support him. Nothing at all.

When John the Baptizer said that Jesus was going to come and

---

* Editor's Note: Dallas discusses this topic more extensively in chapter 4 of *The Allure of Gentleness* (San Francisco: HarperOne, 2015).
** Hebrews 12:29 quotes Deuteronomy 4:24. You can enhance some of the topics in this book by doing your own study of fire, clouds, and whirlwinds as manifestations of God.

baptize, he stated that it would be with fire and spirit: "He who is coming after me is mightier than I," he said. "He will baptize you with the Holy Spirit and fire" (Matt. 3:11). During the Israelites' escape from Egypt, God used both fire and clouds. He shepherded Israel through the wilderness with a pillar of cloud by day and of fire by night, and in Exodus 14 he protected them from Pharaoh with both:

> And the Angel of God, who went before the camp of Israel, moved and went behind them; and the pillar of cloud went from before them and stood behind them. So it came between the camp of the Egyptians and the camp of Israel. Thus it was a cloud and darkness to the one, and it gave light by night to the other, so that the one did not come near the other all that night. (vv. 19–20)

The Lord kept the pillar in place until about two o'clock in the morning, while all of Israel crossed through the Red Sea.

> Now it came to pass, in the morning watch, that the LORD looked down upon the army of the Egyptians through the pillar of fire and cloud, and He troubled the army of the Egyptians. And He took off their chariot wheels, so that they drove them with difficulty; and the Egyptians said, "Let us flee from the face of Israel, for the LORD fights for them against the Egyptians." (vv. 24–25)

God faithfully remained with them as a pillar of fire and cloud for the rest of the trip. We repeatedly see the manifestation of God's glory and power in these ways throughout Scripture.

Envisioning the Invisible

The eleventh chapter of the book of Hebrews opens with another statement that eternal power and divinity are the invisible things of God that are seen in the visible things of creation. God, being invisible, is the source of all that is visible, and we use our understanding of creation to see what cannot be seen with our eyes. The author of Hebrews wrote, "Now faith is the substance of things hoped for, the evidence of things not seen" (Heb. 11:1).

Faith, born out of experience, is the means by which the mind contacts reality. If I hope to have light in a dark room, my faith in the light switch leads me over to the light switch, which I then flip up, and I have what I hoped for: light fills the room.

In verse 3 the writer of Hebrews 11 tells us that it is "by faith we understand that the worlds were framed by the word of God." Now remember, the word of God is energy. Often when you hear people talking about God creating the world they say that God created it "out of nothing." That is actually not what the Bible teaches. The biblical doctrine is that all creation came "out of" the person of God himself, that he spoke and created matter.* God speaking is a form of energy that became matter. While it is true that there was no pre-existing matter involved in creation, there was energy. And matter is energy in a certain form.

In this regard, it is interesting to think about the practice of fasting and what it can teach us about the reality of the word of God coming to us and sustaining our bodies without the intermediary of matter. In John 4, we read about Jesus' friends going into the city of Samaria for food and returning to him saying, "Rabbi, eat." What did he say in response? "I have food to eat of which you do not know. My food is to do the will of Him who sent Me" (John 4:31–32, 34). As C. S. Lewis said, "In God there is no hunger that needs to be filled, only plenteousness that desires to give."[2] Faith that interacts with God draws directly from God and the power that is in the word of God.

When we make contact with God a flow of energy comes to us. That energy is directly the source from which Jesus worked, and we

---

* In addition to Hebrews 11:3, see Genesis 1; Psalm 33:9.

can know it by our experience. Jesus taught us that when we fast we are not to look miserable (Matt. 6:16–18). Do you suppose he was asking us to fake it? Was he saying, "Now, you're going to be miserable, but don't let it show"? No, Jesus understood that when we fast before God we are nourished directly by the word of God, whether spoken or written. Fasting is feasting upon God. This is how Jesus was able to fast for forty days and not die. This is something you only learn by experience, and he wanted us to fast with that expectation. *The availability of this energy is the absolute source of absolute sufficiency.*

What God Can Do You Can Do . . . Sort Of

In Hebrews 11:3 we read that "the worlds were framed by the word of God." You and I are also able to do a little bit of this creative work, but not much. You are able to make a very nice cake from your thoughts, but you also need to have a few other things from the grocery store. Nonetheless, it is your thoughts that go into that cake. If that sounds strange, try making a cake without the thoughts. And they are *your* thoughts. We could say that "by faith we understand that the cake was made from the word of [insert your name here]." Do you see both the parallel and the difference between God's creative work and yours?

You have enough energy to "create" matter, but only in the sense of putting it in a different form. You do it all the time. That's why God put you here on earth. If you read the Genesis creation story, you will see that you were put here to have dominion over the earth (Gen. 1:26–27). God gave you a body to supply you with an extra amount of power in addition to the power in your mind. Your body is your own personal power pack that allows you to exercise your willed actions. God desires that each of us would use our bodies and our minds to rule the earth, together with one another, in love.

When God created us in his image, he created us with the power to act and to create. That is the image of God in man and woman. That power includes the ability to create other persons. A young lady was at a dinner where I was speaking, and she was pregnant. As we were talking about her pregnancy, I said, "Oh, that is wonderful! You are going to make a person!" And it was so interesting to watch her face, which went in several different directions at once. Obviously she had never thought this way about what she was doing. She was going to make a *person*.

Making persons is one of humankind's greatest creative acts. And, of course, we act in a way similar to God in that. How do babies come to us? Most of us don't believe in the stork, but we sometimes act as though babies just get dropped down on us like that. There is often a great expression of unfaith in the way we approach this, but nonetheless when we are having a baby, and when we are raising a child, we are making a person. We are exercising the creative part of the image of God in us.

God's Greatness Seen in History

Not only do we see the invisible characteristics of God in nature, we also see evidence of his activity in history. In the fourth chapter of Deuteronomy, we find Moses relating how God has acted in history, and especially in the history of the Jews:

> For ask now concerning the days that are past, which were before you, since the day that God created man on the earth, and ask from one end of heaven to the other, whether any great thing like this has happened, or anything like it has been heard. Did any people ever hear the voice of God speaking out of the midst of the fire, as you have heard, and live? Or did God ever try to go and take for Himself a nation from the midst of another nation, by trials, by signs, by wonders, by war, by a mighty hand and an outstretched arm, and by great terrors, according to all that the LORD your God did for you in Egypt before your eyes? To you it was shown, that

you might know that the LORD Himself is God; there is none other besides Him. Out of heaven He let you hear His voice, that He might instruct you; on earth He showed you His great fire, and you heard His words out of the midst of the fire. (Deut. 4:32–36)

Notice that again God is referred to in relation to fire. The chapter goes on to relate more of the history of Israel, and through this history the nature of God is revealed as a spiritual, invisible power that is present and moves in the lives of human beings.

What's in a Name?

God's power and personality, then, are perceived in both nature and history. In addition, his character is revealed in his names. Two of the primary names that come to us in the Old Testament are *Elohim* and *Yahweh*. *Elohim* reveals God's great creative and governing power, as in Genesis chapter 1. *Yahweh* (also translated as *Jehovah*) has the primary sense of a self-subsistent eternal being—one who does not depend on anyone else for his existence, but has "life in Himself" (John 5:26).

Abram calls the Lord *Adonai* in Genesis 15:2, which has a personal, possessive sense of "my Lord," and is often used in conjunction with *Yahweh*. *Yahweh Adonai* describes a personal, covenant-making God who holds people as his friends. God also identifies himself to Abram as *El Shaddai* in Genesis 17:1–2, the almighty God, all-abundant to his people. As he progressively reveals himself in the Old Testament, the names of God help us see more of the nature, personality, and character of God.

In the third chapter of Exodus, we find Moses responding to God's assignment to deliver the Israelites from the Egyptians, essentially saying, "So, I'm going to go back down to Egypt, am I? And what is it I am going to do there?" God tells him, and in verses 13 and 14, Moses finally gets around to asking, "*Well, what is your* *name? What shall I say to them?"* God responds with this puzzling statement: "'I AM THAT I AM . . . * Thus you shall say to the children of Israel, 'I AM has sent me to you.'"

This is not just a name like Charlie or Bill or Mary or Tanya. "I AM" is a statement of the nature of God as *being*—self-sustaining, self-sufficing, all-powerful, self-determined being. "I am *that* I am" means, "My being sustains My being." It is something that only God can say. Jesus affirmed this when he declared, "As the Father has life in Himself, so He has granted the Son to have life in Himself" (John 5:26).

So God's essential nature can be characterized in this way:

> God is an immaterial, intelligent, and free personal being, of perfect goodness, wisdom and power, who made the universe and continues to sustain it, as well as to govern and direct it in his providence.[3]

Or consider carefully this description of God by the nineteenth-century Methodist theologian and biblical scholar Adam Clarke:

> The eternal, independent, and self-existent Being: The Being whose purposes and actions spring from himself, without foreign motive or influence: He who is absolute in dominion; the most pure, the most simple, the most spiritual of all essences; infinitely benevolent, beneficent, true and holy: The cause of all being, the upholder of all things; infinitely happy, because infinitely perfect; and eternally self-sufficient, needing nothing that he has made; illimitable in his immensity, inconceivable in his mode of existence, and indescribable in his essence; known fully only by himself, because an infinite mind can only be comprehended by itself. In a word, a Being who, from his infinite wisdom, cannot

---

* Editor's Note: Whereas some translations have "I AM WHO I AM," Dallas considered, "I AM THAT I AM" to be the best and most accurate translation (KJV, ASV, Lexham English Bible, the NET Bible) because God's existence is dependent upon nothing outside of himself. He is self-existent.

err or be deceived; and, from his infinite goodness, can do nothing but what is eternally just, right, and kind.[4]

It is important to embrace that God's moral absolutes as loving, beneficent, and generous *flow out of the plenitude of his being.* Why are we not generous? Maybe we are afraid that we don't have enough. But God is never in that position; his love and his giving are unlimited. They reach beyond any imaginable boundaries because of what he is in himself.

Now please do not lose sight of the purpose of this book. I am pleading with you here to take upon yourself the task of making these realities about God a part of your mind, to understand that God is a certain kind of being; that he existed before the creation of the earth in all his plenitude. God is not now sitting off in some distant corner of the universe like a neglected senior citizen in the cosmos, waiting to see if someone will pay any attention to him. He is surrounded by unlimited glorious beings that he made, who worship him and praise him.

Even more fundamental, there is a constant communion among the great persons of the Trinity itself. Think of the most wonderful, the most attractive, the most thrilling, the most vibrant personal company that you can imagine, and multiply that by a factor of infinity, and you have begun to get a glimpse of what God is doing, where he is, what he was doing before the foundation of the earth, and what he will be doing forever. That is the being upon whom a life without lack relies. Such a life is guaranteed for those whose minds are set upon this God in faith.

Three Glimpses of God's Grandeur

In Nehemiah 9:6 we are given a little glimpse of the grandeur of God. The context is one in which the people of Israel were standing to bless God, saying:

You alone are the LORD;
You have made heaven,
The heaven of heavens, with all their host,
The earth and everything on it,
The seas and all that is in them,
And You preserve them all.
The host of heaven worships You.

You see, the greatest thing you and I can imagine is the fellowship of other loving persons, to love and to be loved, to know, to enjoy, to be with, to adventure, to create. That's what has been going on in heaven forever. There is an everlasting, eternal party that we cannot even begin to imagine. But God has begun to show it to us.

A second glimpse of God's grandeur is in the book of Job. This is a great book to study to get an impression of what God is like and what he did before and after he created the world. There we find Job being challenged by God himself. Job had been uttering his understandable complaints, and the Lord answered him out of the whirlwind, asking Job where he was when God laid the foundations of the earth. "On what were its bases sunk, or who laid its cornerstone when the morning stars sang together and all the heavenly beings shouted for joy?" (Job 38:6–7 NRSV).

This is a description of what was going on before the earth was created—God existing throughout eternity, the self-sufficiency of God to himself, this being of such grand proportions and such infinite complexity, and all his created beings with him. God's greatness in himself goes far beyond anything we can imagine. The earth is merely a tiny fragment of his vast creation.

Recall the first words of the Lord's Prayer: "Our Father who art in heaven" (Matt. 6:9 ASV). Next comes the first request: "Hallowed be thy name." What are you praying for when you pray for that? You're praying that God would be known for who he is. That his name would be cherished and loved. Why? Because once you begin to have an impression of who God truly is, everything else fades into insignificance. When the bountiful sufficiency of God in himself and the glorious realm of his kingdom are continually brought before the mind, it puts everything else in its proper place and opens us to a life in which we find God more than capable of supplying everything we need.

God's Ample Supply

Paul certainly experienced this kind of life, and he drew from psalm-like language in describing his life to the Christians in Philippi in response to a monetary gift they had sent him. He thanked them for their kindness and wrote:

> But I rejoiced in the Lord greatly that now at last your care for me has flourished again; though you surely did care, but you lacked opportunity. *Not that I speak in regard to need, for I have learned in whatever state I am, to be content.* (Phil. 4:10–11)

Paul was talking about what he learned through his experiences with the all-sufficient provision of God: to be content, at ease, free of anxiety. While grateful for the Philippians' gift, he could truthfully say that he did not need what they had sent. Whereas King David wrote "The Lord is my shepherd, I shall not want," Paul wrote "not that I speak in regard to need." They both knew the provision of God that became for them a life without lack.

But how could Paul say that? This man has been dragged through every jailhouse in the Roman Empire. Several times we find him bobbing around in the ocean, trying to survive shipwrecks. It makes me want to say, "What do you mean, you don't have any wants? Couldn't you use a boat?" He would respond, "Well, sure, I'll take a boat, but I don't really *have* to have it, you understand." What kind of man is this? One who has had many lessons, in many different circumstances, that taught him the deep truths of sufficiency. His simple testimony is, "I know how to be abased, and I know how to abound. Everywhere and in all things I have learned both to be full and to be hungry, both to abound and to suffer need. I can do all things through Christ who strengthens me" (Phil. 4:12–13).*

What did David and Paul share that gave them both this confidence? They both knew Jesus, who proclaimed, "I am the good shepherd" (John 10:11). David speaks of being strengthened by the Shepherd's rod and staff; Paul speaks of being strengthened by Christ. It's the same experience. And Paul was convinced that it was an experience that everyone can know. Out of that conviction he could promise the Philippians: "My God shall supply all your need according to His riches in glory by Christ Jesus" (4:19). Notice Paul's statement of *how* God will supply their need—in conformity with his riches in glory in Christ Jesus. God's glory is where his riches are found.

A Vision of Glory

Glory refers to the effulgent nature of God and the realm where he dwells. God's glory includes all the heavenly realms—the heavens and the earth that his word created. That is glory. This same glory was in Jesus, and a central part of his ministry was revealing that glory. He revealed it at a wedding in the Galilean village of Cana, when he turned water into fine wine. Some would prefer to call it grape juice, and that's fine with me. It is just as great a miracle to make grape juice out of water as it is to make a nice Beaujolais. If he turned the water into glue, it would still have been a miracle! But they didn't need glue; they needed more wine.

John summarized the significance of this event as: "This beginning of signs Jesus did in Cana of Galilee, and manifested His glory;

---

* For Paul's description of the kinds of situations in which he experienced God's sufficiency, see 2 Cor. 11:22–28.

and His disciples believed in Him" (John 2:11). The miracle was the first "sign" that manifested his "glory." In other words, the wine was a glimpse into the reality that Jesus was from another place—a beautiful place that shines with glorious splendor—the very presence of God. A place that, because of the infinite resources of God, knows no lack whatsoever. Jesus' glory had obviously been manifested to his mother earlier in his life. That's why she knew who to go to when they ran out of wine. Knowing that Jesus was working out of the abundance of God's riches in glory, she told the servants, "Do whatever he tells you" (John 2:5 NIV).

Again, Paul promised the Philippian believers that God would supply all their needs. This is true for you as well. He will supply all your needs. *All* of them. No need left unmet. And you will find yourself exclaiming, in the words of the Twenty-Third Psalm, "My cup *runs over*" (v. 5). You will have more than enough! God does not have a shortage of anything you can think of. His "riches in glory" are endless. We see it when Jesus multiplied the bread and the fishes. How much did they have left over? Twelve baskets! God is not stingy. He dwells in magnificent abundance, and lovingly provides for our needs out of that abundance.

God is not worried that he is going to run out of something. God is beyond rich. He is overflowing with everything that is good and everything we need. He has so much that he will never run out of any of it. It is so very important to remember this when we are fretting over a perceived need. In such a time we may be tempted to think that maybe, just maybe, God is as stingy and small as we are. He is not. God loves to give. God loves to *for*give. God loves to just gush forth with his goodness (John 4:14). Nothing so delights him as giving to anyone and everyone who will receive. "For God so loved the world that He gave . . ." (John 3:16).

CHAPTER 2

God in Himself, Part 2

Living in Mindfulness of Our Magnificent God

> *First of all, my child, think magnificently of God.*
> *Magnify His providence; adore His power, pray to*
> *Him frequently and incessantly. Bear Him always*
> *in your mind. Teach your thoughts to reverence*
> *Him in every place for there is no place where He is*
> *not. Therefore, my child, fear and worship and love*
> *God; first and last, think magnificently of Him!*
>
> —Paternus, *Advice to a Son*

Psalm 23 begins with what is surely one of the most audacious assertions in the English language: "The LORD is my shepherd, I shall not want." When you first read this thoughtfully you may be tempted to think, *Is this guy living in the real world?* The answer is most assuredly *yes*. Indeed, he is living in the *most* real world, a world where Yahweh is present and available and actively involved in the lives of those who know and trust him. Such people can truly say, "I shall not want," and know it to be true by experience. So can you.

As I have said, the secret to a life without lack is rooted in our knowledge of God. When that knowledge is absent from our minds, everything goes to pieces. Because of that fundamental fact, let me emphasize again the truth we began to look at in the last chapter: *your primary contact with God is through your mind, and what you do with your mind is the most important choice you have to make.* Wherever your mind goes, the rest of your life goes with it. When your mind loses its integrity–through disease, damage, or sin–your actions follow, becoming chaotic and disconnected.[1] They don't make the right kinds of connections with reality. You might even die. Your mind loses contact with the right things, and your body follows.

This is simply a commonsense example of what has happened in the world at large as it has fallen into sin. Our minds are in the wrong place and they are contacting the wrong things. What we place our minds on brings that reality into our lives. If we place our minds on God, the reality of God comes into our lives. That is why there must be preachers and teachers, because until our minds are informed by the right view of God, we cannot put our minds on God in the right way. The problem is so severe that when Jesus came he essentially said to people, "Forget everything you think you know about God, and I'm going to tell you what he is really like."*

It's the problem of wrong ideas. As someone said long ago, "It ain't what we know that hurts us. It's what we know that ain't so."[2] All the things that we know about God that "ain't so" destroy our lives, poison us, throw our lives out of kilter, and throw our bodies out of an appropriate relationship to reality. Wrong ideas about God make it impossible for us to function in relationship to one another. We are not able to love one another because we do not have our minds filled with an accurate vision of God.

Remember what we discussed in the last chapter concerning God's name. In the Twenty-Third Psalm, when we come to the words, "The LORD is my shepherd," the word translated as "The LORD" is actually God's name, *Jehovah* or *Yahweh*. "Yahweh is my shepherd." As I mentioned in chapter 1, the name means "self-subsistent, eternal

---

* Matthew 22:29.

being." It is the divine name most used in the Old Testament because it is the name that is most revealing of God's nature. God is a being who cannot *not* be. You may think that this concept is quite foreign from your ordinary life, but it is not so. You are worried about *being* more than anything else, especially your own being, or that of your loved ones. A little child most commonly discovers the mystery and terror of being when death takes her goldfish, or kitty, or a relative. She is hurt because nonbeing is not natural. Being is natural in a world where there is a God like Yahweh—an eternal, self-subsistent being, so full and great and glorious that it is impossible for him not to be. That is Yahweh.

What You Don't See Is More Important than What You Do See

The single most important thing to remember about God is his total unlikeness in his being from anything that we can see. The great contrast that runs through the entire Bible is the difference between the visible and the invisible. Let me remind you of Paul's statement in Romans 1:20: "Ever since the creation of the world his eternal power and divine nature, invisible though they are, have been understood and seen through the things he has made" (NRSV). There you have it—the invisible made visible by the things that are made. In what way is this true? The nature of Yahweh—a being that *cannot* not be—is revealed through the things that are made, *because* everything that is made is something that could very easily not be, whether it is a solar system, a star, a galaxy, a grasshopper, or you or me. But we humans are beings with an important difference from these others in that we have two sides, for there is a part of us that also cannot *not be*. You are never going to cease to exist. If you are afraid of going out of existence, fear no more. Why? Because God, in creation, has imparted an aspect of himself into you. Being made in God's image means, among other things, that you also are an eternal being and you can create. But, unlike God, you are not self-subsistent; you are dependent upon God for your being.

Your own experience verifies the truth of Romans 1:20. While you know that you are visible to others, you also know that part of you is invisible. It is in your thoughts and feelings (your mind) and, above all, in your ability to choose (your will). You can direct your actions, make plans, and carry them out—this is a function of the invisible part of you. You know, by experience, that your will is the source of the visible things that come to be as a result of your choices. How do you know? By simply observing yourself. That you are reading these words now is a clear example. Earlier in the day, maybe only twenty minutes ago, the invisible part of you—your will—decided to read this book. That decision led to the visible actions of picking up the book, turning to a particular page, and to the further actions of reading, turning more pages, and maybe even taking notes—all visible things. Why did it all happen? I doubt it is because someone picked you up and threw you into a chair and forced you to read. No, you are reading this book now because the invisible side of you decided to do so, directed your body to do the necessary things, and now here you are, reading.

The important point here is that you have *in yourself* the Romans 1:20 experience of the invisible originating the visible. That is why, when you look around at the things that are visible, you can know two things they share in common. First, they came into existence and, sooner or later, will pass out of existence. Second, each of them was created from an invisible source. Again, you know this from your own experience, and you confirm it in others who have the same experience.

If I had to pull all this together in one phrase, I would say it is *the experience of free will*. By making you in his image, God has given you, in your will, *the power of originative action*, the power to create and to bring things into existence. You, then, are the best clue to the nature of God, understanding that while your powers and being are limited and dependent, God's are not. Everything that exists *outside* of God exists *because* of God.

A Big No-No: Confusing Anything with God

When I was a child in Sunday school, the latter portion of the Ten Commandments always made a lot of sense to me, especially the ones that say, "Don't steal" and "Don't lie," because that was right at my level. I knew exactly what they meant. And I liked the one that says, "Don't kill," because it comforted me to know that someone would not kill me. But the first few commandments didn't make much sense to me, in particular the second one about not making idols and not bowing down to them. The second commandment says:

> You shall not make for yourself a carved image—any likeness of anything that is in heaven above, or that is in the earth beneath, or that is in the water under the earth. (Ex. 20:4)

Of all the things that God created, what is not covered here? Nothing. That covers every created being. Another word the Old Testament uses for idols is *vanity* or *vanities*.* This is because idols are vain, empty, worthless things—things that have no spiritual reality or power. In the King James Version, Psalm 24:4 speaks of the person who "hath not lifted up his soul unto vanity." In many contemporary versions, you will find the word *vanity* is now translated as *idol* or *idols*.**

God continues the second commandment:

---

* See Psalm 31:6 and Jonah 2:8. The Hebrew word *shav* is translated in the NRSV as *worthless idols* or *vain idols*, but it is a single term translated in older versions simply as *vanities*.

** Editor's Note: These are the New International Version, New Living Translation, New King James Version, New Century Version, Good News Bible, Today's New International Version. The New International Readers Version uses "the statue of a god."

You shall not bow down to them nor serve them. For I, the LORD your God, am a jealous God, visiting the iniquity of the fathers upon the children to the third and fourth generations of those who hate Me, but showing mercy to thousands, to those who love Me and keep My commandments. (Ex. 20:5–6)

For the contemporary reader, it is better to substitute the word *zealous* for *jealous*, since this more accurately captures the meaning of God's explanation for the commandment, which is his zeal or fervor for the well-being of his creatures, especially for human beings. Then comes the third commandment:

You shall not take the name of the LORD your God in vain, for the LORD will not hold him guiltless who takes His name in vain. (v. 7)

The command to not take God's name in vain is most often misunderstood as relating to swearing or cursing, especially in ways that ask God to "damn" someone or something, or possibly when a person exclaims, "Oh, God!" While that may be a problem, this is not the issue that the command is addressing. Rather it is dealing with any way of using God's real name, *Yahweh*, that is not in accord with God's real nature. Remember, God's name is a reflection of his nature, and the most common way of using it "in vain" is to degrade God to the level of a created being. This is what you have in an idol.

We transgress this commandment any time we refer to God in ways that are not appropriate to the greatness of his being, especially ways that do not take into consideration that God is an invisible and eternal power who has a personality. This is precisely what takes place when people carve a figure out of wood or stone and treat it as if it had Godlike characteristics, when in fact it is nothing but a lifeless, soulless piece of matter. But that is not the only way of being an idolater. Anything that occupies a greater concern in our lives than God qualifies—position, influence, success, wealth, even family. As Paul points out, covetous or greedy persons, those who "worship" the things they desire to possess (*created* stuff), also qualify.* We'll discuss this further in chapter 6.

A Long Education in the Same Direction

The history of Israel is a long, steady education in what it means to obey the commandment against taking the Lord's name in vain, which involved how they thought and spoke of God. In particular, in their escape from Egyptian slavery to their return from Babylon and again from Persia, Israel learned that their God—Yahweh— was literally *out of this world*, incomparable to anything in creation in his self-sustaining power, glory, and goodness. At what point do we finally come to the place where we can use God's name without doing so "in vain"? After we have come to know Jesus Christ. Only after that point are we fully capable of using his name rightly. Why is this so? One way to answer that is to look at what is commonly called Jesus' High Priestly Prayer, found in John 17.

Because of the depth at which Jesus is moving in this prayer, it is seldom addressed in sermons. But it is a wonderful revelation of the nature of God and of God's name. In verse five he prays, "And now, O Father, glorify Me together with Yourself, with the glory which I had with You before the world was." As we saw in the previous chapter, Job 38:7 describes the time before time, which was one of wonderful, joyous celebration, "when the morning stars sang together, and all the sons of God shouted for joy." What do you imagine they were shouting about? What made them so happy? It was the glory Jesus is talking about here, "glory that I had in your

---

* See Eph. 5:5: "Be sure of this, that no fornicator or impure person, or one who is greedy (that is, an idolater), has any inheritance in the kingdom of Christ and of God" (NRSV).

presence before the world existed" (John 17:5 PAR). Jesus continues, "I have manifested Your name to the men whom You have given Me out of the world" (v. 6). That is to say, "I have shown these people what your name really means." God's name is an expression of his nature, and from everything we can glean from Jesus' entire life—his teachings, his healing ministry, how he treated people, and how he prayed—the only conclusion we can draw is that God is a being who is perfectly glorious and perfectly safe. This is what God's name means and why it is "exalted above all blessing and praise" (Neh. 9:5).

Take a moment right now and think of the most wonderful thing you could say about anyone. Consider what characteristics someone might have that would deserve your highest blessing and praise.

Whatever you thought of, God's true blessedness is far above that. God's glory and power and goodness are deserving of infinitely more praise. No matter how magnificent in power or kindness or patience or any other attribute you want to assign to someone, God far exceeds that. So, as you "count your blessings," no matter how many and how wonderful they are, God's name will be beyond them all. And even when you give God your highest praise, he will always be deserving of more. There is absolutely nothing that God lacks. We must understand this, because the overflowing sufficiency that we will experience when Yahweh is our Shepherd lies in *the all-sufficiency of the Shepherd himself.* If we do not understand the all-sufficiency of the Shepherd, we will never experience that sufficiency in relationship to him. What we need, God has—in infinite supply.

To take the name of God in vain, then, is simply to speak or think or imagine God as being less than he actually is. And like Israel, we, too, require a long, steady education in this direction. Those who take time to increasingly come to know and trust God as he truly is, are laying the sure foundation of a life without lack.

Come to Think of It, There's Nothing to Fear

My objective here is to help you think about God, and to do so correctly in accord with the truth about the kind of being God is. I am also asking you to think about yourself and what kind of being you are. I want to help you think things through and come to a correct understanding of matters. This will lead you, together with the Lord, into actions based on this truth.

Jesus taught us not to be afraid of those who can kill the body.* He also discussed other fears people have, each of which he gently and intelligently dismissed. You can live completely without fear. God is the kind of being who, if you will place yourself in his hands, in trust, will ensure that nothing can ever happen to you that will make you say, "I'm afraid" or "I don't have enough."

What do you fear? Whatever came to mind, I want you to know that you have nothing to fear. If you doubt this, I urge you to ask God to give you a peace about this. Let me say it again: no matter what you fear, you can live without that fear. You do not have to be afraid of anything. Nothing. Absolutely nothing—not death, not the loss of loved ones, not being without someone to care for you. (For many people, this becomes an absolute obsession as they become older. They fear that there is not going to be anyone to take care of them. I am saying that this is completely avoidable and unnecessary.) If you will take the time required to come to know and trust God as he is, asking the Lord to give light to your mind, you can come to a place of perfect peace and fearlessness. *Because God is with you, you can live without fear.* This is precisely what the Shepherd Psalm is talking about.

Now, some people may read this and begin to feel guilty for being frightened about something. That is not my intention. You can leave that with God, who understands and forgives. My intention is to

---

* Matthew 10:28; Luke 12:4.

help you realize that fear and worry are worthless—indeed, vain—emotions. If you are frightened or afraid, there is no use feeling guilty about it. What you need to do is fix your mind upon God and ask him to fill your mind with himself. And as your mind is transformed, your whole personality will be transformed, including your body and your feelings. The transformation of the self away from a life of fear and insufficiency takes place as we fix our minds upon God *as he truly is.*

"I Am the Good Shepherd"—Jesus Christ Is Yahweh

In his letter to the Ephesian Christians, Paul spoke of "the boundless riches of Christ" (Eph. 3:8 NIV). At the center of these "riches" is Christ himself, for he is, in fact, that being of complete self-sufficiency we have been focusing upon. He is the Shepherd-LORD of the Twenty-Third Psalm, *Yahweh in the flesh!* In the apostle John's depiction of the events in the Garden of Gethsemane, as Judas arrives with the group of Jewish leaders and Roman soldiers who have come to arrest him, Jesus asks them who they are looking for. When they respond, "Jesus of Nazareth," Jesus' reply is powerful. While most versions of the Bible record Jesus as having said "I am he," the Greek phrase is literally "I am." Their reaction to this self-revelation is telling: they draw back and fall to the ground (John 18:1–8). Jesus knows what he is saying in using this phrase, one that shows up throughout the gospel of John. Jesus is signaling his identity as the great "I AM"—Yahweh, the eternal, self-sufficient creator of all things, and the covenant Lord of Israel.

That is why Jesus, in complete confidence, could just lay down his life. He said, "I lay down My life that I may take it again. No one takes it from Me, but I lay it down of Myself. I have power to lay it down, and I have power to take it again" (John 10:17–18). He was completely and totally without fear. Why? Because he understood his relationship to his Father. Jesus is the first person who ever fully lived Psalm 23:1—"The LORD is my shepherd, I shall not want." His union with his Father was such that he never knew lack or fear. The Father was Jesus' Shepherd, just as Jesus is ours. As Jesus knew no fear, so can we.

Who Jesus Is

To better understand this, and to see how a life without fear is possible, we need to look deeper into who Jesus is. We might as well just jump into the deep end of the theological pool and think briefly about the nature of God as triune. Why the Trinity? Simply put, it is the nature of God's infinite, loving personality to be multiple in itself and in its creative activity. This is why God created the heavens and populated them. What is in the heavens? Mostly persons—wonderful, glorious beings called "sons of God" (Job 1:6; 38:7) or "angels" (Heb. 1:13–14; Rev. 7:11). Why did God create angels? Because he is a personality capable of understanding and of love, and love desires to share itself with others. So God created this grand, marvelous thing called "the heavens" and "the highest heavens" (Deut. 10:14 NIV) in which he dwells with his created angelic beings. Then out of that came his desire to create human beings as another dimension of the opportunity to develop love.

God is personality. He creates other personalities and, *out of the plenitude of his being, he loves them.* When you read the verses in 1 Corinthians 13 that describe love, what is your feeling? Try it. Here is how Paul described agape, divine love:

> Love suffers long and is kind; love does not envy; love does not parade itself, is not puffed up; does not behave rudely, does not seek its own, is not provoked, thinks no evil; does not rejoice in iniquity, but rejoices in the truth; bears all things, believes all things, hopes all things, endures all things. Love never fails. (1 Cor. 13:4–8)

You may have heard that every time the word *love* appears in this passage, you should insert your own name in its place. It would not be surprising if this frustrated you, because that little exercise puts the cart before the horse. Paul is not primarily giving instructions on how Christians should live, but describing what God is like. First and foremost, these words describe God's love, a love that is the fruit of God's absolute self-sufficiency. The key to loving like this is to be "filled with all the fullness of God" (Eph. 3:19). God can love like this because of who he is, and if we are to love like this we need to be fully immersed in who he is.

Most people would agree that if everyone loved like Paul described, nearly all the problems we face in human society would disappear, along with many others that we don't usually connect with human misbehavior. At the center of so many of our difficulties is fear—fear of rejection, fear of failure, fear of death, fear of sickness, fear of not being able to take care of ourselves in old age, fear of what may happen to our loved ones.

There are so very many things to frighten us. What is the answer to all our fears? Love. The love that comes out of plenitude—out of the fullness of God's sufficiency. We read in 1 John 4:18 that "there is no fear in love; but perfect love casts out fear." As the King James Version puts it, "Fear hath torment." To fear is to be tormented, but to be loved perfectly—and to know it—is to be free of fear's torment.

Let 'Er Rip!

My wife and I knew an older brother in Christ who, when he found himself burdened by difficult circumstances, would entrust his situation to God by going out onto his back porch, raising his arms high and crying out, "Let 'er rip! Let 'er rip!" The only way any of us could say that and mean it is by knowing that we are not in control, but that we are grounded in the sufficiency of God the Shepherd.

Norman Vincent Peale's recommendation for those caught in

fear is to imagine that the worst thing they feared had taken place, and then ask themselves, *Where would I be if this actually happened? What would happen to God?*[3] If we were to do this, we would realize that in reality it would not make much difference, since most of our fears are quite trivial. Even severe fears can be faced when we are confident in the strength and generosity of God—and in the fact that his kingdom isn't shaken, and he is not undone by these things. In Hebrews 11, the famous chapter on faith, after cataloging the great heroes of the Old Testament and their various achievements, the author added this:

> Others were tortured, not accepting deliverance, that they might obtain a better resurrection. Still others had trial of mockings and scourgings, yes, and of chains and imprisonment. They were stoned, they were sawn in two, were tempted, were slain with the sword. They wandered about in sheepskins and goatskins, being destitute, afflicted, tormented—of whom the world was not worthy. They wandered in deserts and mountains, in dens and caves of the earth. (Heb. 11:35–38)

How's that for some encouraging words? What is going on here? Is this supposed to boost one's faith? Yes, and in just this way: because of the nature of God and his kingdom, all his created beings and everyone who trusts in him are in a position to say, "Let the worst happen! Let the worst happen, and God and I will go on together in the abundance of his being."

You may say, "If they kill me, who is going to take care of my children?" One of the great martyrs of the Christian church in years gone by, Dr. Rowland Taylor, passed his wife and children on the way to the pyre upon which he was going to be burned. The night before he had written, "God careth for sparrows and for the very hair of our heads. I have ever found him more faithful and favorable than any father or husband." As he passed his family for the final time he said, "Farewell, my dear wife; be of good comfort, for I am quiet in my conscience. God shall stir up a father for my children."[4] He was testifying to God's ability to provide everything we need—no matter what.

What about Jesus in all of this? We have spoken of the sufficiency of God, that God is all around us, that God is love, that God is a social God who creates persons and a kingdom and sustains them. Jesus is a manifestation of that glorious reality. One of the great prophecies of the Old Testament is found in Micah 5:2: "But you, Bethlehem Ephrathah, though you are little among the thousands of Judah, yet out of you shall come forth to Me the One to be Ruler in Israel, whose goings forth are from of old, from everlasting."

Notice the relative insignificance of Bethlehem. It is one of the little clans of Judah, and yet it is from here that the Messiah was to come. This is in keeping with Jesus' teaching about the last being first and the first being last and is primarily a declaration of the limitless kingdom of God. This is why Jesus could pronounce as blessed those who are the religious outsiders, those who are poor, those who are hungry, those who mourn, and those who are persecuted. It is because, in spite of their circumstances, they are living in vital communion with the Shepherd and his kingdom, and they know no lack.[5]

Jesus knew what he was speaking about because, as Micah puts it, his origin is "from of old," from ancient days. Jesus existed long before he made his earthly appearance. This is made clear in John 17:24, where Jesus prayed: "Father, I desire that they also whom You gave Me may be with Me where I am, that they may behold My glory which You have given Me; for You loved Me before the foundation of the world." When did the Father love the Son? "Before the foundation of the world." When you put verses like this and the Micah 5:2 passage together, you begin to get a clearer picture of the greatness of God and life in his kingdom. There are God (Father, Son, and Spirit, all in their sufficiency) and his created beings, enjoying the glory*—the full and wondrous greatness—of the kingdom of God. This is the life that the Son knew before his incarnation. And when he came, although he laid some of his glory aside, he was still able to give us some stunning glimpses of it, glimpses that were meant to provide us with a vision of a life without lack.

Glimpses of Glory and Sufficiency

It is important to realize that God's power is meant to be at the disposal of human beings. This is what we see in the life and ministry of Jesus, and a good deal of his training of the disciples was intended to show how this is done. Jesus had complete confidence in God's power, and he intended to establish that same confidence in his disciples. He did not mean for them to walk in blindness in this regard. One clear example of this took place when Jesus went up onto a mountain in Galilee with three of his most intimate disciples, Peter, James, and John, for a bit of advanced training in kingdom ministry. Luke tells us about that momentous event:

> Now it came to pass, about eight days after these sayings, that He took Peter, John, and James and went up on the mountain to pray. As He prayed, the appearance of His face was altered, and His robe became white and glistening. And behold, two men talked with Him, who were Moses and Elijah, who appeared in glory and spoke of His decease which He was about to accomplish at Jerusalem. But Peter and those with him were heavy with sleep; and when they were fully awake, they saw His glory and the two men who stood with Him. Then it happened, as they were parting from Him, that Peter said to Jesus, "Master, it is good for us to be here; and let us make three tabernacles: one for You, one for Moses, and one for Elijah"—not knowing what he said.

---

* "Glory" is the greatness, the goodness, the awesomely beautiful magnificence of all aspects of God. Jesus shared in that.

While he was saying this, a cloud came and overshadowed them; and they were fearful as they entered the cloud. And a voice came out of the cloud, saying, "This is My beloved Son. Hear Him!" When the voice had ceased, Jesus was found alone. But they kept quiet, and told no one in those days any of the things they had seen. (Luke 9:28–36)

This event fulfilled what Jesus had said a week or so before. He was alone with his disciples at the time, and he asked them what people were saying about him and who they believed he was. The disciples reported several differing opinions, including John the Baptizer, Elijah, or some other of the great Hebrew prophets. Jesus then turned the question on his disciples, asking, "Who do you say that I am?" Peter gave his great confession: "The Messiah of God," and Jesus told them not to proclaim that truth just yet (vv. 20–21 NRSV). Then, after foretelling his suffering, death, and resurrection, and explaining what it takes to be his disciple, Jesus declared, "But I tell you truly, there are some standing here who shall not taste death till they see the kingdom of God" (v. 27).

Notice carefully what Jesus predicted was going to happen to some of the disciples before they died: they would *see* the kingdom of God. Not all of it, but enough of it. That is precisely what took place on what we now call the Mount of Transfiguration. Peter, James, and John were given a glorious glimpse of the reality of God and of his kingdom. It became *visible* to them. It was there all along, but now they *saw* it. When Matthew described Jesus' appearance at this time, he said, "His face shone like the sun, and His clothes became as white as the light" (Matt. 17:2).*

What transpired that day was the revelation of the glory of the kingdom of God. The glory that Peter, James, and John *saw* on Jesus was also on Moses and Elijah, who, by the way, had obviously not

---

* I consider this another manifestation of God through fire: energy being released, as I mentioned in chapter 1.

been rotting in their graves, but enjoying the fellowship of God and the greatness and grandeur of his kingdom. While Peter had a few other lessons to learn, he never forgot this one. In his second letter, he grounded his teachings and exhortations directly in the reality of what he saw that day on the mountain:

> For we did not follow cunningly devised fables when we made known to you the power and coming of our Lord Jesus Christ, but were eyewitnesses of His majesty. For He received from God the Father honor and glory when such a voice came to Him from the Excellent Glory: "This is My beloved Son, in whom I am well pleased." And we heard this voice which came from heaven when we were with Him on the holy mountain.
>
> And so we have the prophetic word confirmed, which you do well to heed as a light that shines in a dark place, until the day dawns and the morning star rises in your hearts. (2 Peter 1:16–19)

Entering in Through the New Covenant

This theme of the invisible and the visible worlds is taken up again by the writer of the book of Hebrews, where we are given another glimpse of the grand reality of heaven. In his defense of the superiority of the new covenant of grace over the old covenant with its laws and regulations, the author contrasted the fearful experience of Moses and the Israelites at Mount Sinai with what is available to followers of Christ:

> For you have not come to the mountain that may be touched and that burned with fire, and to blackness and darkness and tempest, and the sound of a trumpet and the voice of words, so that those who heard it begged that the word should not be spoken to them anymore. (For they could not endure what was commanded: "And if so much as a beast touches the mountain, it

shall be stoned or shot with an arrow." And so terrifying was the sight that Moses said, "I am exceedingly afraid and trembling.")

But you have come to Mount Zion and to the city of the living God, the heavenly Jerusalem, to an innumerable company of angels, to the general assembly and church of the firstborn who are registered in heaven, to God the Judge of all, to the spirits of just men made perfect, to Jesus the Mediator of the new covenant, and to the blood of sprinkling that speaks better things than that of Abel. (Heb. 12:18–24)

That is the reality of heaven! It is where we stand, with God at the center, surrounded by all his perfect and perfected beings, those who have come to God through Jesus, the Lamb of God whose blood does not call out for judgment and condemnation, but for mercy, forgiveness, and the fullness of the grace of God! Indeed, it calls for a "festal gathering" (Heb. 12:22 NRSV)—a grand, eternal, joyous party of praise to the God who makes it all possible!

In the new covenant that Jesus initiated, we are given a foretaste of this reality. The phrase "innumerable company of angels" suggests that there are more angels than there are numbers. Think about how many numbers there are. Actually, you can't do that, since there are innumerable numbers! When you compare the number of human beings to how many numbers there are, there are immeasurably more numbers, right? So when the writer mentioned "innumerable" angels, he was attempting to express the overwhelming abundance of this world in which God exists at the very center, and which he calls us to draw from so we may know a life without lack.

Coming to Grips with the Ineffable God

If we were told that God was in the next room, and that anyone who wanted to do so could just go in and see him, it's doubtful that many of us would accept the offer, especially if we saw bright light coming from around the door and the walls were shaking. That's what was going on in Exodus 19. Mount Sinai was trembling like a massive rocket just before launch. The Israelites were filled with fear and wanted to keep a great distance between themselves and God. Except for Moses. He went right up to where God was and spent forty days in God's presence (Ex. 24:18; 34:28). When Moses came down from the mountain, he was glowing. His face was so bright that it was like looking into a 300-watt lightbulb. The Israelites couldn't take it, and they essentially asked him to get a lampshade and put it over his head (Ex. 34:29–35).

If you're thinking this is weird, you're right. There actually is a direct relationship between weird things and holy things. One use of the word *weird* is to indicate that an experience is strange, uncanny, or has a sense of the supernatural about it. From that perspective, everything I have been describing—from Moses's shining face to Jesus glowing on the mountain—is truly weird. It's supernatural, out of this world. That is what *holy* is, something wholly otherworldly.

Remember that the second of the Ten Commandments states, "You shall not make for yourself an idol, whether in the form of anything that is in heaven above, or that is on the earth beneath, or that is in the water under the earth" (Ex. 20:4 NRSV). God is so "other" that he is literally "out of this world" and should never be identified with any physical thing in this world. It is this total otherness, this holiness, this weirdness that makes most people not want to get close to God. They want to have just enough of God to make their little train chug on down the track, something to fix them up, a cosmic aspirin to help them get on with their own business. So when they see the light and the smoke coming out from around the door and the walls shaking, they say to themselves, "Maybe this is a little too big. I don't think this will fit into my plans."

And, of course, that is exactly right. While we may talk fervently about how we want to be close to the Lord, he does not take us seriously because it's only talk. We often don't really mean it. That may be because we have not had the magnificence and grandeur and glorious reality of God's being brought to our attention. God is not something to be toyed around with. He will not fit into our plans. But we can fit into his, and they are glorious plans indeed.

The Israelites had a hard time learning this. Not long after their liberation from Egypt, as God led them through the Sinai desert, lots of very strange things were happening. Water flowed from rocks and massive flocks of quail appeared, but the Israelites could only think of their former lifestyle with its leeks, onions, garlic, and nice soft beds, forgetting that they were slaves. So God responded with more weirdness in the form of manna, which was quite a strange phenomenon.

Moses reminded the Israelites of this as they were getting ready to cross over the Jordan into the promised land:

> And you shall remember that the LORD your God led you all the way these forty years in the wilderness, to humble you and test you, to know what was in your heart, whether you would keep His commandments or not. So He humbled you, allowed you to hunger, and fed you with manna which you did not know nor did your fathers know, that He might make you know that man shall not live by bread alone; but man lives by every word that proceeds from the mouth of the LORD. (Deut. 8:2–3)

The Israelites knew all about the food of Egypt, but no one knew anything about manna. Ask them about Cairo stew and corn-bread, and they could tell you all about it. But manna was a mystery to them until they trekked across the wilderness. It was strange stuff: the congealed word of God. According to Exodus 16, it did not grow on any shrub; it was not an animal that could be hunted down and served up; it was not a crop that could be sown and harvested. It just appeared every morning lying on the ground for the people to gather before it melted in the sun. They were instructed to gather a one-day supply for each person in the family on Sunday through Thursday each week. And whether they gathered more or less than that, they always had exactly the right amount. That's weird.

If they tried to save some of it for the next day (just in case God didn't provide), it rotted and had to be thrown out. Then on Fridays they were told to gather a two-day supply to last through Saturday, the Sabbath day of rest. The extra day's manna didn't rot. That's weird too. But the Israelites tired of it and whined to Moses, "We're sick of manna! Takes us back to what we were used to in Egypt! At least the food was spicy!" (Num. 11:4–6 PAR).

Of course, this was a litmus test of their hearts, to gauge whether they did, in fact, want nothing more than the God who had rescued them. They didn't. It is the same with us. We are going to be living on weird stuff if we draw near to God. One of the promises Jesus gives, in the book of Revelation, to those who are faithful is that he will give them "hidden manna" (2:17). This connects with the discussion Jesus had with a group of people who were pressing him to prove his credentials as one sent from God (John 6:22–59). They brought up the example of their ancestors whom, under the leadership of Moses, God had provided with manna in the wilderness. The implied question was whether Jesus measured up to Moses, to which Jesus responded:

> Moses did not give you the bread from heaven, but My Father gives you the true bread from heaven. For the bread of God is He who comes down from heaven and gives life to the world. (John 6:32–33)

When they said, *"That sounds great; give us some of that bread,"* Jesus made his disturbing claim:

> I am the living bread which came down from heaven. If anyone eats of this bread, he will live forever; and the bread that I shall

give is My flesh, which I shall give for the life of the world."
(v. 51)

And if that wasn't audacious enough, he went on to shock them with this bit of weirdness:

Most assuredly, I say to you, unless you eat the flesh of the Son of Man and drink His blood, you have no life in you. Whoever eats My flesh and drinks My blood has eternal life, and I will raise him up at the last day. For My flesh is food indeed, and My blood is drink indeed. (vv. 53–55)

This was over the top. Even some of his own disciples essentially said, "Yuck!" They concluded they could no longer follow someone who talked like that (v. 66).

From Glory to Glory

There is no denying it; this is highly unusual behavior. But Jesus was talking about being transformed into a completely new reality, a world of complete sufficiency, where all our needs are supplied by God. If you go to work tomorrow and declare, "I don't need anything," people will probably think you are weird . . . very weird. You are supposed to be in need. You are supposed to lack. That's one of the things that people can use to manage you. But if you go there complaining, griping, groaning, even cursing God, making it known just how much you lack, they will say, "Yes!" They are likely to call you a really good person, the salt of the earth, because complaining is the way of this world.

I am not saying that it is always wrong to complain; each of us needs to work this out in our own way. I am saying that *there is a life in which there is no lack.* Jesus is the example that proves this claim to be true. The good news is that, by his grace, it is a life that each of us can move into by faith. If, by faith, you can now declare, "I have no lack," you will increasingly experience the Shepherd's sufficiency in your life. It will be as Paul described:

> But we all, with unveiled face, beholding as in a mirror the glory of the Lord, are being transformed into the same image from glory to glory, just as by the Spirit of the Lord. (2 Cor. 3:18)

The more we place our minds on God's greatness and self-sufficiency ("beholding . . . the glory of the Lord"), the more we will be transformed from one degree of glory to another. And because our faces are "unveiled" (that is, they have had the lampshades removed) others will see a difference; we will radiate generosity, peace, and contentment. And the reverse is also true; as we associate with others whose faces are "unveiled" and who are growing in their experience of God's sufficiency, their "glory" enlightens us, encouraging us in our own journeys of faith in the Shepherd. It becomes a matter of one person reminding another of the full sufficiency of God.

Notice the word *reminding* in the sentence above. It should really be written *re-minding*, because in these first two chapters we have been talking about getting new minds. Minds that are "on God." In 2 Corinthians 3:18, Paul wrote that we are being "transformed" into the image of Christ. The word translated *transformed* is the Greek word from which we get the English word *metamorphosis*. It literally means a change (*meta*) of form (*morph*), as in changing from caterpillar to butterfly, except we are talking about the form of our minds. They are meant to be God-formed rather than world-formed. That is why elsewhere Paul instructed us to avoid being conformed to the ways of the world (or being "normal" rather than "weird"), but that we should rather "be transformed *by the renewing of your mind*" (Rom. 12:2). This is the key to a life without lack, that we would have the mind of Christ—our Shepherd, who knew first-hand the complete and perfect sufficiency of our magnificent God.

A Brief Meditation

We have just completed two chapters dedicated to the contemplation of the grandeur and greatness of the Shepherd. Before engaging our next topic, it is fitting to pause and reflect once more upon the Twenty-Third Psalm in the glowing light of this awesome being. So please take some time to read the whole psalm—slowly, thoughtfully, and prayerfully—before reading the reflection below.

Psalm 23 is one of those great, wonderful passages of writing that could not possibly have been made up by human ingenuity alone. Our minds do not naturally run at these kinds of heights. Some stories are so real they could never have been made up; the words of the psalmist, David, are like that. They express the experience of a man whose life was rugged, but who came to know the overflowing richness of Yahweh in the midst of it.

In chapter 1, we dwelt on the attributes of God—that completely self-sufficient, eternal being who makes covenant promises with individual human beings. David knew those promises and walked in them, having seen the hand of God in his own life. He experienced firsthand the lavish sufficiency of God in such a way that it simply didn't matter what else happened. Nothing could rob him of the full provision he found in the active and conversational relationship in which he lived with God. Absolutely nothing. In fact, it seems almost everything *did* happen to him: shunned by his family, envied and hated by King Saul, enemies breathing down his neck, and years spent hiding in caves. A failure—and all the while *he had an intimate relationship with God.* The boy who went out and slew Goliath still knew times of great testing afterward.

This psalm reflects David's personal relationship with God, and it is within this kind of relationship that a life without lack is known. *You* can have that kind of relationship and life, as fully as it can be imagined. That is the reason for this book. What is described in the Twenty-Third Psalm is not something reserved for a few peculiar people we read about in the Bible. It is an expression of God's intent for every human being. *Everyone.* And from the human side, the life without lack is simply a matter of having one's mind fully and constantly fixed upon God as he is, confident that he will provide everything that we need.*

As I mentioned earlier, this relates directly to why, in what is known as the Lord's Prayer, the very first petition is, "Hallowed be your name." This is why I find it helpful to reword this verse to, "may your name be cherished and loved" so as to better capture the fullness of its meaning.**

In John 17:6 we are told that Jesus revealed the name of the Father to his disciples. This means that he let them truly know who God is, because biblically the name of God brings with it the reality of God. It is interesting to see the similarity between some of David's prayers and the Lord's Prayer. Jesus and David both knew the hand of God in their lives. Jesus, of course, knew it in a more profound way, because by his hand water turned to wine, the blind were made to see, the raging sea was calmed, the dead were raised, and the poor heard good news.

This psalm reflects the nature of God, and how *the radiant sufficiency of the Shepherd provides the life without lack.* God is an ineffable reality so much greater than anything we ordinarily see around us or come to deal with in human life; he simply has no comparison. We are blessed to live in a world where there is a fully self-sufficient, generous God who wants to provide what is best for us and loves us more than we could ever imagine.

---

* Editor's Note: Dallas here echoes the teaching of Jesus in Matthew 6:25–33, which ends with these words: "Strive first for the kingdom of God and his righteousness, and all these things will be given to you as well" (NRSV).
** For a complete rewording of the Lord's Prayer, read *The Divine Conspiracy,* page 269.

CHAPTER 3

Why There Are People on Earth

I look up at your macro-skies, dark and enormous,
your handmade sky-jewelry,
Moon and stars mounted in their settings.
Then I look at my micro-self and wonder,
Why do you bother with us?
Why take a second look our way?

—PSALM 8:3–4 THE MESSAGE

The Shepherd Psalm is a reminder of God's care, protection, and provision for his children; the preciousness of his creatures. It is one thing to understand how our Shepherd is capable of providing for all our needs; of course such an all-powerful, self-sufficient being *can* take care of us. But what is it about humans that would motivate God to do so? Have you ever wondered why there are people? Not just the abstract question about people in general, but also the specific, personal question, "Why am I in the world?" Your concern and mine is to understand why *we* are here. Do you have an answer to this question?

The answer is not always immediately clear, even to the writers of the Scriptures. Take Psalm 8:1 for example: "O LORD, our Sovereign* how majestic is your name in all the earth! You have set

---

* Literally the Psalm begins, "O Yahweh, our Adonai." Most versions translate *Adonai* as "Lord" or "Sovereign" (as in this NRSV translation).

your glory above the heavens" (NRSV). This verse gives the psalmist's impression about the nature of God, what God is in himself. He set his glory "above the heavens." The heavens themselves merely *reflect* the glory of God. He then goes on to pose a question about the purpose of human beings:

> When I look at your heavens, the work of your fingers,
> the moon and the stars that you have established;
> what are human beings that you are mindful of them,
> mortals that you care for them?
> Yet you have made them a little lower than God,
> and crowned them with glory and honor.
>
> (Ps. 8:3–5 NRSV)

Next comes the answer:

> You have given them dominion over the works of your hands;
> you have put all things under their feet,
> all sheep and oxen,
> and also the beasts of the field,
> the birds of the air,
> and the fish of the sea,
> whatever passes along the paths of the seas.
>
> (vv. 6–8 NRSV)

Then he returns to the main theme, "O LORD our Sovereign, how majestic is your name in all the earth!" (v. 9).

What is the heart of the passage? The psalmist is essentially asking God, "In light of the good work you have done—the excellence and greatness of your creation—what good is man?" So I ask you the same question: What good is man? Quite apart from what the Bible says, we know the answer. We believe that people are valuable. But why? Why are *you* valuable? Why are you something that ought to exist, and why is it right that others should help you exist and reach your potential? And why would the magnificent God who created the universe want to be in a personal relationship with you and be your Shepherd?

A World of Good

As we enter into the topic of why there are human beings, it is important to recognize how often the word *good* appears in the first two chapters of Genesis.* What is the first thing that was called good in this story? Light. Would you say that light is good? I think everyone agrees that light is good. Actually, I think that light is wonderful! I'd even go so far as to say it is one of God's better inventions. Light is not something simple; it is very complex, and there are many kinds of light. And with light comes, literally, all the colors of the rainbow. Light is good!

Next came the dome that divided the waters above it from those beneath it.

> Then God said, "Let there be a firmament in the midst of the waters, and let it divide the waters from the waters." Thus God made the firmament, and divided the waters which were under the firmament from the waters which were above the firmament; and it was so. And God called the firmament Heaven. (Gen. 1:6–8)

The word *firmament* here refers to whatever holds up the water above us. There really is water up there. And sometimes it falls, right? We call that rain. God divided the waters, and if they were not divided, we would have a hard time. So rain and water, like light, are good.

I could go on and on about God's creation. He made so many

---

* "Good" in Scripture (*tob* in Hebrew and *kalos* in Greek) conveys excellence, inner and outer beauty, and fulfillment of purpose.

amazing things. Dry land was a great idea. Herbs, grass, and fruit as well. Then came the sun and the moon, which are quite wonderful devices. The sun is good. The moon is good too. As are all the lights in the sky. I find myself agreeing with the writer; it is all good!

Verses 20–25 describe the creation of all the creatures in the sea, in the sky, and on the dry land. Think about the beauty, majesty, and variety of the creatures God made. Notice the way we are drawn to go see them at zoos and aquariums. When I look at them, I find myself thinking of adjectives that go well beyond *good*—especially concerning whales and elephants.

You see, all these creations are good. *Being* is itself good. Being is better than nonbeing. One of the most depressing thoughts you can think is *just nothing*. Occasionally I will get involved in a philosophical discussion with someone who suggests that it would have been better if God had not created anything. In such instances I know I am dealing with someone who is focusing upon some particularly bad thing, like famine or sickness, and the sorrow and pain humans suffer in this world. But, if you weigh all the pain and the suffering against all the joy and the strength you find in human life, it is still good.

And then, after all else, God came to create human beings:

> Then God said, "Let Us make man in Our image, according to Our likeness; let them have dominion over the fish of the sea, over the birds of the air, and over the cattle, over all the earth and over every creeping thing that creeps on the earth." So God created man in His own image; in the image of God He created him; male and female He created them. (Gen. 1:26–27)

God put human beings in charge of the earth. That is, we are to be responsible for the earth and life upon it. It is an assignment that we are still working on today, whether we believe in God or not. If you look at human history, from its most rudimentary form to its most complex, you will see that this is what human beings have always done and continue to do. Although we forget about God in many cases, which is why things often don't work so well, we are still on the project. We are, in our nature, perfectly fitted for what Moses wrote down as the charge that God put on us when we were created: "Be fruitful and multiply; fill the earth and subdue it; have dominion over the fish of the sea, over the birds of the air, and over every living thing that moves on the earth" (v. 28). The charge to humankind was to rule the earth for good. And it was good that it should be so. This is affirmed in verse 31: "God saw everything that He had made, and indeed, it was *very* good."

Yet many people who like the things that creep and crawl around the zoo have some doubts when it comes to human beings. They wonder if the world might not be better off if God had stopped before he created people. Whether this is true or not is the point of this chapter, which seeks to address the challenge by answering two questions: What did God create when he created human beings, and what is especially good about them?

What Are Human Beings?

God created human beings to be different from everything else. We were created to have a special relationship with God and to do our work *in that relationship*. We were to work in a power that was not our own. It is a pretty big job to have dominion over the earth, especially when some of us have a hard time having dominion over a small backyard! A lot of things are at work out there, and it is rather hard to control them.

Genesis 2 describes "a garden eastward in Eden," where the first human beings were placed, being in union with God (v. 8). There was *in* humanity that which was *of* God. "And the LORD God formed man of the dust of the ground, and breathed into his nostrils the breath of life; and man became a living being" (v. 7). The term translated as "living being" is the same word that was used earlier to refer to the whales. The man did not become a moving creature and *then* become a human being. This occurred only in conjunction with God's special creative infusion of something that was like God—*spirit*.

The "breath of life" in verse 7 is not the stuff around us that we breathe in and out. God did not make a little mud baby and get down and give him mouth-to-mouth resuscitation. God does not *literally* breathe; he does not have lungs. But he is spirit, and he infused this special creation with spirit. That's what makes human beings unique, and what gives us our special value. This is what makes each of us unique, and this uniqueness allows us to relate to God and participate in his governing of the earth.

Beyond Belief

It is hard for people to believe that they are spirit-infused beings with such power, privilege, and responsibility. You may feel like you are very far from being in the business of governing the earth. We have accepted an image the world has imposed on us that is in direct opposition to Jesus' teaching and hinders us from stepping into the dignity of the sons and daughters of God. Every human being is a special creation of spirit, living in the hands of God. As Jesus said, all children have guardian angels looking after them—*every child*. When he said this, it was in a context where children were being denigrated, and he said we would be better off being thrown into the depths of the sea with a millstone hung around our necks than offend against a little child.*

But what happens? A child comes into the world and is treated as anything but a precious, wonderful creation. One of the hardest things for us to do—and this is true even for Christians—is to keep

---

* Matthew 18:6–8, 10–14.

this preciousness and wonder in our minds as we approach every human being we deal with. To be sure, people do not always look or act like they are very precious. Perhaps they are filled with hostility and quite dangerous to be around. We hurt one another in so many ways.

There was a hand lotion commercial many years ago that featured a lovely lady who was at a social gathering. She put out her hand to a man, and just as he was going to take it, her hand turned into a cactus. All too often we are like that, prickly to one another, guarding against one another, so much that even a little child can be perceived as a great threat and danger to us.

Here is my point: just as we have a tremendously difficult time conceiving of or imagining what God is like, so we have a tremendously difficult time imagining what people are really like. When the psalmist asked God, "What are human beings that you are mindful of them?" he was expressing this difficulty (Ps. 8:4 NRSV). He had realized that, given the way that God fawns over human beings, we must be something much greater than what we appear to be.

I find it curious that we often speak about people thinking too highly of themselves. I don't think that I have ever met a person who thought highly *enough* of himself. One bit of fallen wisdom claims that we can help people by "keeping them humble," which often means humiliating them. If you watch what happens, you learn that humiliating someone is a sure way *not* to make him humble, in the same way that you cannot make people lovable by hating them, or kind by being cruel to them.

There are many difficulties involved in how we think of ourselves. We cannot envision anyone placing much value on us just for who we are. Think of it this way: imagine that you are a slave on the trading block, and someone is going to make an offer based on your worth. How much do you think he would be willing to pay for you? How you answer that question has a lot to do with how your own society values people in general, since you breathe that same cultural air. Given the way of this world, many of us would not think we would raise much of a price at auction.

Jesus understood this situation when he said, "For what will it profit them if they gain the whole world but forfeit their life? Or what will they give in return for their life?" (Matt. 16:26 NRSV). *You* are the one Jesus was talking about. That is why he put it the way he did. You are the only one who can decide what your soul is worth—what *you* are worth—and trade it for something you deem more valuable. So I ask you, what would *you* trade for your soul? How much are you worth? You are the only one who can decide this and exchange your self for anything.

Where Our Greatness Lies

What is it that makes human beings so precious? It is this: they are capable of being faithful to God and committed to the promotion of good in the world. They are capable of giving their lives for these things, even to the point of dying for them. "No one has greater love than this," Jesus said, "to lay down one's life for one's friends" (John 15:13 NRSV).

Once we understand the greatness of the human soul, we can embrace God's love for us in the giving of his Son. As the apostle Paul put it, "God demonstrates His own love toward us, in that while we were still sinners"—that is, while we were still in rebellion against God—"Christ died for us" (Rom. 5:8). People are valuable even if they're doing nothing; we do not have to *earn* our value. Nevertheless, God put us here to make a difference. Jesus confirmed this with these words, "Let your light so shine before men, that they may see your good works and glorify your Father in heaven" (Matt. 5:16). That one verse encapsulates why there are people—to shine, doing good works and glorifying God—and it is an active process as we live out our lives in the world before God in such a way that people see the goodness of our lives and acknowledge God as the source of that goodness.

Life is made even more valuable because of the sacrifices made by those who give themselves up to God and for God, and for every good thing God has made. That is what God put us here for. That is why we treasure faithfulness, loyalty, and heroism in people. There is something about faithfulness and loyalty between people that is precious and beautiful because it is a reflection of what is possible between man and God. The potential of men and women to give up their lives for the glory of God and for the good that God has created is precisely what makes human life great.

Human life is a process of transition and transformation. We go through life in a belt of time and space with one another, and we have the opportunity to be everything God intended us to be in relationship to him and to those around us. We have the potential to create something incredibly precious and good, and God is going to bring it to pass. If we miss our chance to participate with him, we miss our chance, but he is not going to be defeated in this. He is going to create a community of loving, creative, intelligent, loyal, faithful, and powerful human beings, and they are going to rule the earth. It is going to come to pass. If you want to be a part of that, just get on board.

Let Your Good Works Shine

We are put here on earth and we are given bodies so we can work to bring more good into existence. We are put here to work, for the image of God within us goes far beyond the grand use of our intellect. Some people talk about God as if he just sits around and does mathematical equations or contemplates some exalted form of truth. But God is an *actor*. He is one who acts, one who creates. His essence is seen not just in thought, but also in intelligent action that creates good. This is our calling as well, though in a more limited way.[1]

God created us very like himself (in his image), but every one of us is unique. An original, not a copy. We each are made to assume the role of a particular child of God, and our uniqueness ties in with our unique purpose. God has ensured us a special place and purpose, giving us tasks that he specifically wants us to accomplish in our time and in our place. To this end, God also intended that we should have the freedom to love and serve him—the independent power by which we can choose to give ourselves to him, even, as I have said, to the point of death.

The challenge for us in the creation of good is not usually some big religious issue as we commonly think of it, but in the ordinary stuff of life—our day-to-day living in families, at work, at play. The obviously well-kept secret of the "ordinary" is that it is made to be a receptacle of the divine, a place where the life of God flows. Phillips Brooks, in his book *Best Methods of Promoting Spiritual Life*, acknowledges the role of special religious practices, activities, and experiences. But he goes on to emphasize that to limit our spirituality to these is to omit most of our normal life from spiritual living. To promote spiritual life, he says, is not to be more religious where one is already religious:

> It is to be religious where he is irreligious now; to let the spiritual force which is in him play upon new activities. How shall he open, for instance, his business life to this deep power? By casting out of his business all that is essentially wicked in it, by insisting to himself on its ideal, of charity or usefulness, on the loftiest conception of every relationship into which it brings him with his fellow man, and by making it not a matter of his own whim or choice, but a duty to be done faithfully because God has called him to it. . . . God chose for him his work, and meant for him to find his spiritual education there.[2]

Brooks closes his sermon with these words: "The Christian finds the hand of Christ in everything, and by the faithful use of everything for Christ's sake, he takes firm hold of that hand of Christ and is drawn nearer and nearer to Himself. That is, I think, the best method of promoting spiritual life."[3]

Corrie ten Boom confirmed this in her reflections about working in her father's workshop: "I experienced the miracle that the highest potential of God's love and power is available to us in the trivial things of everyday life."[4]

This steady stream of Christian spirituality through our calling, vocation, and ordinary life flows down through the ages. We have only to step into it, to set ourselves to learn it, and we will see its radiant power at work on the "job," where we are. Our challenge is to fill our hours, minutes, and actions from day to day with the appropriate amount of love for God's creation and creating, and then work to produce more of the good he has put in this world. This is every person's calling.

The Importance of Our Work

Many people believe labor is something to be avoided. (My brother used to joke that he wasn't afraid of work; he could lie down right next to it and go to sleep.) But if we do not work, our lives are wasted because God designed work as a fundamental structure of love in the kingdom of God—something that is meant to bring people together in loving community for mutual benefit and support. What's more, work is a good thing, and it is a natural disposition of human beings from early childhood on. Work is simply human creativity, a special type of causation through which goodness and blessing can be promoted.

Simply put, work is the expending of energy to produce good in various forms and ways. God did not originally intend our work to be difficult—for us to sweat, to grind ourselves back into dust. When Adam was given work to do in the garden, I believe Adam worked the way that Jesus did when dealing with the fig tree that did not bear fruit (Matt. 21:18–19). Jesus didn't say, "Peter, go get the chainsaw." No, he spoke, and it withered away. This is the way Adam worked before the fall. The sweating came because, in disobedience, we broke ourselves off from God and each other and from the energy that would accomplish the good we intend.

If humanity were united under God in love and understanding, we could, with ease, achieve wondrous things far beyond what we can now achieve or imagine (Eph. 3:20). Without such harmonious cooperation we are thrown back on ourselves to do what we can to work and grind out a living on our own. This feeds into our isolation, pride, egotism, and antagonism with others. This is clearly not what God desires.

Your work is the total amount of lasting good that you will accomplish in your lifetime. That might include your job, but for many of us, our families will be the largest part of the lasting good we produce.

Today much that is called work is not the use of energy to produce good. In our fallen world we must distinguish between a job and work, because many "jobs" can produce evil. Your job is what you get paid to do, and it might or might not contribute to lasting good. Of course, some of you may be at a point in your life where you do not have a job or do not want one. That's all right. You still have work to do; you still have the opportunity and responsibility to produce good in the world.

I have a lot of students who do not want a job that requires work; what they want is a *position*. A position is where you have recognition and get paid whether you do anything or not. Additionally, many people base their identity on their work and their job—that is, they think they are what they do. This is problematic because they will identify their jobs with their lives and their personal sense of worth. Then they are apt to draw terribly mistaken conclusions, such as, "Since I do not have a job I am a nobody."

Our work may be of many kinds. It might include having and raising children, developing good personal relations, being artistically creative, leading politically, working in the church of Jesus Christ to spread the truth, building houses, running trains, doing all the necessary work available to human beings as they live together in this world to produce what is good. But regardless of our specific work, the real challenge to every person's faith is that we do everything to the glory of God, even in the smallest actions of our days. And this will certainly entail making sure we do not sacrifice our families to our ministry or jobs.

Here is a truth you must never forget: God is more interested in your life than he is in any of the other things listed above. He's more interested in the person you are becoming than in your work, or your ministry, or your job. And the surest way to realize the full potential of your God-designed self is to live in eternity while you are in time, conscious of the loving gaze of your all-sufficient Shepherd, in whose care nothing of the good you do is lost. It is stored up in your own self and in the lives of others you have touched.

The Challenge of Personal Relationships

The greatest challenge to creating good and living as God has appointed us to live lies primarily within our most intimate personal relationships. This is very difficult to talk about because this is the primary area of human failure. When Satan came to tempt mankind, he tempted us in a way that would, in one blow, rupture the relationship of trust between man and God, and also between man and woman. Then, once this trust was ruptured, the relationship between brothers quickly followed, and we had our first murder. It is a sad story.

The serpent sowed the seed of doubt in Eve's mind and led her to question and mistrust God. That seed of doubt moved her to take action that was contrary to his will, to provide for herself and try to survive. The effect was that she and Adam immediately understood their position; they hid when God came to find them, and the first thing we see is the blame placing that went on in Genesis 3. God calls, "Adam. Adam, where are you? Why are you hiding?" Adam replies, "I was naked and I hid myself" (v. 10 PAR)

We need to be careful here and understand that this reference to nakedness is not chiefly about a lack of clothing. It's true that God allows man to hide, and clothes are no doubt very important. God himself made them, after all (v. 21). Nakedness here, however, refers primarily to human vulnerability. I believe that before the fall, Adam did not see himself as naked and did not realize his vulnerability, because he was surrounded by a glow of light like the one that encompassed Moses on Mount Sinai and Jesus on the Mount of Transfiguration.*

Because of the glow from the light of God resting upon him, Adam did not realize his finitude—he did not realize where he ended and everything else began. Then, after his sin, he certainly did know, and in his vulnerable state he sought to protect himself. He had accepted Eve's invitation, but who did he think was to blame for that? Not *Adam,* surely! And not really the woman. Adam accused *God*, charging him with wrongdoing: *"The woman* you *gave me got us into this!"* Then Eve said, *"Well, the serpent tricked me and I ate the fruit"* (Gen. 3:12–13 PAR). (Interestingly, the serpent is the only one in the story who does not try to pass the buck.)

What Sin Begins

Something momentous and world-changing has now been set in motion. You will see this same pattern in the next chapter of Genesis in the story of Abel and Cain, where mistrust and anger lead to murder (Gen. 4:1–15). The effect of the rupture that sin created in the relationship between the man and the woman is this: mistrust, anger, and disappointment became the standard quality of human

---

* Exodus 34:29–35; Matthew 17:1–5.

life. Even among those of us who have experienced the grace of God, it is rare to find any man and woman who are bound together in marriage who are truly trustful in every respect, and confident, pleased, and satisfied with each other. Rather, there is a constant testing that goes on, and it is a very serious problem.

For example, though it is not as true now as it was in other times, men are often responsible for the financial well-being of a couple's life together, but not many men are smart enough to succeed in that. So the wife is tempted to think, *You know, if this guy were just a little smarter, I'd be a lot better off!* It becomes very easy to get into the posture of doubting the ability of the man, and carrying that sort of mistrust into the midst of the relationship. Correspondingly, most women in our society live with the idea that there is a real possibility that they will be traded in for someone younger and more beautiful. Women often live under a constant threat and wonder, *When is the axe going to fall?* These are just two characteristics of this sin rupture in American society.

It is rare to find a marriage relationship that truly has the grace of God in it to such an extent that both people are completely at home and confident, never in doubt, and full of love and concern for each other. The threats of abandonment I just mentioned hover over most relationships, and people are so busy protecting themselves that they cannot love each other. That violation then spreads down to their children, who also struggle with attacks and withdrawals, doubts and questions that are always there. It is not uncommon that, when a parent leaves due to divorce or death or any of the other things that are beyond the child's responsibility, the first thing the child thinks is, *I am to blame; I am the one responsible,* even though it's entirely out of their hands.

The element of mistrust makes it impossible for people to confidently step forward in the grace of God and realize the goodness that God intended them to have in their relationship to one another. The apostle Paul believed that the grace of God, as it came in Jesus

Christ, was sufficient to heal the relationship between men and women. Yet it was still necessary for him to teach about it; the healing does not happen automatically without effort on both parts.

Portrait of a Healed Relationship

In Ephesians we find the teaching of mutual submission and the responsibilities of the husband and of the wife. Please note that submission is *not* assigning our responsibility to others, abandoning our own judgment, or allowing others to simply dictate to us. It is setting aside our own ideas as supreme and our own will as ultimate, freeing us from the burden of having our own way and of being all-wise in our own eyes.* Saint Paul's instruction about submission comes within the larger teaching about the community of love:

> Wives, submit to your own husbands, as to the Lord. For the husband is head of the wife, as also Christ is head of the church; and He is the Savior of the body. Therefore, just as the church is subject to Christ, so let the wives be to their own husbands in everything.
>
> Husbands, love your wives, just as Christ also loved the church and gave Himself for her, that He might sanctify and cleanse her with the washing of water by the word, that He might present her to Himself a glorious church, not having spot or wrinkle or any such thing, but that she should be holy and without blemish. So husbands ought to love their own wives as their own bodies; he who loves his wife loves himself. For no one ever hated his own flesh, but nourishes and cherishes it, just as the Lord does the church. (Eph. 5:22–29)

This is the central point I was making above concerning the calling of human beings to give themselves to the good, even up to

---

* Hebrews 13:17.

the point of dying for it. Paul is saying here that we are to give ourselves up. The husband is to give himself up for the wife as Christ gave himself up for the church. I doubt that there are many wives in the world who confidently feel their husbands have loved them in that way. Some have. The pity is that many times, even if they have been loved this way, it is impossible for them to be confident about it because of their own lack of appropriate self-image. In such cases it is quite beside the point whether the husband loves the wife that way or not; it would be impossible for her to be confident about it and receive it. Those aspects of doubt and mistrust about ourselves lead us into the games we play in love relationships as we try to get the other person to prove their love. Of course, this always flows from a completely neurotic feeling of worthlessness that no human "proof" can dissuade.

Notice the parallel Paul made between marriage and the church. In the case of the church, whose members have these same feelings of worthlessness and other problems, Christ intends to present it to himself as glorious nonetheless. That is why he came. Likewise, the husband is to think of the wife in this same way, that she would be glorious, and that he would help her to be glorious. The wife, too, would think in the same way regarding the glory of her husband. It almost makes your heart break with grief as you think about the way human relationships actually go and how far short of this they fall.

The Glorious Potential of the Human Race

Remember, I am using the example of husbands and wives to illustrate *why there are people*. People exist to love as Jesus loved. Indeed, the aim of God in human history is the creation of an all-inclusive community of loving persons with himself at the center of that community—as its prime sustainer and most glorious inhabitant. In Jesus' life and death on behalf of all human beings, we behold God's estimate of our worth and the fervency of his desire to create that glorious community. We are made for love, and God was willing to send his own Son to die that he might secure it for us (Rom. 8:32).

The greatest thing God will be showing off in eternity is this society of redeemed persons. This is what Paul was saying in his letter to the Ephesian Christians. In the third chapter, Paul talked about the mystery of the Gentiles being included in the grace of God, and the plan of God for the ages. Then he wrote,

> To me, who am less than the least of all the saints, this grace was given, that I should preach among the Gentiles the unsearchable riches of Christ, and to make all see what is the fellowship of the mystery, which from the beginning of the ages has been hidden in God who created all things through Jesus Christ; to the intent that now the manifold wisdom of God might be made known by the church to the principalities and powers in the heavenly places, according to the eternal purpose which He accomplished in Christ Jesus our Lord. (Eph. 3:8–11)

More than anything else, what will display the wisdom of God throughout eternity is his people redeemed in Jesus Christ.

One final point. You may remember how, when the sons of God came before God in the first chapter of Job, God said to Satan, "Have you considered my servant Job?" (1:8). God was proud of Job. Indeed, he was justly proud of him, even though Job had a long way to go. There is nothing that makes God happier than human beings, redeemed by the grace of God, devoting their lives—the moments and hours of their days—to the good of others and of creation, to the glory of God. That is our privilege, and the reason we are here. That is what humans are, why God pays attention to us, and why God abides with us. The answer to the psalmist is clear: "What are human beings that you are mindful of them, mortals that you care for them?" (Ps. 8:4 NRSV). Just God's greatest treasure in all his created works.

CHAPTER 4

Why Such Lack and Evil?

The fact that "devils" are predominantly comic
figures in the modern imagination will help you. If
any faint suspicion of your existence begins to arise
in his mind, suggest to him a picture of something
in red tights, and persuade him that since he cannot
believe in that (it is an old textbook method of
confusing them) he therefore cannot believe in you.
—UNCLE SCREWTAPE'S ADVICE TO WORMWOOD,
C. S. LEWIS'S *THE SCREWTAPE LETTERS*

For most of us, the thought of a life without lack is unimaginable because we live in a world so obviously full of lack—lack of kindness, fairness, and compassion, all of which are more precious because they seem so rare. So much is going wrong all around us: injustice, oppression, natural disasters, broken relationships, perversity, selfishness, pride, and apathy, so much pain that it seems we would need to block it all out and pretend that all is well to have any hope for a semblance of safety and sufficiency. Yet it is not pretense we need, but understanding.

We live in a world under the care of a wholly good God with unlimited power, who lacks nothing and intends only good for his creation. Why, then, is there so much lack and evil? What has gone wrong? Many people believe that the source of these problems rests with humanity alone, but we must acknowledge the activity of Satan here. His presence in the world accounts for the seemingly unlimited extent of human wrongdoing that goes far beyond what humanity (made in the image of God) would generate on its own. He has humanity in his grasp through the ideas, beliefs, and bastions of wickedness he has developed throughout history, and he intends to keep them there. He works in the realm of the heart and ideas, in their individual as well as social forms, to control the major structures and processes of human life upon the earth.

As we will see in the next chapter, the secret to a life without lack is faith in God and in God's full capacity and willingness to meet all our needs—and more. But what is faith? It is simply an understanding of how things are, wedded to a commitment to live one's life in light of that understanding.

Part of the problem with our faith today is that we do not truly believe in the reality of the spiritual, either the good side or the evil side. In our world people maintain their sense of respectability by rejecting everything except what they can see in the natural world. To accept that there is more than that threatens their self-identity as proper, intelligent citizens of the modern world. But the perspective of the modern world is not the perspective of the Bible, and it is from the biblical perspective that I will be addressing the primary source of lack and evil in the world today.

Our understanding of how things are must include belief in the devil and knowledge of his character and intentions. If you know enough about him and understand him, you will find that you can have faith in him too. People who engage in explicit devil worship understand this; they know it to be true. But we who do not worship Satan also need to have faith that he will do exactly what he is intent on doing. You'd better be ready for it.

Do you know where the devil is now? He's in heaven, engaged in warfare right now. The Bible speaks of three heavens: the heaven of the air around us, the heaven of the angels, and then the heaven of heavens, the place where God himself dwells.[1] According to Paul, Satan's realm is that first heaven where he is "the prince of the power of the air" (Eph. 2:2). John also called him "the prince of this world."*

As we see in the story of Job, Satan also occasionally goes into the highest of the heavens into the presence of God. Why would God allow that? God is demonstrating to all the citizens of the heavens that he has an agenda. As we have seen, that agenda involves creating a community of free beings who have the power to act contrary to God and to undergo temptation. Satan is serving God's purposes on earth as part of that arrangement.

Satan: The Early Years

Satan is described to us in Scripture as a special angel who at one time oversaw what we now call the earth, and possibly the entire solar system. This is what Paul was referring to when he called Satan "the prince of the power of the air" (Eph. 2:2). At first this rule would have been a benevolent one, overseeing a part of God's good and perfect creation. At some point, however, he desired to be like God and fell away from God. We see a description of this in the fourteenth chapter of Isaiah. As is often the case in the Hebrew prophets, we find Isaiah dealing with a situation specific to his time, and then suddenly his words project beyond that to another time and place. As the chapter begins, Isaiah is clearly discussing the earthly king of Babylon. But then, suddenly, in verses 12–13:

> "How you are fallen from heaven,
> O Lucifer, son of the morning!
> How you are cut down to the ground,
> You who weakened the nations!

---

* John 12:31; 14:30; and 16:11.

For you have said in your heart:
'I will ascend into heaven,
I will exalt my throne above the stars of God.'"

Given that the heaven of the stars and the angels is lower than the heaven of heavens, God's dwelling place, Satan is essentially saying, "I'm going to put my throne right in there where God's throne is." His prideful boast continues in verses 13 and 14:

"I will also sit on the mount of the congregation
On the farthest sides of the north;
I will ascend above the heights of the clouds,
I will be like the Most High."

This sounds very much like the serpent's temptation of Eve: "You will be like God" (Gen. 3:5).

The prophet Ezekiel further described Satan's rebellion against God. In the beginning of chapter 28, Ezekiel is dealing with a specific historical situation involving the king of Tyre. But then verse 13 states, "You were in Eden, the garden of God." Surely the king of Tyre couldn't have been in the garden of Eden. Once again, as in Isaiah, we find the shift that so often happens in the prophetic books, and suddenly another figure begins to emerge. Ezekiel continues:

"You were the anointed cherub who covers;
I established you;
You were on the holy mountain of God;
You walked back and forth in the midst of fiery stones.
You were perfect in your ways from the day you were created,
Till iniquity was found in you.

"By the abundance of your trading
You became filled with violence within,

And you sinned;
Therefore, I cast you as a profane thing
Out of the mountain of God;
And I destroyed you, O covering cherub,
From the midst of the fiery stones.

"Your heart was lifted up because of your beauty;
You corrupted your wisdom for the sake of your splendor;
I cast you to the ground,
I laid you before kings,
That they might gaze at you.

(vv. 14–17)

Then the language gradually comes back to the human king of Tyre in the verses that follow.

We may learn from both accounts that in his original form, Satan had a primary role in relation to the earth, undoubtedly the role of the governor of the earth. We have no information on what else that may have meant in terms of the solar system. He was a powerful being, and many were with him.* In rebellion against God he fell from his exalted position and became the tempter of human beings.

The only way the devil can hurt God is through humans, and so he focuses upon us. His strategy is to try to frustrate God's purpose for humanity, beginning at "the beginning" in the garden of Eden. Through deceit and temptation he succeeded in diverting the plan of God for Adam and Eve and their descendants. But you must understand this: Satan can do nothing about God's unshakable kingdom *directly*, but only indirectly through human infirmity and rebellion. His way of doing that is to persuade, and to tempt, and to deceive humanity.

---

* According to Revelation 12:3–9, Satan's rebellion included one-third of the angels in heaven.

In God's Crosshairs

If we look at Satan's work from beginning to end in the Bible, from the opening chapters of Genesis to the concluding chapter of Revelation, we see a clear pattern: Satan's constant deception of human beings. This means, if God is going to achieve his ultimate purpose for human beings, the defeat of Satan is of central importance. Jesus came into the world to this end.

As 1 John 3:8 says, "He who sins is of the devil, for the devil has sinned from the beginning. For this purpose, the Son of God was manifested, that He might destroy the works of the devil." In the gospel of Matthew, when Joseph learned that Mary was pregnant and considered divorcing her, an angel appeared to him and said, "Joseph, son of David, do not be afraid to take to you Mary your wife, for that which is conceived in her is of the Holy Spirit. And she will bring forth a Son, and you shall call His name Jesus, for He will save His people from their sins" (Matt. 1:20–21). To save people from sin is to destroy sin, which in turn is to destroy the works of the devil.

Satan, then, is God's primary target, for he is the one who bears the primary responsibility for all that is wrong with the world. Now you may say that I am not giving humans enough responsibility in this. Well, we do bear sufficient responsibility, for we make choices and we bear the consequences as we live with the mess that is human history. But the reality of evil and lack in our world makes it impossible to place the full blame on human ingenuity or action. While it is true that much of the pain and suffering in the world could be avoided if human beings would not just lie down and accept it all, the question is, why don't they actively resist it?*

---

* Editor's Note: On this point the words of Henry David Thoreau quoted in *The Spirit of the Disciplines* are apropos: "Thus men will lie on their backs, talking about the fall of man, and never make an effort to get up." Quoted in Dallas Willard, *The Spirit of the Disciplines: Understanding How God Changes Lives* (San Francisco: Harper & Row Publishers, 1988), 11.

The answer is, because Satan deceives and misleads people and thereby prevents them from making the kind of connection with God that would work against the effects of sin in the world.

Each year at Christmastime we celebrate the event known as the incarnation, when the Son of God took on a human body. Why was this necessary? In Hebrews 2:14 we are given an answer:

Inasmuch then as the children have partaken of flesh and blood, He Himself likewise shared in the same, that through death He might destroy him who had the power of death, that is, the devil.

Satan had the power of death, the power to separate people from God and to use death as an instrument for repressing and managing human beings. It is of fundamental importance to understand that, while he has plenty of helpers, there is one principal agent of evil in the universe, Satan, and his intent is to thwart God's purposes by manipulating the minds of human beings. That is his intent, and he has been quite effective at achieving it.

It is hard for many of us to believe in the reality of the devil, but the apostle Paul certainly thought such belief was correct. He wrote to the Christians of Ephesus:

Finally, my brethren, be strong in the Lord and in the power of His might. Put on the whole armor of God, that you may be able to stand against the wiles of the devil. (Eph. 6:10–11)

Notice that he did not say "the wiles of your neighbors," which is where we might think all the world's problems lie. The real danger lies not with other people; they are not the enemy. Paul continued,

For we do not wrestle against flesh and blood, but against princi-palities, against powers, against the rulers of the darkness of this

age, against spiritual hosts of wickedness in the heavenly places.
(v. 12)

Notice that curious phrase, "spiritual hosts of wickedness." Today the word *spiritual* is used mainly to mean something good. We speak of a person being spiritual and mean it as a compliment. But from a biblical perspective this is not the case; there are evil spiritual beings in the heavenly realms. These beings, led by Satan, are the ultimate enemies both of God and of all humanity. When we seek to understand and destroy evil in the world, we must realize that we are dealing with something far beyond our natural capabilities, and we need to address evil with that realization. It is no less true when we are speaking about the Christian life; if we are to succeed in walking in the way of Jesus and knowing the life without lack, it is essential that we understand and believe the devil is real and at work.

Satan's Three Weapons of Temptation

In his letter to the believers in Ephesus, Paul describes the general condition of their lives prior to placing their faith in Christ:

> And you He made alive, who were dead in trespasses and sins, in which you once walked according to the course of this world, according to the prince of the power of the air, the spirit who now works in the sons of disobedience, among whom also we all once conducted ourselves in the lusts of our flesh, fulfilling the desires of the flesh and of the mind, and were by nature children of wrath, just as the others. (Eph. 2:1–3)

We must take what Paul says here very seriously, for he is revealing the answer to our questions concerning why there is such lack and evil in the world, and why human beings are caught up in it. Here are the essential points we must grasp:

- Satan is a spiritual being who is the primary ruler in the domain called the "air."
- The "air" is not far off, but all around us.
- Satan, then, is immediately present in this world as its "prince" and chief influencer.
- Prior to placing their faith in Christ and being given new life in him, people are "dead in trespasses and sins" and are, whether they know it or not, under the influence of Satan.
- This is what the phrase "sons of disobedience," means; like father, like son (or daughter).

If we are to know the abundant provision of God's unlimited resources, we must also understand how Satan works to rob us of that experience. He does so by deceit. You may have heard the saying that the way to know if certain people are lying is if their lips are moving. This is absolutely true of Satan. Jesus referred to him as "a liar and the father of lies" (John 8:44 NRSV). Indeed, his whole kingdom is based on lies; he works by deceiving. Why? Because he does not have direct power over our will. Therefore, if he is to get us to do his bidding, he has to fool us. He cannot *make* us do anything we do not *want* to do. If it is true that a person can be the devil's puppet, the strings are Satan's lies.

Satan uses three primary weapons to oppose God and derail our experience of God's sufficiency, all of which are forms of temptation. In the first of the apostle John's short letters, he urges us not to love "the world" (1 John 2:15). John is not referring to the created world of nature, with all its magnificence and beauty, nor even to the many good things that make up the world of human culture. He is referring specifically to those aspects of our world, especially our cultural and social practices, that are under the control of Satan and, thus, opposed to God. This "world" is marked by three spiritual dynamics that John identifies as "the lust of the flesh, the lust of the eyes, and the pride of life" (1 John 2:16). We often associate the word *lust* primarily with sexual temptation, and that certainly is a powerful one. But there are many other kinds of lust, so a better word is probably *desire*—wanting something that appears to be good for some purpose or pleasure.

Satan, then, tempts us through deception, and this deception comes in the three forms the apostle John mentions above: the desires of the flesh, the desires of the eyes, and the pride of life. If we look again at the story of Adam and Eve in the garden, we can clearly see this ploy in action. Here is how the scene is described: "So when the woman saw that the tree was good for food, that it was pleasant to the eyes, and a tree desirable to make one wise, she took of its fruit and ate. She also gave to her husband with her, and he ate" (Gen. 3:6). Satan is laying on the temptation by lying, as is his nature. Notice there are three things about the tree that caught Eve's attention. It was (1) good for food, (2) pleasant to the eyes, and (3) desirable to make one wise. Look how these line up precisely with John's three characteristics of "the world":

It is not a mere coincidence that these two lists match. We are presented here with fundamental dynamics of the human condition under Satanic delusion. Observe how it worked on Eve: "So

EVE'S TEMPTATION	THE WORLD
Good for food	The desire of the flesh
Pleasant to the eyes	The desire of the eyes
Desirable to make one wise	The pride of life

when the woman *saw that the tree was good for food*." Here we see the woman looking at something that appears good to her. It is this *appearance of being good* that is at the center of temptation's power. It wasn't truly good, of course, but *seemed* so to Eve. When she succumbed to the temptation she was, in fact, obeying Satan, who always works by saying, *"Oh, wouldn't you like this?"*

And we respond, "Well, yes, I would like that."

To which Satan in turn replies, *"Go for it! Have it your way!"*

Adam followed suit, believing that what's good for the goose is good for the gander. In fact it was not good for either of them.

Tempted in All Ways Like Us

When Jesus began his ministry immediately after being baptized by his cousin John, his first challenge involved undergoing severe temptation at the hands of Satan.

God's Spirit led him into the wilderness for that precise purpose. The testing took place over a period of forty days, during which time Jesus was confronted with three kinds of temptations. First, with Jesus experiencing hunger pangs from fasting, Satan suggested a way of proving that he is the Son of God: turn hard stones into edible bread. Jesus' response? "It is written, 'Man shall not live by bread alone, but by every word that proceeds from the mouth of God'" (Matt. 4:4).

Next, Satan urged Jesus to prove his bona fides by leaping off the pinnacle of the Jerusalem temple so people could watch angels catch and gently set him on the ground. Jesus' response: "It is written again, 'You shall not tempt the LORD your God'" (v. 7).

Finally, the devil tempted Jesus to worship him in exchange for becoming king of the world. Jesus silenced him with these words: "Away with you, Satan! For it is written, 'You shall worship the LORD your God, and Him only you shall serve'" (v. 10).

Notice how Jesus' temptations align with both those of Eve in the garden and John's threefold description of "the world" (the Satanic system of life).

Now it is easy to see that the first items on each list coincide. But what about the devil's challenge that Jesus throw himself off the pinnacle of the temple? What does this appeal to? Notice that this temptation involves Satan saying, "If you are the Son of God"

JESUS' TEMPTATION	EVE'S TEMPTATION	THE WORLD
Turning stones into bread	Good for food	Desire of the flesh
Jumping off the temple	Pleasant to the eyes	Desire of the eyes
Political power and glory	Desirable to make one wise	The pride of life

(v. 6). That is a messianic title. Wouldn't Jesus have been a big shot around Jerusalem if he had come fluttering down from the temple? Everyone would have said, "Oh, you must be the Messiah!" That is about *appearance.* It touches upon the human desire to look good in other people's eyes, to be well thought of. We all know the tug. But is that really an example of "the desire of the eyes"? As in the case of Eve, we usually think this refers to things we look upon and find appealing. But *wanting to look good to others* is also a form of the desire of the eyes.

When Satan's third attempt was to offer Jesus all the kingdoms of the world and their glory, he was hoping Jesus would yield to what he, Satan, knew so well: the temptation of the big ego—pride of one's own power and accomplishments. Imagine being the king (or queen) of the world. What power! What glory! Now that would be something. Jesus didn't take the bait.

Temptation always comes in those three forms. Satan's way of dealing with people is to catch them up in these three patterns and then make them think they are doing what *they* want to do. He causes them to obsess over the immediate things they want, and he assures them that all will be well. There's no need to be concerned about the consequences. He whispers, "Everything is going to be okay. Don't worry; be happy. Get in there and go for it! Come on, Eve. Come on, Jesus. Come on, Dallas." The pull can be nearly ir-resistible. As you admire some wonderful thing, Satan comes along to provide you with an armload of reasonable explanations of why you are justified in having it, and how it would be quite all right after all, moral qualms aside.

Masters of Justification

You can be sure that when Cain committed the first murder recorded in the Bible, his killing of Abel, he was completely justified in his mind. When God came around afterward and asked, "Where is Abel your brother?" Cain's retort was, "I do not know. Am I my brother's keeper?" (Gen. 4:9). Do you see the avoidance in that answer? The wheels in Cain's head were grinding away, mass-producing excuses and evasions. He had his answers ready. Why did he say he didn't know where Abel was? Surely he was lying right on the ground where he left him. Maybe Cain said to himself, *Well, I am not 100 percent certain where he is. After all, the vultures might have devoured him and he could be nowhere to be found.* He knew exactly where his brother was, but since he had justified the murder in his mind, he would have said anything to avoid the truth.

We are no different; we, too, are masters of self-justification and deception. The foolishness of it all is obvious if we stop to think about it. But Satan counts on our *not* stopping to think about it. Satan hooks us by deceiving us and leading us into all these foolish ways of thinking about our desires: to dominate others, to look good, to enjoy what our body cries out for. These become preeminent in our minds, the driving force in our behavior, and the source of so much of the evil in the world.

There is nothing wrong in itself with looking good. Jesus said, "Consider the lilies of the field, how they grow: they neither toil nor spin; and yet I say to you that even Solomon in all his glory was not arrayed like one of these" (Matt. 6:28–29). People will labor day and night to have their bodily parts modified, twisted and turned in the right directions—all to try to look good. It's fine to look fine. The questions are: *Why* do we want to look good? What is our motivation? And what are we willing to do to accomplish it?

Likewise, there is nothing wrong with eating, but if you are *living to eat*, then your god is your belly. Power is good in the same way. We need to exercise power because we were created to do so. We need to have a responsible effect on the world in which we live. At times we need to guide others, to direct them, or to tell them what to do. We may even need to lean on them a little bit to do something. That's all right if it isn't our egos trying to manipulate them for our own purposes. The whole strategy and system of Satan is at work to get us to do just that, which is why there is so much lying, deceit, manipulation, and domination in our world.

And so much fear.

Fearing for Our Desires

Satan uses not only our desires to deceive us but also our fears. Fear that we will not get what we desire can provide the motivation for actions that cause so many of our problems. When you compare the three main sources of temptation—desires of the flesh, desires of our eyes, and the pride of life—with the things we fear, you will find that nearly all our fears are grounded in our desires.

Depending upon our circumstances, we are frightened that our needs for physical things will not be met. But truth be told, most of us would rather die of starvation than look bad. And we are also afraid of what other people will do to us—that they will either hurt us physically or hurt us in other ways, such as thwarting our career goals. Given the world in which we live, these are not unfounded fears. Not a day goes by—not a minute—in which someone is not harmed in one way or another by a fellow human being.

We will deal with this issue more in the coming chapters, but if we are to experience a life without lack as we go out into the world every day, we must, by the grace of God, deal with these fears—or we will be in bondage to Satan. We will be bound both in terms of fear and the temptation to meet our needs in a way that is not right before God, which reveals our lack of faith in him and lack of trust in his all-sufficient care and strength.

Thoughts of the Heart

After Satan pulled his original trick on Eve in Genesis 3, we see one person after another falling in lock step behind the great deceiver. By the time of Noah, things on earth had reached a crisis point. While we do not have a lot of information, what we do know is dreadful. So dreadful, in fact, that when God viewed the human condition he essentially said it was all but hopeless. We are given a mournful and fateful description of the situation in Genesis 6:

> Then the LORD saw that the wickedness of man was great in the earth, and that every intent of the thoughts of his heart was only evil continually. And the LORD was sorry that He had made man on the earth, and He was grieved in His heart. So the LORD said, "I will destroy man whom I have created from the face of the earth, both man and beast, creeping thing and birds of the air, for I am sorry that I have made them." (Gen. 6:5–7)

What a tragic commentary! How did things get so bad with what God once declared to be so "very good"? The short answer, which should no longer be surprising, is Satan. It is revealing that right before we read of God's decision to destroy all human and animal life on earth (one family notwithstanding) we find these words: "Then the LORD saw that the wickedness of man was great in the earth, and that every intent of the thoughts of his heart was only evil continually" (v. 5).

When God looks at human wickedness, he is not looking

exclusively at our actions, but at our minds and hearts, our thoughts and intentions.* God looks on the heart for two reasons: (1) our heart is the source of our actions and life,** but more important here, (2) our thoughts are where Satan plies his trade.*** He governs through images, through ideas, through feelings and fears. From this complex arena of our minds and hearts come most of our actions, so this is the arena where Satan focuses his work.

Again I remind you, human beings cannot be forced to do evil. They cannot be forced to do good either. They must choose to do evil or good. How do they choose? By being persuaded that one course of action is better than another. So Satan works upon the heart through the mind, as he did with Eve, and as he will with us today.

Of First Concern

As Solomon warns us to "keep your heart with all diligence, for out of it spring the issues of life" (Prov. 4:23), our first concern must be for our hearts. The heart is our point of contact with God's unlimited capacity to protect and provide, which flows to those who choose to keep their minds fixed on him. Remember Paul's words to the believers in Rome, when he said that the downward spiral of history began with humanity's choice not to retain God in their knowledge (Rom. 1:28). This choice still leads downward today.

Deciding to fill our minds with God is how we keep our hearts. To listen to his Word and nourish our whole beings with it is not a nice thing we might do occasionally. Our very lives depend upon it. The psalmist gave us the prescription for life when he declared, "Your word I have treasured in my heart, that I might not sin against You" (Ps. 119:11 NASB). God speaks life-giving truth to us in his Word, which is living and active and able to judge the thoughts and

---

* 1 Samuel 16:7.
** Proverbs 4:23.
*** Matthew 16:23; 1 Chronicles 21:1; 2 Thessalonians 2:9.

intentions of the heart (Heb. 4:12). We need to cultivate a readiness to listen.

When the prophet Samuel was a young boy, Eli the priest gave him unerring advice on listening for the voice of God. It is a simple but profound prayer: "Speak, LORD, for Your servant hears" (1 Sam. 3:9). When we get up out of bed in the morning, among our first thoughts should be this: *Lord, speak to me. I'm listening. I want to hear your voice.* This is not because it's a nice way to start the day, but because the only thing that can keep us straight is being full of God and full of his Word. If you don't do something like this, *you do not have the option of having a neutral mind.* Your thoughts cannot be empty. As the old saying goes, nature abhors a vacuum. If you are not entertaining God's truth, you will be entertaining Satan's lies. This is what happened to each one living in the days of Noah when "every intent of the thoughts of his heart was only evil continually" (Gen. 6:5). Now contrast that with Jesus.

A Lesson from the Victorious One

When Satan confronted Jesus, he did not pick him up and throw him off the pinnacle of the temple. Nor did he turn the stone into a loaf of bread and stuff it in Jesus' mouth. He did not have the power to do that. He had to appeal to Jesus and then wait for Jesus' response. What was that response? It was not, "Who do you think you are? Do you know who *I* am? I am the Son of God, you pip-squeak! Now scram!" No, Jesus responded with the Word of God. Rather than speak on his own behalf, he used the Scriptures to respond to Satan. He spoke them directly to him, using the authority of God's Word to defend himself against Satan's attempted deceptions.

All three temptations received the same response: "It is written. It is written. It is written." Satan did not argue back. He simply left Jesus alone—at least temporarily. We are told that after the final temptation in the wilderness "[the devil] departed from Him until an opportune time" (Luke 4:13). We are not told when, but the implication is that he came back. Indeed, you can be sure that Satan was Jesus' constant companion during the days of his flesh. He was never very far away.

Satan was fully aware that only Jesus could break his grip on the human world, devoted as it is to power and deceit, and only Jesus could deliver human beings from the mire of sin and evil in which they floundered. He knew Jesus to be the only truly radical person to enter human history, for he would refuse to use evil to defeat evil. He would set alight a new order that does not employ the devices evil persons use to try to secure themselves and get their way.

Everything rested upon Satan's defeat of Jesus. If Satan could prove that it was impossible for a flesh-and-blood human to do the will of God, he would have defeated God's great project that began with creation. He would have shown that the idea of creating an even more glorious universe by bringing God's church to fullness was impossible, a divine pipe dream. And perhaps—just perhaps, for it's hard to read Satan's mind—he thought tricking Jesus would give him a few more millennia before he met his final destiny. Whatever he thought, he was sorely disappointed by Jesus, who later told his disciples in the Upper Room just before his arrest in Gethsemane, that "the ruler of this world is coming, and *he has nothing in Me*" (John 14:30).

The Battle Plan in the Garden

How Satan wanted to find something in him! He wanted to be able to get inside Jesus' mind in the same way he got inside Eve's mind. That is what the Garden of Gethsemane was about; it was the final struggle between Satan and Jesus. From the beginning of Jesus' earthly life, Satan had tried to destroy or deflect him. And in the final hours before the cross, Satan tried to break Jesus down by pressuring him with the hopelessness, in human terms, of what

Jesus was attempting. Satan's aim was to prevent the redemptive act of crucifixion—the one thing that would open the doors to deliver humanity from the grasp of evil by demonstrating the power of good over evil—and he brought all his demonic power to bear upon Jesus.[2]

Jesus' will was invincible, but the victory was not without a great struggle. Indeed, he sweated great drops of blood from withstanding Satan's effort to turn him away from the cross. We sometimes see Jesus portrayed in the Garden of Gethsemane as cowering in the face of upcoming death, begging God to allow him to live, and unable to do anything about what would be done to him. He is depicted, in short, as a pathetic victim. But in light of who he was—and is—we would err badly if we were to accept this interpretation. There is no indication anywhere in the Scriptures that Jesus was afraid to suffer and die. He was not trying to avoid the cross. He was overcoming Satan. Once this was accomplished and the way to the cross was clear, Jesus was as serene as anyone you can imagine.

With humanity under his direction, Satan used people to torture Jesus. His goal was either to see Jesus die in the beating or to provoke Jesus into asserting his miraculous powers against those who were harming him. In either case, Jesus' progression toward the cross, and the radical act of redemption in world history, would be prevented, and Satan would continue his rule. But to Satan's chagrin, Jesus himself was in charge of the events and people involved in the story. He had "set his face" toward this goal—like a football player who sees the whole field and anticipates every move—to achieve his end of blowing open a carefully prepared but tiny cultural enclave of redemption and stepping upon the stage of world history (Luke 9:51). As he said at a crucial turning point in his career: "I, when I am lifted up from the earth [in crucifixion], will draw all people to myself" (John 12:32 NRSV). We need to see clearly the profound wisdom of his chosen path toward his goal. This was the Trinity's winning strategy to break down the rule of Satan, and with its accomplishment Jesus stands quietly at the center of the contemporary world, as he himself predicted.

The events of Christ's death and resurrection demonstrated to his followers and other observers that what Jesus said about the kingdom and its availability was and is true. To live through and beyond torture and the cross in resurrection life shows the presence of God among men. Knowledge of this presence and the unfailing availability of God to those who trust him led Jesus to say all the beautiful things that we wistfully acknowledge but hardly believe to be true: all those things about birds and flowers being in the care of God, and about how we need never be anxious or afraid, no matter what comes, even crucifixion.

Jesus' basic idea about this world—with all its evil, pushed to the limit in what he went through going toward and nailed upon the cross—is that this world is a perfectly good and safe place for anyone to be, no matter the circumstances, *if* they have placed their lives in the hands of Jesus and his Father. In such a world we never have to do what we know to be wrong, and we never need be afraid. Jesus practiced what he preached, even as he was tortured and killed. And multitudes of his followers have chosen to do the same.

If at First You Don't Succeed . . .

Jesus' victory over Satan in the garden was such that we do not hear of any further encounter between them in the gospels. Perhaps Satan stayed around to see what happened, but when Jesus was nailed to the cross and soon cried out, "Father, into Your hands I commit My spirit" (Luke 23:46), Satan knew he had been defeated and his attention now was to be focused on those who believed in Jesus. For millennia this has been his primary engagement—his effort to defeat Jesus' followers—and it will continue to be so until the end of human history. His ultimate destiny is described in the book of Revelation:

Then I saw an angel coming down from heaven, having the key to the bottomless pit and a great chain in his hand. He laid hold of the dragon, that serpent of old, who is the Devil and Satan, and bound him for a thousand years; and he cast him into the bottomless pit, and shut him up, and set a seal on him, so that he should deceive the nations no more till the thousand years were finished. But after these things he must be released for a little while . . .

Now when the thousand years have expired, Satan will be released from his prison and will go out to deceive the nations which are in the four corners of the earth, Gog and Magog, to gather them together to battle, whose number is as the sand of the sea. They went up on the breadth of the earth and surrounded the camp of the saints and the beloved city. And fire came down from God out of heaven and devoured them. The devil, who deceived them, was cast into the lake of fire and brimstone where the beast and the false prophet are. And they will be tormented day and night forever and ever. (Rev. 20:1–3, 7–10)

This is Satan's ultimate destiny. It's a done deal, and he knows it. He and his minions all know where they are headed, as evidenced by Jesus' encounter with two demon-possessed men near the Sea of Galilee (Matt. 8:28–34). The demons, of course, recognized Jesus and shouted at him, "What have we to do with You, Jesus, You Son of God? Have You come here to torment us before the time?" (v. 29). They are referring to the time of their demise. They knew what was going to happen to them, and their only joy, if you can call it that, was in serving Satan until the end. That service, in which they are now engaged, is the deception of the nations, tricking people into thinking they are in control, that they know what they are doing, when all the while they are on the dancing end of Satan's strings.

A Whirling World of Ideas

The spiritual world is a populous place, and the Bible presents us with a picture of ongoing warfare between the forces aligned with God and those with Satan. If you look at passages such as Daniel 10:13–20, you will see that there are various levels of evil spirits under Satan's command, at work in the world and at work on us. At the same time there are vast numbers of "holy ones" (Dan. 4:17), God's angels doing his bidding, serving his purposes. While we should be aware of this constant interaction of spiritual forces, we must remember that *the primary means Satan uses to keep the evil pot boiling are the ideas that govern society's individuals.* Of central importance are the ideas about what is good and what is right, and how things should be done.

Ideas are subtle things. As with the motion of the earth, which occurs without our noticing it, we are normally unaware of the ideas moving us. We are hurtling through space in an incredible sort of whirligig way at a tremendous speed. If you think about it much, it might make you want to lie down and hug the earth! The ideas that govern our lifestyles are even more disconcerting, for they cause people to behave in ways that undermine their own well-being. In the words of Paul, without knowing it, people are "tossed to and fro and carried about with every wind of doctrine, by the trickery of men, in the cunning craftiness of deceitful plotting" (Eph. 4:14). And behind all that trickery and craftiness is the great trickster, the devil.

Satan governs nations by the way people understand themselves. One example of this is found in the United States, where we talk about "the American way" of life. There is certainly something good in that, and in the foundational principles upon which the country was built. But by the time it gets presented on television, in newspapers, and through other media, or even sometimes in our churches, it has been turned into something tremendously destructive. For example, most Americans think that they ought to be able to do what they want to do whenever they want to do it. This understanding of freedom is often identified with the American way of life. That is as crude and straightforward a statement of Satan as you will ever find. If there is anything you ought *not* to do, it is to do what you want to do whenever you want to do it.

Of course, there is a true value to freedom, and our country was in large measure founded by people who understood how essential and costly freedom is to the moral development of genuinely good persons. They had no way of understanding that by the twenty-first century it would be transformed from the freedom to pursue virtue into a freedom from moral restraint. The pursuit of happiness, and the security of life and liberty, as the Founding Fathers understood it, are very good things and very much a reflection of ideals that express the kingdom of God. But those ideals have been perverted over time.

The Vision Dims

Such perversion is not unusual. All good ideas—true ideas—that have been in the stream of human history for a while become perverted. Why? Precisely because Satan is at work on them, distorting their meaning. It is no different with the church.

If you go to the town of Assisi in Italy, you will find many people who talk a great deal about Saint Francis, many monuments to him, and many businesses thriving by selling memorabilia. But you will not find anyone who carries in himself the fire that Francis carried. No doubt many fine folks are there, but they do not have the character of Francis, nor do they do the deeds of Francis, nor have his effects.

Take any church you wish—Catholic, Methodist, Presbyterian, Quaker, or Baptist—and compare its founding culture with what it has become. The mission or missions that have been set afoot begin a subtle divergence from the vision that gripped the founder, and before too long the institution and its mission has become the vision. This may be something that happens within the lifetime of individuals, or it may occur across a few generations—rarely more than a few—as with the degeneration of the kingship in Israel from David, through Solomon, to Rehoboam. The power, beauty, and effectiveness that was so vibrant in the beginning dissipates, and the movement becomes unrecognizable when compared with its beginnings.

Why does this happen? Why the decay? Why do good churches go bad?[3] It happens because someone in control of ideas is pursuing this result. And it happens—surprise, surprise!—primarily through the desire to look good and the desire to be wise. After all, it is important that our preachers are known to be wise and look good. So we send them off to schools where they get wise and come back looking good.

I have been around theological schools a great deal, and in my observation, the number one concern of all theological schools is looking good and being respectable. It is no less true of our secular institutions. The pursuit of knowledge in universities has now come to the place that if you talk seriously about truth and righteousness with faculty members of leading universities, you will be laughed at. If they do not laugh, they will smile condescendingly at your quaint moral naiveté. Because, of course, we all know that there is no such thing as truth! On the outside of Mudd Hall of Philosophy at the University of Southern California you will read that "Truth shall make you free." But universities no longer engrave words of any significance on the walls of their new buildings; they simply display the names of the millionaire donors who paid for the buildings.

Truth does exist, but it does not come easily, if at all, to those trapped by Satan's deceptions about what is desirable. A society can lose the truth it once possessed simply by no longer desiring truth above reputation, pleasure, and power. Jesus once spoke to a group of religious leaders who thought they were wise but refused to believe in him. He put his finger right on their problem when he asked, "How can you believe, who receive honor from one another, and do not seek the honor that comes from the only God?" (John 5:44). When looking good takes precedence over *knowing* the good, Satan wins the battle, if not the war.

Destroying the Citadel of Satan

To know the enemy and his strategy is half the battle. Satan is our chief enemy, and his primary target is our knowledge of and trust in God. Satan's constant assault is aimed at our belief in God's goodness and power, that God will supply all our needs, and that we can trust God to be sufficient in all ways. When our minds are on God, and our thoughts are formed by our knowledge of God, such sufficiency will flow to us. Thus Satan's main task is to keep our minds elsewhere, anywhere but on God.

Sadly, and tragically, we make this task relatively easy for him. Unknowingly we are the devil's playground. He takes our thoughts, he takes our feelings, he manipulates us through the ideas that dominate our society. As Paul put it, people generally live their lives "in the futility of their mind, having their understanding darkened, being alienated from the life of God, because of the ignorance that is in them, because of the blindness of their heart" (Eph. 4:17–18).

When Paul was dealing with a struggling group of believers in the ancient city of Corinth, he knew what their main problem was, and how it needed to be addressed. He knew that we are engaged in a spiritual struggle with Satan. Thus he wrote,

> For the weapons of our warfare are not carnal but mighty in God for pulling down strongholds, casting down arguments and every high thing that exalts itself against the knowledge of God, bringing every thought into captivity to the obedience of Christ. (2 Cor. 10:4–5)

Strongholds. Arguments. High things exalting themselves against the knowledge of God. This is the citadel of Satan. We are to bring the clear and full teaching of the gospel against this demonic stronghold, as Paul's words to his apprentice, Timothy, make clear:

> And a servant of the Lord must not quarrel but be gentle to all, able to teach, patient, in humility correcting those who are in opposition, if God perhaps will grant them repentance, so that they may know the truth, and that they may come to their senses and escape the snare of the devil, having been taken captive by him to do his will. (2 Tim. 2:24–26)

So we occupy a world in "the snare of the devil." It is the world of ideas, images, feelings, and beliefs that allow people to be manipulated through their desires, through their feelings about what is wise and what looks good.

It is also the world that, nevertheless, God loves, and to which he sent Jesus. Only the gospel of Christ can take back what Satan controls and can reclaim the mind and heart of every human being held captive by his deceit. *It is, indeed, a battle of hearts and minds*, and you cannot overcome the citadel of false beliefs and images and feelings—the very things that rob us of knowing the life without lack—except by the power of God. This power comes to those who have been trained to keep their minds on God—in Paul's words, "bringing every thought into captivity to the obedience of Christ" (2 Cor. 10:5). This involves coming to think about God as Jesus thought about him, and to trust God as Jesus trusted him—moving from having faith *in* Jesus to having the faith *of* Jesus. To do so is to know the life without lack. We will focus upon this central truth in the next chapter. But before turning there, take a few moments to read and then pray these words:

Lord, minister to me by your Spirit.

Come into my heart and mind,
and release me from all inward tension and anxiety.
Hold before my mind the truth that I have nothing to fear
    from Satan
for you have defeated him;
all I must do is fill my life and my mind with you.
Remind me often, especially in the midst of difficulty,
that you, who are in me,
are greater than he who is in the world.
Help me to carry this truth with me
as I contemplate the awesome reality of the spiritual battle
    taking place,
a battle that, perhaps in our time, is moving perceptively
    closer to its climax.
Give me the vision of you who are:
our Father who art in heaven,
the Shepherd in whose presence there is no lack,
so I may have the confidence and power to love and to live as
    Jesus lived.
In his name,
    amen.

CHAPTER 5

Trust in God: The Key to Life

Faith don't come in a bushel basket, Missy.
It come one step at a time. Decide to trust
Him for one little thing today, and before you
know it, you find out He's so trustworthy you
be putting your whole life in His hands.

—LYNN AUSTIN

We have now come to the important matter of how we embrace God, who is the holy center and wellspring of a life under the Shepherd's care. This chapter and the two that follow will each focus on one of the three things that must be working within us before we can truly experience the sufficiency of God: faith, death to self, and agape love. These three combine to create a triangle of sufficiency in our lives. When faith, death to self, and love are alive in you, you will find that hope and joy pervade your entire life as a natural result. Each one is a gift from God, and our privilege and calling is to become the kind of people who can receive these gifts and work with God to develop them as we learn to live a life without lack.

Faith—*trust*—is the key that unlocks our readiness to receive God's sufficiency in our lives. Given how we commonly use these words today, it is helpful to replace all occurrences of *faith* in the

Bible with *trust*. For example, "For by grace you have been saved through *trust*" (Eph. 2:8). To have faith in God is simply to trust God, to rely upon him in the face of all fears.

The best-known definition of faith in the Bible is this: "Now faith is the substance of things hoped for, the evidence of things not seen" (Heb. 11:1). *Substance* means what stands under something (sub-stance or under-standing). Faith is the substance of things hoped for in this way: when we have faith, we act in relationship with God to bring what we hope for into reality. Faith is also "the evidence of things not seen." What are the "things not seen"? In the same passage, a few lines later, we are told that "the worlds were framed by the word of God, so that the things which are seen were not made of things which are visible" (v. 3). The phrase "things not seen" refers to the word, or even energy, of God in action. When we have faith, that is sure evidence that the word of the unseen God is active in us. Faith is a gift; God creates it in our hearts.

Just Enough Faith

In chapter 2, we talked about the Mount of Transfiguration and the dramatic effect it had on Peter's faith.* Jesus had taken Peter, James, and John up on a high mountain, and while they were up there Jesus began to shine like the sun, Moses and Elijah showed up for a chat, God spoke from heaven, and the three disciples found themselves flat on their faces, overcome by the glory of it all. Once things had returned to normal, Jesus led them back down the mountain only to encounter a great commotion involving his other disciples, some religious leaders, and a man with a son troubled by a demon. The man had brought his boy in hopes that Jesus would heal him. In his absence, Jesus' disciples had

---

* Matthew 16:28–17:3; Mark 9:1–8; Luke 9:28–36.

given it a try without success. Jesus asked the man how long his son had suffered. "Since childhood," was his response, followed by the desperate plea, "If You can do anything, have compassion on us and help us" (Mark 9:22).

Then comes the part where most of us want to crawl under a chair and hide. Jesus told the man, *"If you can believe, all things are possible to him that believes"* (v. 23). *All* things? Really? Does this mean all things are possible to us too? Yes, it does. And we should feel free to speak right back to Jesus the words of the desperately hopeful father, "Lord, I believe; help my unbelief!" (v. 24). This was not a coldly analytic report about his cognitive state. We are told that he cried it out "with tears." This beautifully expresses our condition.

A great part of faith lies in the intensity with which we want something, and the father's tears expressed his deepest heart. I never worry about someone who wants to believe, because I know they already believe enough to want to believe more. If they did not already believe a great deal they would not even want to believe. That is why God says to us through the prophet Jeremiah, "You will seek Me and find Me, when you search for Me with all your heart" (Jer. 29:13). Why? Because only faith would lead you to seek God with all your heart.

The nature of faith involves love and the desire for good. When the father begged Jesus to heal his son, that was faith—love and desire—in action. When with tears he cried out, "Lord, I believe," he did believe. He had just enough faith to make a fool of himself by coming there in the first place. You know what they were all saying back home: *"Yeah, yeah. Old Josh. He took his kid up to see this wild preacher . . ."* Yes, he did just that. With a great deal of desperation and tears he cried out, "I believe. Help my unbelief." And Jesus did help, by healing his boy. The cup of the man's faith only had a few drops in it, but you can be sure he left with a whole lot more. All things are possible to him who believes.

The Power of Words

All relationships and kingdoms work by words, and the first act of faith is to speak. *If you have enough faith to speak it, then you may have enough faith to do it.* That's why praise is so important. Praise the Lord in every situation; speak it out even if it is a struggle because things are so bad. Think about God's creation, or things he has done for you in the past, and speak praise to him for who he is and what he's done. Try to think of even one thing you can say. And if you try, God will meet you where you are.

You are primarily a mind with a will in a body, and that will is the center of your being. So if you will remember the cry of this desperate father, and follow his example in words and action, you will know the all-sufficient love and power of God. If you do that, proceeding in this way, your heart will gradually be strengthened. This is what Jesus knew when he responded to the devil in the desert; he was in a time of duress, and he used the words of Scripture. He affirmed the truth of those words. He spoke them out.

Clearing Up the Confusion About Faith

Many people misunderstand faith; it often falls into the category of mystery or superstition. This is especially true for many who go to church regularly, where we hear how important it is to have faith. You may feel some degree of pain or guilt because you think you do not have enough faith. A deeper understanding of faith can help you gain a greater peace and confidence about your own faith and how you are growing in it.

Faith, however, is not a mystery. We experience it day in and day out. In its most basic aspect, faith is simply reliance upon something in both attitude and action. It may or may not involve reliance upon God. I have faith in my car, even though I am not driving it at the moment. This frees me from worrying about how I am going to get home later. If I did not have faith in my car, I would have trouble concentrating on what I'm doing, wondering how I was going to get home. I would probably stop and give someone a call to see if they could come and pick me up. My attitude (concern to get home) would affect my action (making the call). Again, *faith is reliance (trust/confidence) revealed in attitude and action.*

Attitude can be understood as a continuing posture we have in life, our basic way of being in the world. It is here, in our fundamental posture toward life, where the real spiritual goods are needed most of all. Take love as an example. We need to love in attitude as well as in action. The person who only acts in a loving way, but does not actually love, is deficient in character. He needs to get the love into his heart, into the very fibers of his being. From Jesus' perspective, the person who merely acts righteously falls into the category of being pharisaical or legalistically righteous. The righteousness of the kingdom of God, however, is righteousness of the heart (Mark 7:6). It is an attitude, and therefore an aspect of faith.

You cannot escape faith. There's no way to get through life without it, because you have a future. You make plans for your future, and making plans involves having confidence—*faith*—that things will be a certain way and what you desire will come to be. The only way you can deal with your future is by some kind of faith. It may not be faith in God, but it is still faith.

Now faith has two main parts: one is *vision* and one is *desire*, or will. *Vision* is *seeing* reality as it is, or in the case of the future, as it could be for us. *Desire* is *wanting* reality to be as it is, or as we hope it could be. To have the faith necessary to live into our hoped-for future is to trust with the psalmist that "goodness and mercy shall follow me all the days of my life" (Ps. 23:6).

Sometimes we speak of someone being "under conviction." When this happens, it means that a person has a vision of how things could be different, but is resisting it. She *sees* that she should change something in her life; that is her vision. At the same time, she lacks the desire for her life to be different than it is. She desires—*wills*—something other than what she sees would be best, and thereby lives in denial of her vision. This, in turn, leads her to *act* in ways that are in accord with her desire, but not her vision. She knows that the romantic relationship she is in is not healthy (her *vision*), yet deeply wants to be with this man (her *desire*). So she chooses to remain in the relationship, yet is not at peace with her choice. This is the experience of conviction. We might say this is an example of bad faith, but it is an act of faith nonetheless.

The vision or perception of reality upon which we base our faith may often come to us by means of a spoken or written word. You may have an accurate opinion about a person you have never met because you read about him in the newspaper. You may trust a babysitter based on the word of a friend. Of course, advertisers know the power of a good recommendation, and they will spend great sums of money to hire a well-known individual to endorse their product in order to create an attitude of faith in your heart. To what end? So you will *act* on that attitude and buy their widget. This is how faith works. It is the same with the kingdom of God; faith comes to us as a result of hearing the truth about that kingdom. As Paul put it, "Faith comes by hearing, and hearing by the word of Christ" (Rom. 10:17 NASB).

In summary, you cannot live without faith. Faith is tied to the future. Faith has the elements of desire and vision. The element of vision comes from our contact with reality or words about reality, which in turn brings about a certain attitude and action. We are now going to see how faith is transformed, growing richer through our contact with the greatest reality of all—God.

The Three Faiths of Job

One of the finest examples of transformation of faith that leads to a life without lack is seen in the life of the ancient figure Job. When we first meet Job, he is a fine fellow who is doing quite well in his life.

> There was a man in the land of Uz, whose name was Job; and that man was blameless and upright, and one who feared God and shunned evil. And seven sons and three daughters were born to him. Also, his possessions were seven thousand sheep, three thousand camels, five hundred yoke of oxen, five hundred female donkeys, and a very large household, so that this man was the greatest of all the people of the East. (Job 1:1–3)

That is a ringing endorsement of a good and great man who was enjoying the blessings and approval of God. He was, we can be certain, a man of faith. But Job went through a deep transformation in his understanding and relationship to God. It is important to recognize that Job *maintained his faith* throughout his excruciatingly difficult trials, yet *that faith was transformed*.

Job's journey of faith moved from ritual to relationship. He began with what we may call the faith of propriety, moved through the faith of desperation, and finally arrived at the faith of sufficiency—the faith that says, regardless of what happens, "It doesn't matter. I have God, and that is all I need." We can learn much from Job's journey through the maturing of his faith as we move forward in our own.

Before looking at each of these three kinds of faith, keep in mind that I am not devaluing any of them, and I am not saying that there is something wrong with you if you are not at the third stage yet. One thing we must always keep in mind is that faith is a gift from God, and we need to understand both its nature and how God transforms it. True, sometimes the way it is given can be a little rough, and the path difficult. Nonetheless, faith is a gift.

There is a good reason for this. If faith is something I can have and exercise all on my own, and if faith is as powerful as Jesus said it is, what do you think is likely to happen? The universe would probably be out of control quite rapidly. There would be mountains bouncing around, fig trees withering all over the place, and mulberry trees flying out of the ground and into the sea!* God is more concerned with who you are becoming than in what you can accomplish with your faith. He desires that you become the kind of person who can joyfully and easily receive an abundance of faith and power—the gift of great faith from God, who knows when, what kind, and how much to give us.

The Faith of Propriety

The story of Job is not a fairytale someone made up. Job lived in the land of Uz, which is essentially the land of Jordan today, running south and north up into Syria on the eastern side of the Jordan River. He was a man of reputation, power, and wealth. Job trusted God to be good to him if he lived a proper and upright life. He had obviously heard that if you do good things, God would be pleased and would provide for and protect you.

His main problem seems to have been with his family, his sons in particular. Apparently they did not have much to do beyond throwing parties: "And his sons would go and feast in their houses, each on his appointed day, and would send and invite their three sisters to eat and drink with them" (Job 1:4). That his children spent their time like this was probably worrisome to Job, a good man living with the faith of propriety, concerned about the benefits that come from serving God. In response to his family's activities we are told, "So it was when the days of feasting had run their course, that Job would send and sanctify them, and he would rise early in the morning and offer burnt offerings according to the number of them all. For Job said, 'It may be that my sons have sinned and cursed God in their hearts.' Thus Job did regularly" (v. 5). Personally, I would do that too. I would also get them a job!

---

* Matthew 21:21; Luke 17:6.

As the story goes, one day a company of angels came into the presence of God. Along with them came Satan. God asked him where he had been, and Satan replied, "From going to and fro on the earth, and from walking back and forth on it" (v. 7). Does that sound familiar? Remember from the last chapter that Satan is the prince of the power of the air (Eph. 2:2). He presides over the thought patterns, the social organization, the forces of human society, trying to move them in opposition to God. That is precisely what he had been up to.

So God asked him, "Have you considered My servant, Job, that there is none like him on the earth, a blameless and upright man, one who fears God and shuns evil?" (Job 1:8). Now Satan is not dumb—just the opposite, he is cunning and crafty and understands human beings. But he may have missed Job in his comings and goings on earth. When he heard God's glowing description of Job, he went right to the heart of the matter, questioning the sincerity of Job's faith:

> So Satan answered the LORD and said, "Does Job fear God for nothing? Have You not made a hedge around him, around his household, and around all that he has on every side? You have blessed the work of his hands, and his possessions have increased in the land. But now, stretch out Your hand and touch all that he has, and he will surely curse You to Your face!" (vv. 9–11)

Eventually we see that Satan was wrong about Job. His faith was sincere. God was right in bragging about Job. He was a man of faith who never cursed God. He was, at this point in the story, a man of the faith of propriety. Yet, while it is genuine, this kind of faith is essentially superstitious and relies heavily on ritual, for it believes that it must get everything just right to reap the benefits. It involves a vision of God that has him up in heaven looking down to see if you are going to make any mistakes. If you do, you are in real trouble.

As we'll see, Job worried about this (3:25). A lot of folks have the faith of propriety, and I want to tell you that it's not all bad. It is the faith of the typical Pharisee, and I mean that descriptively, not critically. John the Baptist and Jesus gained many of their followers from among the Pharisees (Acts 15:5). There are worse things than being a Pharisee.

Of course, if some Pharisees have been "admonishing" you recently, you'd probably disagree. They try to live good, moral lives, and make sure others do the same. Pharisees have the faith of propriety, believing that if you get it just right, all will go well. So, like Job rising early every morning to offer burnt offerings on behalf of his sons, the faith of propriety is intent on living life, as we say, "religiously." Job got out there and did it just right, and the Lord was pleased with that and blessed him for it. God will bless that kind of faith because God likes to bless people. Satan knew this, and decided to challenge this arrangement.

Death of Propriety

After God told Satan that he had permission to go after Job, all hell broke loose, and the limited nature of the faith of propriety became apparent. That Job never lost his faith is obvious in his response to his wife's urging that he should give up on God:

> So Satan went out from the presence of the LORD, and struck Job with painful boils from the sole of his foot to the crown of his head. And he took for himself a potsherd with which to scrape himself while he sat in the midst of the ashes.
>
> Then his wife said to him, "Do you still hold fast to your integrity? Curse God and die!"
>
> But he said to her, "You speak as one of the foolish women speaks. Shall we indeed accept good from God, and shall we not accept adversity?" In all this Job did not sin with his lips. (Job 2:7–10)

Job did not sin, but we soon learn that he also did not have peace in his faith. After his well-meaning friends sat with him for a week trying to comfort him while he scraped his boils, Job cried out his first lament. While he did not curse God, he did curse the day he was born (Job 3:1), pouring out his deep regret for having lived to see the days of his suffering. Then, at the end of his inconsolable groaning, we see it: "The thing I greatly feared has come upon me, and what I dreaded has happened to me" (v. 25). What was it that Job dreaded and feared? Just this: that God was going to take down the hedge of protection. That God would take away his blessings. His faith, as sincere and genuine and good as it was, was mixed with great fear. Why? Because he was trusting in his own propriety rather than trusting in God.

Job never gave up on propriety, and that's good. There's nothing wrong with wanting to do the right thing. But there are problems with propriety, not only because we tend to make bad choices and bring difficulties upon ourselves, but because things can go badly even when we do everything right. Sometimes God even *allows* those bad things to happen because he has something better for us, just like he had something better for Job.[1]

One of the things you find in people who have not suffered much is their tendency to believe in propriety. But when they have the saw-dust knocked out of them a few times, they lose their great faith in propriety. I have known quite a number of pastors who believed that divorce was something you could never really get over. But then their children experienced it, and they were liberated from that belief. This is not hypocrisy. It is the transformation of their faith. They went through a painful process and came to understand how the blessing of God goes well beyond failure, disappointment, and tragedy.

That is what happened to Job. His friends kept saying, "Come on, 'fess up, Job. You did something wrong." They were still working from the perspective of propriety that says, "If you own up to your sin and correct it, God will put you right back where you were."

But God did not want Job back where he was; he wanted him in a far better place. Which is precisely how the book ends. There God says to Job's friends, "You fellows didn't know what you were talking about. I want you to make sacrifice, and I want you to get Job to pray for you. I'll forgive you when Job prays for you" (Job 42:7–8 PAR). It would be a humbling experience to ask someone, "Would you pray for me?" after you had wrongly advised them and accused them of sinning. Of course, Job did pray for them, because he had the right kind of heart.

The Faith of Desperation

I am confident that when God called Job to Satan's attention in the first place, God knew what was in Job's heart. But Job did not know what was in his own heart. That kind of knowledge comes only through experience. God knew Job had faith, and it was now maturing from the faith of propriety to the faith of desperation. Like the faith of propriety, the faith of desperation is a wonderful thing. I have seen it in many people lying in bed sick, or losing their possessions, or watching what they cherished in their hearts go down the drain. With grim faces, they say with Job, "Though He slay me, yet will I trust Him" (Job 13:15). Not everyone is able to do that. There are a lot of people who say, "Well, if God's not going to give me the goodies, I'm not going to trust him!"

A large church had a big blowup and many of its members never got over it. Years later they were still sulking, still blaming God, saying, "Well, if you are not going to make the church work right, then I'll just stay home and watch football. I'm not going to have anything to do with church." Not everyone handles setbacks like Job did. He held on, clamped down his teeth, and said, "Whatever comes, I will trust him."

That word *trust* is very important. I am glad Job did not say, "I'll faith him." The word *faith* is a real problem in our time. It has become "respectable." How many churches do you know that have the word *faith* in their name? How many with the word *trust*? Trust is sloppy. It's out there on the street, in the field of battle. Trust is where Satan and God are struggling for the soul of man! But faith . . . faith is quite nice, isn't it? Very prim and decent—proper even.

There is a family of words in the New Testament that are variously translated as belief, faith, and hope, and what they all have in common is the notion of reliance, confidence, and trust. It is trust that puts you in contact with God so you can draw upon his unlimited and inexhaustible resources. Unfortunately, many folks have their faith lined up in such a way that they do not need to rely on God. They do not need to trust God. They have a proper faith in terms of what they need to believe to go to heaven when they die, but they hope that God is never going to put them in a position of needing to actually *trust* him before they go there.

Run with Perseverance

The faith of desperation—trusting faith—digs in, holds on, clings tight, and says, "I don't care what's going to happen, I am holding on to God!" As the psalmist put it, "God is our refuge and strength, a very present help in trouble. Therefore, we will not fear, even though the earth be removed, and though the mountains be carried into the midst of the sea" (Ps. 46:1–2). For those of us who live in Southern California with our frequent earthquakes, that is a very relevant verse!

Desperate faith is all about trusting God when the shaking begins and everything crumbles around you. Through the prophet Haggai, God speaks of shaking "heaven and earth, the sea and dry land" (Hag. 2:6), and the writer of the book of Hebrews picked up the cataclysmic theme, explaining that this "indicates the removal of those things that are being shaken, as of things that are made, that the things which cannot be shaken may remain" (Heb. 12:27). What remains is the kingdom of God that cannot be moved, and by trust, and trust alone, we enter it.

Often God allows us to reach the point of desperation so we can learn how to trust. It is a hard lesson, but an essential one. The life without lack is known by those who have learned how to trust God in the moment of their need. *In the moment of need.* Not before the moment of need, not after the moment of need when the storm has passed, but *in* the moment of need. For it is in that moment, when everything else is gone, that *you know the reality of God.* That moment may be a blood-stained one, as with the faithful martyrs of Hebrews 11 or the stoning of Stephen from Acts 7, but it will also be a God-drenched one.

This may sound outrageous to you, but I think that while these people did not receive deliverance from their sufferings, what they did know, in the very moment of their pain, was the abundant provision of God. They were without lack *in that moment.* Some of you may say, "You know, if I had known he was going to define *lack* and *sufficiency* that way, I wouldn't have bought this book!" I understand, but a life without lack is all about knowing the unlimited sufficiency of God in the moment of need.

When you're betrayed, abandoned, lied about, and scandalized; when you are sick with a fatal disease; when your finances are going down the drain; when you see your loved one walk through the doorway of hell; that is the moment to trust. And in trusting you will know God. Your point of desperation will likely not involve being sawn in two or wandering about destitute in sheepskins, but it might. Regardless, when you have nowhere else to turn except to God, *and you turn to him,* your faith of desperation will meet the fullness of God, and you will taste the life without lack as you discover the depths of the faith of sufficiency.

The Faith of Sufficiency

After Job's three friends gave up on him "because he was righteous in his own eyes" (Job 32:1), a young man named Elihu stepped forward to reprimand them for their ineptitude in answering

Job, and to offer his own wisdom. He recognized where Eliphaz, Bildad, and Zophar were wrong, even though he was not yet clear on what was correct. Elihu believed Job was mistaken to hold God accountable for what was happening to him.

But the truth is God was responsible for it. Job was right. In the final analysis, God is responsible for everything. God, in fact, led Job into his troubles. Does that bother you to read? If so, remember that Jesus teaches us to pray that God would not "lead us into temptation" (Matt. 6:13). Jesus is not talking about temptation to sin. God will not do that.* We are to pray that God would not put us to the test and that he would deliver us from bad things. It is the kind of prayer a child would pray, an admission of our weakness and vulnerability. It is a prayer for protection and deliverance from the trials and the evil that would overwhelm us. When we do pray like this, most of the time he will do just that—deliver us from evil. But sometimes God does not deliver us immediately. This is what happened with Job, and he was on the verge of experiencing something deeper than anything else he had known up to that point.

Even though Elihu was a smart man, he did not understand this, and he engaged in a very long discourse extending through six chapters (Job 32–37), in which he sought to correct Job's assumption that God was accountable for his troubles. While he was in the midst of declaring the goodness and majesty of God, he suddenly stopped speaking, never to be heard from again. Job did not respond to him. He was simply gone. What happened? I believe there is a clue to be found in the last three sentences of Elihu's speech:

> He comes from the north as golden splendor;
> With God is awesome majesty.
> As for the Almighty, we cannot find Him;

---

* James 1:13: "No one, when tempted, should say, 'I am being tempted by God'; for God cannot be tempted by evil and he himself tempts no one" (NRSV).

He is excellent in power,
In judgment and abundant justice;
He does not oppress.
Therefore men fear Him;
He shows no partiality to any who are wise of heart.

(JOB 37:22–24)

Those are Elihu's final words. Then silence. Why? I suggest it is because he suddenly saw the Lord coming to answer Job "out of the whirlwind" (Job 38:1). He saw God coming on the scene, "from the north." In the Bible, the term "the north" can refer to the dwelling place of God. We saw this in chapter 4 in Isaiah's description of the fall of Satan, as he quoted Lucifer saying:

"I will ascend into heaven,
I will exalt my throne above the stars of God;
I will also sit on the mount of the congregation
on the farthest sides of the north;
I will ascend above the heights of the clouds,
I will be like the Most High."

(ISA. 14:13–14)

Likewise, the prophet Ezekiel envisioned judgment coming from "the north," that is, from God:

Then I looked, and behold, a whirlwind was coming out of the north, a great cloud with raging fire engulfing itself; and brightness was all around it and radiating out of its midst like the color of amber, out of the midst of the fire. (Ezek. 1:4)

Notice what it is that is coming out of the north: "a whirlwind." The whirlwind is a primary epiphany of God. This term is often used in conjunction with God's presence and especially his presence in judgment, as in these words of Jeremiah: "Behold, a whirlwind of the LORD has gone forth in fury—a violent whirlwind! It will fall violently on the head of the wicked" (Jer. 23:19). When Elijah was taken up into heaven at the end of his life, he went up in a whirlwind (2 Kings 2:11). This is the biblical writer's way of saying that God came and took him. The whirlwind signifies God showing up. A similar event happened to Jesus' disciples on the day of Pentecost. When the Holy Spirit came there was a rushing, mighty wind (Acts 2:1–4).* *When you think "whirlwind," think "God is coming."* And this is exactly what happened to Elihu and to Job.

Immediately following Elihu's speech we read, "Then the LORD answered Job out of the whirlwind" (Job 38:1). Now we know why Elihu stopped talking. He saw God coming. Apparently he no longer had anything to say to Job and had no desire to hear from God. He saw this whirlwind coming and said, "I'm out of here!"

But Job stayed right there. Although he was silent, he did not flee from God, for God had granted him his deep desire. Repeatedly throughout his ordeal he had cried, *"I would like to appear before God. Where is God? I want to talk to God!"* If you want to talk to God and you pursue that desire, God will grant you that talk. He will decide when it's appropriate and under what circumstances, and if you persist, you will see God. You will have your talk. It is likely to be a humbling, enlightening, and *faith-deepening* experience as it was for Job.

In Your Presence Is Fullness of Joy

God's first words were not words of comfort, empathy, or encouragement, and certainly not an apology for letting it all happen. No, God's first words to Job were in the form of a question: "Who is this who darkens counsel by words without knowledge?" (v. 2). This

---

* *Mighty* in this verse can also translated as *violent*. Editor's Note: Dallas also noted that the connection between wind and Spirit is "very rich," as in John 3, and points out that Spirit and wind are the same Greek word: *pneuma*.

is followed by what is essentially a command to keep quiet, listen carefully, and be prepared to respond: "Now prepare yourself like a man; I will question you, and you shall answer Me" (v. 3). So that is how the conversation began, with God saying, *"My friend, you don't really understand what you are talking about. So I need you to pay close attention to what I am about to say."* Then God began to talk, and Job took it all to heart. Job made only two responses, both of which are pertinent to our discussion about faith.

After two chapters of withering questioning that revealed the limitations of Job's understanding, God posed another question and request: "Shall the one who contends with the Almighty correct Him? He who rebukes God, let him answer it" (Job 40:2). So Job did answer, with these words: "Behold, I am vile; What shall I answer You? I lay my hand over my mouth. Once I have spoken, but I will not answer; Yes, twice, but I will proceed no further" (vv. 4–5). The word *vile* is an old English term that has come to mean something different from what it once did. *Vile* now has the idea of something evil or despicable, but this is not what the Hebrew word *qalal* means. A better word would be *insignificant* or *unworthy*. Job had been humbled to the point of being speechless. He realized the foolishness of everything he had said, and he simply responded, "I have spoken but I will not answer. I will go no further."

God continued to question Job, who then responded,

> I know that You can do everything,
> And that no purpose of Yours can be withheld from You.
> You asked, "Who is this who hides counsel without knowledge?"
> Therefore I have uttered what I did not understand,
> Things too wonderful for me, which I did not know.
>
> (JOB 42:2–3)

Keep in mind that God did not say that Job was wrong in what he said, but that he did not understand what he was saying. We are often like this—correct in what we say, without understanding its meaning or significance. Teachers know what it is like to have a student who has the right answer, but does not have the foggiest idea of what he is saying. As Job came to this realization, he said to the Lord, "I have heard of You by the hearing of the ear, but now my eye sees You. Therefore I abhor myself, and repent in dust and ashes" (vv. 5–6).

We must live through things like Job did, and become desperate as Job was. What made the difference for Job was that he hung in there and his faith of desperation carried him to the point where God showed up and Job could say, *"I've heard about you, but now I've seen you."* It was an undeniable experience of God, and it changed his life. His vision of God was now so great that he realized what had happened to him didn't matter. That is the deep faith of sufficiency.

In this new place of faith in God, Job said, *"I repent."* How did he repent? He stopped pressing his case with God. He stopped trying to get God to make everything right. Having seen God, he let go of desperation. He saw that whatever needed to be taken care of would be taken care of. Job saw the greatness of God, and in that vision he was able to rest in the all-sufficiency of Yahweh.

This is why we need to live in clear view of the cross. When we look at what Christ did for us on the cross and keep that at the center of our vision, there are not many things that will bother us, or even matter at all. When we realize that Christ went willingly to the cross on our behalf, trusting in the greatness of his Father, it casts a transformative light on our own sufferings. That's what Job saw. Job beheld the greatness of God.

Lessons on the Road from Desperation to Sufficiency

One of the fundamental changes that takes place as we move from the faith of desperation to the faith of sufficiency is that we take our minds off ourselves and place them on God. This is what happened to Job. It is interesting to note what Job did not say after seeing God. In almost all the other epiphanies in the Old Testament, when someone saw God they would cry out, "I've seen God; now I'm going die! No man can see God and live!" Not Job. He simply said, "I've seen God, and I've seen myself." We cannot truly see ourselves until we see God, but as long as our eyes are fixed on ourselves, we cannot see God. We must focus on God if we are to know the sufficiency of God.

Desperation can help in this regard. There are many examples in the Bible, such as the Syro-Phoenician woman, the little lady from Lebanon, who came to Jesus distraught over her demon-possessed daughter.* She came to Jesus and said, "My daughter needs your help." Jesus was trying to take a little retreat at the time, but she begged him repeatedly to cast the demon out of her daughter. Finally, Jesus replied—with words that seem so cruel: "Let the children be filled first, for it is not good to take the children's bread and throw it to the little dogs" (Mark 7:27).

On the face of it, that is one of the cruelest things ever said in the Bible. Yet she came back with an answer that is so wonderful: "Yes, Lord, yet even the little dogs under the table eat from the children's crumbs" (v. 28). Jesus said, "For this saying, go your way; the demon has gone out of your daughter" (v. 29). What's going on here? Is Jesus just toying with her? No. This seemingly cruel act was meant to bring this woman to the place where she could clearly see what she was looking for. It was the same with Job. It is the same with us. Faith requires vision, and a fuller faith requires a fuller vision.

Then there is Jacob. Jacob the supplanting deceiver, Jacob the crook. Not an admirable fellow, to be sure. But Jacob loved God. He loved him, and he learned to love—*and trust*—him more in a time of desperation. He was returning to his father's house after many

* Mark 7:24–30; Matthew 15:21–28.

years away and learned that his brother, Esau, was coming to greet him with four hundred men. Certain that Esau was going to kill him for having deviously taken his rights as the firstborn son and the blessing of their dying father, Isaac, Jacob sent his herds and his wives and children on ahead to Esau, hoping to soften up his older brother's heart.* Jacob stayed behind in a lonely place, and in his desperation God came to him:

> Then Jacob was left alone; and a Man wrestled with him until the breaking of day. Now when He saw that He did not prevail against him, He touched the socket of his hip; and the socket of Jacob's hip was out of joint as He wrestled with him. And He said, "Let Me go, for the day breaks."
>
> But he said, "I will not let You go unless You bless me!"
>
> So He said to him, "What is your name?"
>
> He said, "Jacob."
>
> And He said, "Your name shall no longer be called Jacob, but Israel; for you have struggled with God and with men, and have prevailed."
>
> Then Jacob asked, saying, "Tell me Your name, I pray."
>
> And He said, "Why is it that you ask about My name?" And He blessed him there. (Gen. 32:24–29)

In the ancient Near East, names were reflective of a person's nature or character. To ask a person his name was like asking, "Who are you? What kind of being are you?" So here we have this being asking Jacob that question, and Jacob asking the same of him. Because of Jacob's behavior, especially toward his brother, his name came to be associated with "one who displaces another," a "cheater" or "deceiver." The "Man" said to him, "Your name shall no longer

---

* If you are unfamiliar with the story of Jacob and Esau, you can read it in Genesis 25:19–33:17.

be called Jacob, but Israel; for you have struggled with God and with men, and have prevailed" (v. 28). From "cheater" to "one who prevails with God"—that is quite a transformation! In some manner, the being revealed himself to Jacob after that, for in verse 30 Jacob says, "I have seen God face to face."

Jacob, fearful of what his brother might do, had refused to let go of God until he blessed him. It was an act of desperate faith; he had come to the end of his schemes, and all he could do was to trust God (*note the attitude*) by asking God for a blessing (*note the action*). God, knowing that some fundamental change had taken place in Jacob, gave him a new name and the requested blessing.

What that blessing was we are not told, but I believe he gave him something of what he was asking for. We can surmise that it had to do with protection from Esau. We can be certain, however, that Jacob's faith had moved from desperation to sufficiency. After all, when he asked God to tell him his name, God's reply was essentially, "Why do you want to know?" Jacob said no more and moved on with his life, not knowing for sure what would happen with Esau. It would turn out well, but he did not know that until later. When they finally met, Esau tried to refuse the generous gifts of servants and livestock that Jacob had brought him. Jacob's response tells us much about his increased faith:

> And Jacob said, "No, please, if I have now found favor in your sight, then receive my present from my hand, inasmuch as I have seen your face as though I had seen the face of God, and you were pleased with me. Please, take my blessing that is brought to you, because God has dealt graciously with me, and because I have enough." (Gen. 33:10–11)

Behold the heart's confession of the faith of sufficiency: "God has dealt graciously with me, and I have enough." The Lord is my shepherd; I shall not want.

Now It's Your Turn

One of our problems—and I am particularly speaking to those of us who spend a lot of time in churches—is that we think that experiences like these are only for very special people. But that is not so. Such experiences are for everyone. God will reveal himself to you. All of us can come to trust God as Job did, if we want it and if we seek it. In this regard, it is important to recognize that Job, Jacob, and the Syro-Phoenician woman did not arrive at their relentless faith in God's all-sufficiency simply by trying to trust in the greatness of God. It was the result of two things: they sought the Lord *and* the Lord showed up.

It is the same with you and me. You should not try to do this in your own power. Seek the Lord and wait for him to show up. Set time aside to devote yourself to prayer and other spiritual disciplines that will strengthen your faith and prepare you to receive from him. Listen for God when you pray. Watch for him and wait on him throughout the day. If the Lord does not show up when and how you think he should, you must not be upset with him or with yourself. Just keep seeking. When we begin to seek the Lord, some things must change—some outside of us and some inside of us—before we can bear the vision of God. These changes can take time, and God, in his mercy, gives them time.

We have this promise from Jesus: "If anyone loves Me, he will keep My word; and My Father will love him, and We will come to him and make Our home with him" (John 14:23). Jesus means that he and the Father will be moving through and about us in our lives. He will speak to us. He will act on our behalf, and we will know the presence of God in our lives. If you are in doubt about this I beg you not to say, "Oh, well, I'm just supposed to believe." Do *not* do that. Seek the Lord. Ask him to reveal himself to you and give you the faith of sufficiency that knows no bounds.

Of course, it may be that you will not recognize him as you

begin. We all have certain expectations and ideas about God and what it would be like for him to show up. This is what Jesus was getting at when he asked his disciples, "Who do men say I am?" When they gave the various answers, he then put the light on them: "But who do *you* say that I am?" (Mark 8:27, 29). He asks this same question of us, and does so by revealing himself to us in ways we do not expect. Who do you think he is? God will not try to fit within your expectations, but he will reveal something precious to you.

If you want to have a deeper, more trusting faith, seek God and be prepared to go with him. He will bring you into a faith of sufficiency as he reveals himself uniquely to you. No more of this "I heard about it with my ears." That is where faith begins, but not where it ends. As with those who lived in the little Samaritan village of Sychar, we can move from a faith based on hearsay to one based on experience (John 4:1–42). They had been told that Jesus was a prophet and possibly the Messiah by a woman who had encountered him at a well. Intrigued, they went to him and found out for themselves with this result:

> And many of the Samaritans of that city believed in Him because of the word of the woman who testified, "He told me all that I ever did." So when the Samaritans had come to Him, they urged Him to stay with them; and He stayed there two days. And many more believed because of His own word.
>
> Then they said to the woman, "Now we believe, not because of what you said, for we ourselves have heard Him and we know that this is indeed the Christ, the Savior of the world." (John 4:39–42)

Faith based on what we hear or read is central and necessary; the beginning of faith does come by hearing. But God wants to lead you on to the point where you can say, "Now I've seen it with my own eyes and it's all clear." It's clear because you are convinced that all will be well, and you shall not want. This kind of faith comes from spending time in the presence of God. It does not have to be in a whirlwind. Indeed, we most clearly see the presence of God in the face of Jesus Christ. As Jesus told his disciple Philip, "He who has seen Me has seen the Father" (John 14:9). Do you know what Philip had just said to him? "Lord, show us the Father, and it is sufficient for us" (v. 8). *Sufficient.* I would much rather have Jesus than a whirlwind, but if it takes a whirlwind, let it be a whirlwind. The important thing is to be in the presence of God, for that is the birthplace of the life without lack.

We must beware of pretense. It is crucial that we do what we can to avoid *acting as if* everything is fine, when in fact we are suffering. *Faith and complaining are not mutually exclusive.* Even if you have strong faith, you may still complain to God. While Job never cursed God or accused him falsely, he did complain. He complained and he moaned and he groaned. When bad things happen, you can do that too. If you doubt this, just read the psalms! Tell it to God! Let him hear from you. He is not nervous, he is not insecure, he is not worried. It will not upset him to hear you complain. It is one of the ways that we seek God. One lesson Job teaches us is that we can seek God *by* complaining. He said, "Oh, that I knew where I might find Him, that I might come to His seat! I would present my case before Him, and fill my mouth with arguments" (Job 23:3–4). He carried on and complained. It was his faith of desperation speaking, but it was faith. If with Job we say, "Though he slay me, yet will I trust him," and hang on, we will grow into the faith of sufficiency (Job 13:15).

The Social Context of Faith

There is also a social dynamic to faith. When we're with a group of people, the flow of faith occurs separately through each individual as well as through our fellowship. Even Jesus, in his finitude, was limited in some measure by the attitude of others. On one occasion when he was visiting his hometown of Nazareth, he was met with a great deal of skepticism on the part of the folks living there. In fact, the resistance was so great that he was not able to perform many miracles, "and He marveled because of their unbelief" (Mark 6:6). Faith is not just an individual matter.

On another occasion, when Jesus was getting ready to raise the daughter of Jairus, who everyone knew was dead, he sent everyone but Peter, James, and John outside (Mark 5:21–24, 35–43). He did not want to fight the unbelief that was present among the people.

Unbelief and belief are real forces in the world, and they are polarized so that one takes away from the other. I have seen people blessed with my ministry, even when I did not have faith, because their faith was so strong. I can remember one woman who was allergic to bee stings. She was stung, asked me to pray for her, and then she had no allergic reaction whatsoever. I'm still astonished! I had no sense of doing much of anything. But she had faith that God would use me and that was enough.

The story of a paralyzed man whose friends brought him to Jesus provides us with another example of the group dynamic of faith (Mark 2:1–12). You may remember that because of the crowd they could not get close to Jesus and so decided to climb up on the roof, dig a hole, and lower their friend down to Jesus' feet. Notice what happened next: "When Jesus saw their faith, He said to the paralytic, 'Son, your sins are forgiven you'" (v. 5). Whose faith did Jesus see? "Their" faith—the faith of the friends, not just the man, who may or may not have had faith.

When faith begins to move, it moves on groups. When you are with other people, your faith is affected by the totality of the faith present. Sometimes when you go to pray with people you will find yourself totally drained in your efforts because they do not have faith. So an important part of our growth in faith involves the people with whom we associate. This is why the writer of the book of Hebrews, as he was encouraging his readers to draw close to God in faith, instructed them with these words:

> And let us consider one another in order to stir up love and good works, not forsaking the assembling of ourselves together, as is the manner of some, but exhorting one another, and so much the more as you see the Day approaching. (Heb. 10:24–25)

God uses others to transform our own faith.

Ask, Seek, and Knock . . . but Don't Pretend

While I have mentioned three kinds of faith—of propriety, desperation, and sufficiency—there are in fact many degrees of faith, and many stages through which we pass. It is a continual progression as we experience more of the reality of God; our faith grows according to our vision. In turn, as our vision grows, our will—our ability to decisively act—grows, and we become increasingly capable of choosing and doing the good. We must never forget that faith is a gift. Like any gift, faith must be received. It must be wanted. God very rarely just dumps it on people who do not want it.

There is a distorted teaching about the gift of grace in which grace is just randomly poured out on whomever God chooses, regardless of the receptacle. This teaching makes me think of the RC Cola plant I worked in when I had just finished high school in Missouri. There was a long conveyor belt on which the bottles traveled. As a bottle moved along, it would come under one machine that would squirt water into the bottle, and then the next would squirt syrup, and the next one would place the cap on it. I think a lot of people believe that's how God dispenses faith, grace, and other blessings. They think that is what a church service ought to be—just bring your empty bottle (yourself), sit down, and wait for the pastor to squirt it full of whatever it is you need. Then you leave all full of juicy, fizzy stuff that will hopefully last until the next Sunday.

That is not the way of God. It is asking, it is seeking, it is knocking.

The truth of God's grace is that we never merit the good that is done to us. Grace is opposed to earning, but it is not opposed to effort, because effort is action and earning is attitude. That point is important. You cannot do justice to the teachings of Scripture unless you understand that if you do not rise and go after God's blessing, God will rarely just give it to you. I say "rarely" here because at times God does decide he's going to pour something good on you without being asked. But that's unusual, and if we want to work with God, we must determine what is normal for him in dealing with people and set our expectations realistically. When we aim for the unusual and glorious things to happen, that can damage our faith. We must take the faith we have, act on it, and grow toward the faith of sufficiency.

Increase Our Faith

If you want faith, ask God for it. And when you ask God, be willing to let him take you through what is necessary to prepare you for it. Take this opportunity to join with the psalmist in saying, "Examine me, O LORD, and prove me; Try my mind and my heart" (Ps. 26:2). You may find yourself saying, "Wait a minute, God! I didn't count on this!" That's all right; I guarantee that once you've gone through it, you will never regret it. Job never regretted it. Job wanted God; he wanted to trust God. He persevered and came out trusting.

Because faith is a gift given by God as we are ready, it comes to us without any kind of strain, or hype, or exaggeration. We simply know, beyond a doubt, that "the LORD is my shepherd, I shall not want." We are not trying to impress anyone, most of all not ourselves. We just believe. David seems to have been blessed with that kind of faith. He trusted God deeply, even though he did not receive everything he asked God for. This shows up powerfully in the death of his child in 2 Samuel 12. He prayed for a week, lying prostrate on the ground, fasting and weeping. He really bent God's ear. But when the child died, David arose, cleaned himself up, went to the tabernacle to worship God, and then had a meal.

His servants were perplexed by this. David explained himself this way: "While the child was alive, I fasted and wept; for I said, 'Who can tell whether the LORD will be gracious to me, that the child may live?' But now he is dead; why should I fast? Can I bring him back again? I shall go to him, but he shall not return to me" (vv. 22–23). That is a beautiful demonstration of having a "no-lack faith." It's the real thing.

And it can be your thing too. You can ask that it be your experience. Here is Jesus' promise:

> So listen: Keep on asking, and you will receive. Keep on seeking, and you will find. Keep on knocking, and the door will be opened for you. All who keep asking will receive, all who keep seeking will find, and doors will open to those who keep knocking.
>
> Some of you are fathers, so ask yourselves this: if your son comes up to you and asks for a fish for dinner, will you give him a snake instead? If your boy wants an egg to eat, will you give him a scorpion? Look, all of you are flawed in so many ways, yet in spite of all your faults, you know how to give good gifts to your children. How much more will your Father in heaven give the Holy Spirit to all who ask! (Luke 11:9–13 THE VOICE)

Faith is a gift that is yours for the asking. Striving or pretending is not the way to faith. Nowhere does the Bible say that you should *make* yourself have faith, or that you can have faith if you *say it*, or that you *ought* to have faith because you are a Christian. Remember, faith is "the substance of things hoped for" (Heb. 11:1). When you have faith that you will have something you are hoping for, it is because God has created that confidence in your heart, and he is going to bring it to pass in partnership with you. God is running the show, and we can rest in that knowledge. The problem comes when we believe we ought to be able to have faith simply because we want to have faith. It is not possible. What is possible is asking, seeking, knocking . . . and then waiting on God.

It is also possible—and necessary—to be honest with ourselves and with others. Where we do not believe something, we should not act as if we do. Acknowledge your doubts openly and honestly and wait until faith comes. Seek God and ask him to give you the gift of faith. Faith is something you can identify in yourself. You know when you believe something, such as your belief in the sun rising tomorrow, or your belief in the chair you're sitting in, or your belief in the loyalty of a close friend. You know you believe it. No faking or forcing is necessary. You simply believe it. You also know what you do not believe. Please, do not *try* to believe anything. Simply say to God, "Lord, give me faith. I am ready for it. Take me through whatever I need for it." That is the way forward to the faith of sufficiency.

CHAPTER 6

Trust Completed in Death to Self

*Self-denial means knowing only Christ, no longer
knowing oneself. It means no longer seeing oneself,
only him who is going ahead, no longer seeing
the way which is too difficult for us. Self-denial
says only: he is going ahead; hold fast to him.*

—DIETRICH BONHOEFFER

For faith to serve as a channel of God's provision to our needs, two more conditions are necessary: the first has to do with our relationship to ourselves, and the second with our relationship to others. The latter, which will be discussed in chapter 7, may not surprise you, for it involves the central Christian virtue of love, though how it relates to our experience of God's sufficiency may be new to you. But first we will look at how the very important concept of *death to self* directs us toward a life without lack.

In a day and age in which we hear far too much about self-fulfillment and self-promotion, this topic may not sound inviting. So it is essential at the start to notice that we are dealing with "death *to* self" not "death *of* self." The distinction between these prepositions is vital to maintain. Death to self is not ultimately a negation, but a rising up into the very life of God (2 Peter 1:4). Thus our lives are saved by his life (Rom. 5:10). This is essential.

One problem that has hindered this teaching in the past is that those presenting it have not carefully drawn the distinction between death *to* and death *of* self. As a result, people view death to self as if it means getting rid of yourself. That is not at all what it involves. You were not put here on earth to get rid of yourself. You were put here to *be* a self, and to live fully as a self. The worth of the self—*your* self—is inestimable, and God's intent for you is that you become a *fully realized* self as you make the grace-fueled movement from the old self to the new (Col. 3:9–10).

Some of Jesus' teachings might lead you to think otherwise. Take Matthew 16:24, for example: "If anyone desires to come after Me, let him deny himself, and take up his cross, and follow Me." What does it mean for someone to "deny himself"? We must be very careful how we understand this kind of teaching, especially remembering that God's adversary, Satan, works to confuse and misdirect our minds. Does denying your self mean denying that you exist? Of course not. Does it mean that we should consider ourselves as worthless? This hardly makes sense, given what Christ went through to save us. So what does it mean?

One clue is found in the paradoxical character of what Jesus goes on to say:

> "For whoever desires to save his life will lose it, but whoever loses his life for My sake will find it. For what profit is it to a man if he gains the whole world, and loses his own soul? Or what will a man give in exchange for his soul?" (Matt. 16:25–26)

The Greek word translated as "soul" here is also translated as "life" in other passages because the soul encompasses and "organizes" the whole person, interrelating all dimensions of the self, and both terms take us back to the *self.*

Jesus clearly states that if you try to save your own life you will lose your soul. How does that work? How does a person lose her soul? You may have met people who say, "I have lost my life" or "my life is over" because they have pursued the wrong things. Jesus is speaking to a common human condition, the feeling that you have exchanged your soul—your self—for something far less valuable. It is a real danger that we all face.

Jesus himself was faced with it. Six days before he would be crucified, two of Jesus' disciples, Andrew and Philip, asked him if he would talk with some Greek-speaking Jews* who heard he was in Jerusalem and requested an audience with him. It seems these Greek Jews had come to ask Jesus to go back with them to their homeland to teach, and it is clear that everyone knew Jesus was going to be killed if he did not leave Jerusalem. Jesus used the occasion as an opportunity to speak to the heart of Christian discipleship:

> Jesus answered them, saying, "The hour has come that the Son of Man should be glorified. Most assuredly, I say to you, unless a grain of wheat falls into the ground and dies, it remains alone; but if it dies, it produces much grain. He who loves his life will lose it, and he who hates his life in this world will keep it for eternal life. If anyone serves Me, let him follow Me; and where I am, there My servant will be also." (John 12:23–26)

Jesus, fully conscious of what his choices were, made the choice to lay down his life, to give his life on the cross. He knew firsthand what it was to die to self, and that choice represented his obedience to this fundamental biblical teaching: "Unless a grain of wheat falls into the ground and dies, it remains alone; but *if it dies, it produces much grain*" (v. 24). The positive aspect of "if it dies" is that it *"produces much grain."* The death he chose was for the sins of the world. It was not just to lose life, but also to give

---

* These were Jews who lived in what is known as the Diaspora, the dispersion of the Jews among Gentile nations after the Babylonian exile.

life. This is what keeps his death, and Christian death to self, from being morbid. It was for the "joy that was set before him" that he "endured the cross" (Heb. 12:2). If we miss this truth and fail to incorporate it into our own experience, we will miss the route to life without lack.

The nature of the death-to-self experience is that, if we have had the kind of revelation of God that Job had, it happens naturally. Imagine what it would do for us if we could get a glimpse of what Job saw. He experienced the grandeur and greatness of God and was left knowing that what he had suffered to that point simply did not matter anymore in light of his new understanding of reality. Remember his statement of his own insignificance: "Now my eye sees You. Therefore I abhor myself" (Job 42:5–6).

You will not meet many people who have experienced God as Job did. People generally do not pursue God that tenaciously or expect God to meet with them in that way. Most people do not want God to meet them in that way because they are afraid of losing something they value. The human heart is very complex, and the fact that someone trusts God at one level does not mean they have fully surrendered their life to him. But we seek God to work through those things and come to the place where we are ready to lay it all down.

The gospel is presented today with very little connection to the complete surrender of our lives to God. This leads to the real possibility that we will miss the central necessity of dying to self. Christianity tends to be presented as if God is our servant, instead of us being his, and God's greatness and love are not made manifestly clear for the hearer.

Anyone who has had a very deep experience of the gospel—plainly having set forth in his mind and heart the death of Christ on the cross, his resurrection, and his glorious present ministry in his people—is likely, in a very unconscious way, to move toward the liberating truth of the death-to-self teaching.

Paul and Death to Self

Paul knew the truth of Jesus' teaching about self-denial and death to self, and his letters are full of references to this principle.* One of the most impressive examples appears in 2 Corinthians 4. While you will profit greatly by reading the entire chapter, here are the highlights:

> But we have this treasure in earthen vessels, that the excellence of the power may be of God and not of us. We are hard-pressed on every side, yet not crushed; we are perplexed, but not in despair; persecuted, but not forsaken; struck down, but not destroyed—always carrying about in the body the dying of the Lord Jesus, that the life of Jesus also may be manifested in our body. . . .
>
> Therefore we do not lose heart. Even though our outward man is perishing, yet the inward man is being renewed day by day. For our light affliction, which is but for a moment, is working for us a far more exceeding and eternal weight of glory, while we do not look at the things which are seen, but at the things which are not seen. For the things which are seen are temporary, but the things which are not seen are eternal. (vv. 7–10, 16–18)

Perhaps as in no other place, Paul is expressing his confidence in God and demonstrating the way in which he lives, looking in hope to the eternal life of God. Then, out of that confidence, the conviction of what was basic Christianity for Paul bursts forth a few verses later:

> For the love of Christ compels us, because we judge thus: that if One died for all, then all died; and He died for all, that those

---

* Colossians 3:1–5; Romans 6:1–14; Galatians 2:20; 2 Corinthians 5:14–15 and 6:4–10.

who live should live no longer for themselves, but for Him who died for them and rose again. (2 Cor. 5:14–15)

This is the essence of the death-to-self life: that we should no longer live for ourselves, but for him who died for us and rose again.

To this we add Paul's words from Galatians 2:20, where we see again that paradoxical way of presenting the believer's relationship in Christ:

I have been crucified with Christ; it is no longer I who live, but Christ lives in me; and the life which I now live in the flesh I live by faith in the Son of God, who loved me and gave Himself for me.

This echoes the example of Jesus not loving his own life (as in *protecting* it), but giving up his life as the foundation of our own lives in him. Then, later in the same letter, Paul describes what should be the normal Christian life: "And those who are Christ's have crucified the flesh with its passions and desires. If we live in the Spirit, let us also walk in the Spirit" (Gal. 5:24–25). We see here the contrast between what Paul referred to as "the flesh" and the Spirit is the same as the contrast between living to the self and living to Christ. But what is "the flesh"?

Fleshing Out "the Flesh"

The first thing to be said is that "the flesh" is not bad in itself. Simply stated, the flesh is merely the natural powers of the human being, based in the human body—our capabilities, wants, and desires as they are in themselves, unaided by divine assistance or guidance. The flesh is not identical to human nature, but simply one aspect of it. It is not to be thought of as being essentially sinful, "fallen," or bad; our bodies are intended to be "members of His body," and our life in the flesh lived "by faith in the Son of God, who loved me and gave Himself for me" (Eph. 5:30; Gal. 2:20).

For example, we read in Galatians that Abraham's servant, Hagar, gave birth to their son, Ishmael, "according to the flesh" (4:23)—that is, in the way that normal human reproduction takes place. This contrasts with the birth of Isaac, whose birth was through "promise" (v. 28). This was God's promise to Abraham that the child would be born of Sarah through the action of God in combination with the normal abilities of Abraham and Sarah.* Human beings have natural abilities, and those abilities are good when they are used in accordance with God's designs and desires.

The problem with the flesh lies in its weakness and lostness when uncoupled from God's Spirit, which is precisely the condition of humanity apart from Christ. To live in the flesh, to live with uncrucified affections and desires, is simply a matter of putting them in the ultimate position in our lives. Whatever we want becomes the most important thing. This is what happens when we are living apart from God; we make our desires ultimate because they are all we have. We look to them as if they were everything in our lives; thinking of *my* worth, *my* glory, *my* appearance, thinking of *my* power to sustain *my*self.

Desire and Spirit

Desire is essentially the impulse to possess or experience something. It cares for nothing else other than its object. Desire proclaims, as the old song puts it, "I want what I want when I want it."[1] There is nothing wrong with wanting or desiring. Desire is a fine thing, and it is one of the things that keeps us alive, but desires are terrible masters. The objects of desire may differ; I may want to eat or sleep, I may want to dominate others, I may want great wealth. Taken

---

* Genesis 15:1–3; Romans 4:18–21.

by themselves, desires are inherently chaotic and deceitful (James 4:1–3; Eph. 4:22). In our natural state, apart from God, our "fleshly lusts . . . wage war against the soul" (1 Peter 2:11 NASB). Here "soul" should be understood as the whole person, and the war involves the very center of the person, the human heart, will, or "spirit."

Our spirit is different from unrestrained flesh with its singular focus on satisfying desire. The spirit is able to consider *alternatives*, and God prompts us to have an interest in what is better and best. It is our God-given ability that gives us an interest in what is better and best. It takes a broad view of the possibilities before us, not just of one desire and its object, but of other desires and goods. That is where *choice* comes in. Choice involves deliberation between alternatives, with a view to what is best. The conflict between the flesh and the human spirit is the conflict between desire—what I want—and the will for what is best. It is, in fact, the conflict between desire and *love*, for love is always directed toward what is good, and not at simply having my desires satisfied. Love is the will-to-good of its object.

The relationship between the good that love seeks and our fleshly desires is revealed in Jesus' teaching about anger and cultivated lust in the Sermon on the Mount (Matt. 5:21–30). The *desire* embedded in both anger and sexual lust is not at all concerned with the good of the object, but only with its own satisfaction. In the case of anger, it is the desire to have the object suffer in some way.* In the case of sexual lust, it is the desire that the object provide sensual pleasure. Desire says, "Let's have sex." Love says, "A greater good is at issue here: the purity of human love and faithfulness toward other human beings." In both anger and lust, love—which is the essence of all the laws of God and which is to be the driving motive in all our actions—is absent, and the "flesh" is enthroned.

---

* For a more thorough discussion of Jesus' teachings on anger, contempt, and malice in the Sermon on the Mount, see Dallas Willard, *The Divine Conspiracy* (San Francisco: HarperSanFrancisco, 1998), 147–154.

Our Willy-Nilly Wills

We might also think of the flesh in terms of our confidence in our own power—what is sometimes called "willpower." The basic nature of sin is to trust only oneself. When you turn from God, your will becomes blind and helpless before the hammerings of desire. Even when we do not have confidence in our own powers, we put our trust in them because we think they are all we have.

When our abilities are the only things we know to trust, and when we are living with them as ultimates, we are living "in the flesh." We are living in dependence upon the God-given drives of our human personalities rather than in the God who gave them to us. That is life in the flesh, the frightful story of which the apostle Paul described repeatedly.*

That is a strong claim. *As long as our desires are paramount in our lives, we cannot have faith in God.* As we saw in the last chapter, faith is a gift of God. If faith is a gift of God, and God gives me faith while I am still treating what I want as my ultimate concern, what will I do? I will use my faith to get what I want. That would be my ultimate point of reference. I would not be thinking about the good of others or the glory of God. I would be thinking simply of getting what I want. If my desire is to have people recognize the good that I do or think well of me, and I am destroyed if they do not, then I would use my gift of faith to glorify myself. If I have faith and I want to dominate others above all else, then I would use my faith to do just that.

That is why God does not give us significantly more faith until we have come to terms with death to self. An individual can have only a very small amount of faith until he has come to a very clear resolution of the place of his desires, his glory, or his power to dominate. Until these are settled, he is not going to have much faith. This

---

* Romans 1:18–32; 7:14–25; Galatians 5:19–21.

was certainly Jesus' belief. In John 5 we find him talking with some very proper people. They had the faith of propriety in abundance. These proper folks—the same ones who were going to kill Jesus—claimed to know God, and to be able to do the works of God. Jesus disagreed:

> You search the Scriptures, for in them you think you have eternal life; and these are they which testify of Me. But you are not willing to come to Me that you may have life. I do not receive honor from men. But I know you, that you do not have the love of God in you. I have come in My Father's name, and you do not receive Me; if another comes in his own name, him you will receive. (John 5:39–43)

Jesus was describing a very common practice in his day. They welcomed people who came with their own attainments, saying, "Look what I've done," hoping to be received on the basis of those accomplishments. What is the effect on our faith of this concern for self-attainment and recognition? Jesus put his finger on it with the question we encountered in chapter 4: "How can you believe, who receive honor from one another, and do not seek the honor that comes from the only God?" (v. 44).

These folks had not settled the fundamental issues. What was uppermost in their life was the honor of others in their group. Their desire for such honor was keeping them from believing, because you cannot hold the esteem of *others* to that degree of importance and at the same time believe that God is who he is. It is not possible. As long as people are hung up on honor from other people—reputation, appearing well—they cannot truly believe and trust God. The connection between faith and death to self—or conversely, the failure to have both faith and death to self—is one we must come to terms with or we simply cannot enter into a life without lack.

The Insatiable and Its Satisfaction

Human desire is infinite by its nature; it cannot be satisfied. You must take your stand against it because you cannot satisfy it. You can never get enough money, if you want money. You can never get enough power, if you want power. You can never get enough love, you can never get enough glory. It is impossible. So fundamental is this truth that every person who wishes to follow Christ must understand it. He spoke directly to the point: *"Unless you lose your life for my sake, you cannot follow me. Unless you take up the cross, you cannot follow me"* (Matt. 16:24 PAR). The cross means the acceptance of limitation on desire. Without establishing this for yourself, there can only be frustration and worse, for you simply cannot satisfy desire.

As Solomon wrote, "The eye is not satisfied with seeing, nor the ear filled with hearing" (Eccl. 1:8). This is a fundamental truth that Satan twists and uses to trap people. Surely it is true of sexual desire, as its many perversions reveal. But the object of desire may be comfort, possessions, talent, money, or reputation in a profession. If you watch people in the sports or entertainment industries, you will see a magnificent display of vanity. It is likewise in literature and in many of the arts. There is incredible vanity that can never be satisfied: an itch that simply cannot be sufficiently scratched. No matter what you do, there will always be a cry for more. If we are going to live a life of abundant sufficiency, we must be focused and intentional in standing against these dreadful roots of the self-life. Until we have done that, we will be incapable of entering by faith into the life God longs to give us.

Desire is infinite partly because we were made by God, made for God, made to need God, and made to run on God. We can be satisfied only by the one who is infinite, eternal, and able to supply all our needs; we are only at home in God. When we fall away from God, the desire for the infinite remains, but it is displaced upon things that will certainly lead to destruction. As we pursue this desire for self-gratification and self-satisfaction, life becomes just as Paul described:

> Now the works of the flesh are evident, which are: adultery, fornication, uncleanness, lewdness, idolatry, sorcery, hatred, contentions, jealousies, outbursts of wrath, selfish ambitions, dissensions, heresies, envy, murders, drunkenness, revelries, and the like; of which I tell you beforehand, just as I also told you in time past, that those who practice such things will not inherit the kingdom of God. (Gal. 5:19–21)

James speaks of two kinds of wisdom in comparing the flesh and the spirit, using language that is also characteristic of many other portions of Scripture:

> Who is wise and understanding among you? Let him show by good conduct that his works are done in the meekness of wisdom. But if you have bitter envy and self-seeking in your hearts, do not boast and lie against the truth. This wisdom does not descend from above, but is earthly, sensual, demonic. For where envy and self-seeking exist, confusion and every evil thing are there. (James 3:13–16)

Pure Wisdom

Where there is envying and self-seeking, the old self with its practices and habits (Col. 3:9) is still alive, insisting on having its own way. Otherwise there would be no envying, no self-seeking, but simply satisfaction in God's appointments for our lives. We will not be striving with others about anything. We may speak the truth. We may calmly present what we believe to be good and right, but there will be no envying, there will be no self-seeking, there will be no bitterness, there will be no confusion.

In contrast to the "earthly" wisdom rooted in the elevation of our desires as ultimate, there is another wisdom to be possessed:

> But the wisdom that is from above is first pure, then peaceable, gentle, willing to yield, full of mercy and good fruits, without partiality and without hypocrisy. Now the fruit of righteousness is sown in peace by those who make peace. (James 3:17–18)

Notice how this "wisdom from above" is described: It "is first pure." Purity. That is something noticeably lacking from much of the wisdom of the world. I have often been discouraged, while hobbing and nobbing with people who think they are something great in the academic world, to find that they are as impure as anyone you can imagine. They saw no connection between their supposed moral sophistication and the depravity of their actual lives. There have been university professors among my colleagues who thought it was open season for sex with any student or person with whom they associated. If you said something to them about it, they'd smugly reply, "Well, what's wrong with it? It's fun." Impurity abounds, not just in sexuality, but in many other ways as well.

Besides being pure, heavenly wisdom is also "peaceable, gentle, willing to yield, full of mercy and good fruits, without partiality and without hypocrisy." What a list! These beautiful qualities are marks of persons who have learned in their heart of hearts the great freedom of death to self, and out of their peaceful lives comes everything that is right and good: "Now the fruit of righteousness is sown in peace by those who make peace." Such people no longer promote themselves; they no longer exalt their wants and their way as the condition of getting along with them. They are not trying to dominate others. They are ready to simply stand for the truth, to speak what they see to be right in a peaceable, pure, gentle way, and to let it rest with that. As a result of that, God gives them a life of beauty and power that is obvious to others. I assure you, he does.

Playing by the Rules

One of the interesting—and most common—things you will see when you become like this is that people struggle to believe you are real. Lust, envy, domination, and self-seeking are so pervasive that purity shocks people. We all know people who readily give up what they want, but they make sure you recognize them for doing so. Or they may be using it as a technique of domination, in effect saying, "Look, I've given all this up, so you should do what I want you to do." The prophet Jeremiah pointed to this dynamic when he wrote, "The heart is deceitful above all things, and desperately wicked; who can know it?" (Jer. 17:9). Of course the answer is, God can know it. Not only that, but God can make the condition of our own hearts known to us, and he can give us new hearts marked by the wisdom from above. The requirement on our part is to die to self.

What that will involve in your own life is a matter only you can decide. No one can spell this out for you or test you on it. People have played all sorts of games with this and created even more misunderstanding. Think of all the things that have been presented as dying to the flesh: we shouldn't wear lipstick or cowboy boots, or drive certain kinds of cars. When I was in college, one of the Bible professors bought a bright, shiny new red Ford. How he was criticized! *Red?!* A black one would have been much less ostentatious and self-serving.

When we try to make rules for dying to the flesh, we are likely to miss the core problem, which is not our behavior but what is in our hearts. There are many reasons we get caught up in the things we do. For example, many people maintain a posture of defiance. Perhaps they have been hurt in some way, so now they are going to have their way no matter what. They may be Christians, but that doesn't mean they are going to be doormats for Jesus! Others are just lost in the desires themselves. They enjoy the glory or the domination or whatever it is they want. Again, there is nothing inherently wrong with wanting things or with having things, but we should attempt to receive whatever God wishes to give us so we might use it to his glory.[2]

What *is* wrong is when not getting what we want propels us into a state of bitterness, irritation, impatience, and anger, and we depend upon our own tricks and devices, our confidence in our own power, to get the things that we want. The right thing would be simply releasing it all and saying, "All right. God knows. I'm living in his world. He can give me what he wants. I will not put these things in the place of God." Putting things in the place of God is the central issue.

According to Paul, a covetous person is an idolater: "Therefore put to death your members which are on the earth: fornication, uncleanness, passion, evil desire, *and covetousness, which is idolatry*" (Col. 3:5). Someone is an idolater not because he carves little idols and bows down to them, but because he wants things to such a degree that he is dominated by those wants. He wants things that others have, resents them for having those things, and desires to take them. Simply desiring to have a house is not covetous—it's desiring to have *someone else's* house. The covetous idolater is prepared to see other people suffer in order to have his own way.

A covetous person is an idolater precisely because he has put his desires, rather than God, in the ultimate place in his life. Right or wrong, there is no limit to what he will do to get what he wants. When living at this level of the self-life, he is prepared to do what is wrong to gain what he desires. That is always the mark of the person in whom the flesh is alive—who has not died to self.

Another Day in the Life of the World . . . and the Uncrucified Self

If you pay attention to news outlets, you see far too many examples of people in whom the flesh is very much alive. You may often find yourself saying, "The world has gone mad!" And it has. But it is also functioning just as we should expect given its estrangement from God. The chaos of the world we live in reflects the chaos of the untethered and uncrucified self. Paul described how people reach such a state in his letter to the Ephesians:

> This I say, therefore, and testify in the Lord, that you should no longer walk as the rest of the Gentiles walk, in the futility of their mind, having their understanding darkened, being alienated from the life of God, because of the ignorance that is in them, because of the blindness of their heart; who, being past feeling, have given themselves over to lewdness, to work all uncleanness with greediness. (Eph. 4:17–19)

One of the effects of "being past feeling" is that the normal restraints upon our desires are cast off. Paul continued by comparing the effects of learning the way of Christ with the fruits of a life in the flesh, "which grows corrupt according to the deceitful lusts" (v. 22). If you wonder what qualifies as a "deceitful lust," think about how addictions operate. Desire whispers in your ear: "Just once more. That's all you need." The corruption of human lives that has come from listening to that sinister voice is beyond telling.

This is our world . . . and our selves . . . in a nutshell. If you ask yourself why people do the things they do, why they engage in the kinds of destructive behavior that goes viral on YouTube, it is because they have decided that they must have their way. This lies behind the shootings we continuously hear about, for example. Someone's will gets crossed. That someone becomes angry, which is the normal "fleshly" response toward those who have interfered with our will. That anger is transformed into the hunger for revenge, and soon a body lies dead on the street. All because someone didn't get what he wanted. These people are caught in a system where what they want—and what they are willing to do to people who do not give them what they want—is the focal point of their lives.

It is very important to understand that "they" are not the only ones. Our desires are the roots of the self-life in *all* of us. And until we, in conjunction with the grace of God, have made an intentional decision not to allow our desires to be the center of our lives, we can never have the kind of faith that will lead us to the life of abundant sufficiency in God.

It is not uncommon for people to hear this message and think, *The Christian life is going to be a long, dry haul. So much for a life without lack!* Not at all. The reality is that the long, dry haul is when you are trying to manage your life by always getting what you want. This is what Jesus was teaching when he said, "If you try to save your life, you'll lose it" (Luke 17:33 PAR). Why will you lose it? Because you will miss out on the provision of God. Choose death to self, however, and you will have it. Think again of Job. Did he miss out on God's provision? He certainly went through a hard time, but he came out far ahead of where he had been. In the end Job tasted the lush provision of God's sufficiency.

You may recall the time when Jesus shocked his disciples by telling them it was quite difficult for a rich person to enter the kingdom of God (Mark 10:23–27). Peter responded by pointing out that he and his friends were certainly not in that category. The scripture says, "Peter *began* to say," so apparently he was just getting started when Jesus zeroed in on his (and our) central concern:

> Then Peter began to say to Him, "See, we have left all and followed You."
>
> So Jesus answered and said, "Assuredly, I say to you, there is no one who has left house or brothers or sisters or father or mother or wife or children or lands, for My sake and the gospel's, who shall not receive a hundredfold now in this time—houses and brothers and sisters and mothers and children and lands,

with persecutions—and in the age to come, eternal life. (Mark 10:28–30)

Jesus always teaches in a way that gets your attention and makes you think. In this case, he did not mean that if you give up one sister you are literally going to receive a hundred sisters. But on the other hand, that may be how it turns out when you are immersed in a community where these kinds of relationships are given to you in the grace of God.

Notice that Jesus includes persecutions at the end of that list. This is simply part of the deal. But when you release all your concerns and desires, and God becomes your ultimate concern, the persecutions will not matter that much. When the self has been put to death—that is, when our wants have been placed in their proper relationship to God—it is not a matter of a mere "grin and bear it" existence. That is not what the Shepherd Psalm tells us. It speaks not of lack, but of abundance, of *a cup overflowing with sufficiency* for those who are willing to let loose of all the lies about what we need and what we can achieve on our own.

This is difficult for those who depend on themselves and their own abilities, and are unwilling to let go of themselves and trust God. They are unable to say, "I don't have to dominate. I don't need to have my way. I can live without all the little pleasures I was taught that I needed in order to avoid being a failure." Such are the truly miserable. Such are those who lose their souls in pursuit of the things that are set before them by the inclinations that are in the world—the lust of the flesh, the lust of the eyes, and the pride of life. Jesus made it clear that to pursue these things in reliance upon ourselves is the surest way to lose our souls. It is more than we can possibly manage on our own; we end up compromising our health and our relationships, all that is truly good in life, and we find ourselves crushed rather than conquering.

Only when we are prepared to let go of the things that tempt us to keep life under our own control are we prepared to give up our lives—even to the point of death. Jesus was very clear about that. He told his disciples, "I've taught you how to love one another. Real love is when a person is prepared to lay down their life for their friends" (John 15:12–13 PAR). That is the ultimate self-denial, to be sure. But those who walk in the kingdom of God, and know his sufficiency, are ready to give and forgive without limitation.

Self-Control and Other-Control

One of the greatest temptations that we have at this level of the self-life is trying to keep our loved ones under control. Jesus understood this, and so warned us: "If anyone comes to Me and does not hate his father and mother, wife and children, brothers and sisters, yes, and his own life also, he cannot be My disciple" (Luke 14:26). He is, of course, using exaggeration here to drive home his point. Too often our "love" for family members is domination in disguise. We learn this from our elders, many of whom have tried to control us since childhood. They may identify their own well-being with what we do. Often when a child does something wrong (or at least wrong in a parent's opinion), the parent says, "How could you do this to me?" Their foremost thought is *how they appear as parents* and their need to be in control of things.

But death to self includes our desires about our husbands, our wives, our children, our parents—any whom we love. We must put those desires on the cross as well and take our hands off them. This does not mean we don't seek to do the good and loving things that we can for them; it simply means we do not confuse their well-being with our own sense of self-worth.

Crucified with Christ

We must put all our desires on the cross. Once again, Jesus could not have been more clear:

If anyone desires to come after Me, let him deny himself, and take up his cross daily, and follow Me. For whoever desires to save his life will lose it, but whoever loses his life for My sake will save it. For what profit is it to a man if he gains the whole world, and is himself destroyed or lost? (Luke 9:23–25)

Deny your self and follow Christ, or deny Christ and follow your self. Those are the options. The results? Saving your life or losing it. "For whoever desires to save his life will lose it, but whoever loses his life for My sake will save it" (v. 24).* If we are going to follow Christ and gain our real life, we *must* take up our own cross. That is, we must experience our own crucifixion.

Crucifixion is an interesting thing. It is hard to do by yourself. In fact, it is impossible. You might be able to nail one hand to the cross, but what are you going to do when you get to the next hand? The crucifixion of the self is a cooperative affair between us and the Lord. We cannot die to self without the help of God's grace, for only God can satisfy our ultimate desire, and only God can convince our hearts that, when we die to self, he will raise us up. Death to self means releasing all our desires, our reputation, our glory, and having our way with other people. Everything. A dead person does not continue to have just a little life left in him. So, when it comes to our death to self, we have to say, "Lord, give it to me. I will take it. I will lay it all down for you."

Our task is *to understand* what death to self is and to understand that we cannot live in the Shepherd Psalm—a life without lack in the kingdom of God—until we have accepted it, recognized it, and said, "Lord, give this gift to me."

Christ was not crucified so that we wouldn't have to be. He was crucified so we could be crucified *with him*. He did not die so that we wouldn't have to die; he died so we could die *with him*. In death

---

* Matthew 16:24–26; Luke 14:25–33.

to self you are crucified *with* Christ (Gal. 2:20). It might help you to embrace this if you were to imagine Jesus on the cross and then imagine yourself being superimposed on him, hanging with him on the cross. As you do, repeat, "I am crucified with Christ," slowly several times.

Roots of Bitterness and Other Obstacles

You are likely to face some struggles after taking a stand like this. This has been true in my own experience. There may be times when you have to renew your commitment to release what you want, how you look, and especially what you are doing for the Lord. Much of our effort to do things for the Lord is really the resurgence of our desire to dominate and make things happen in our own strength.

We need to be watching for this. One good way to check our motives when doing something for the Lord is to see how sweet and patient we can remain when it does not go the way we want it to. If we believe we are acting out of love toward someone, but we become angry if the other person does not reciprocate, that indicates there is something beyond love motivating us. When something like that happens, we surrender again, saying, "Lord, here it is; I made a mess of it. I need your help." Paul said, "I die daily" (1 Cor. 15:31). We must do the same.

Even though we cannot do it alone, dying to self is still something *we do*. It is an act we intentionally perform. I encourage you to take time to study some of the wonderful passages about the identification of the believer with Christ, such as Romans 6:1–14 and Colossians 3:1–5. This "dying" will mean different things to different people. Some are troubled by what others say about them. Some are troubled by fears of lack. I knew a woman who became extremely uneasy and irritable if her refrigerator and cupboards were not packed with food. She had grown up in conditions of near starvation, so her exercise in death to self involved allowing her shelves to be sparse at times. Others have to work through bitterness regarding a past relationship. There may be resentment from being passed over for a promotion or the shame of being shunned by the popular ones at school. We have different backgrounds that come with different challenges and points of struggle.

Many of us carry deep, hidden scars of hurts that constitute what the Bible calls "a root of bitterness" (Heb. 12:15). These memories nearly always take hold in the realm of the self-life, and it is a real challenge to release them into God's hands. This kind of bitterness can take root in people who are truly devoted to Christ in almost every aspect of their lives, but they have been unwilling to crucify just this little bit. I say "unwilling," but the person who is wrestling with this is much more likely to use the word *unable* because it can feel like an impossible task.

This is where so many distressing stories come from about people in the ministry. Anyone who is attempting to help others in the way of Christ needs to *have* the life they are describing. They must have peace, purity, patience, and the other fruit produced by following Jesus. They must have a willingness to see others praised, while they are overlooked. They must die to the idea that what they want has any importance at all.

If death to self should bring us eye-to-eye with physical death, what do we say at that point? We say the same thing we would say about giving up an ice cream cone, or a job, or anything else. When we give up the smaller, everyday things we are training for times when greater sacrifice is required. This prepares us to say with Abraham, "Shall not the Judge of all the earth do right?" (Gen. 18:25). And we learn how to join Job in saying, "Shall we receive the good at the hand of God, and not receive the bad?" (Job 2:10 NRSV). That is, shall we receive the things we want and not the things we don't want? We can receive the things we do not want—or give up the things we do want—*if* we have decided, by the grace of God, that we can trust God to take care of us.

Death to Self and Life's Inevitabilities

But what about pain, failure, sickness, helplessness, or injury by others? Unfortunately, most Christians today have not been trained in how to meet these inevitable realities of life. So instead of rejoicing in tribulation, as we are instructed in James 1, they give up and sulk, closing themselves off from God. The self remains alive and on the throne of our lives as long as we take what happens to us as the ultimate point of reference. Instead, we need to engage in honest and thoughtful prayer, letting God know what we are going through, listening for his calming assurance that all will be well, then acting in trust against the lack or threat while praising God as we move forward with our lives.

We have a marvelous example of this in the life of Jehoshaphat, the ancient king of Judah, when he was attacked by an overwhelming number of enemies. He was a man of deep faith, responsible for much-needed reform and revival among the people. He had instructed the judges of the land with these words: "Thus you shall act in the fear of the LORD, faithfully and with a loyal heart" (2 Chron. 19:9). This is precisely how he acted when faced with the great threat from his enemies. When the report came to him of the impending invasion, we are told that "Jehoshaphat feared, and set himself to seek the LORD, and proclaimed a fast throughout all Judah" (2 Chron. 20:3).

Notice Jehoshaphat's response. First, he was honest about his fear. Next, he "set himself to seek the Lord"; that is, he purposed in his heart to seek God's help. Then he acted, proclaiming a national fast, enlisting the help of others, and directing them to seek the Lord as well. This is precisely what they did, with people coming from all over Judah to Jerusalem. When they were assembled, Jehoshaphat acted again by pouring out his heart to God in a prayer of desperate faith:

O Lord God of our fathers, are You not God in heaven, and do You not rule over all the kingdoms of the nations, and in Your hand is there not power and might, so that no one is able to withstand You? Are You not our God, who drove out the inhabitants of this land before Your people Israel, and gave it to the descendants of Abraham Your friend forever? And they dwell in it, and have built You a sanctuary in it for Your name, saying, "If disaster comes upon us—sword, judgment, pestilence, or famine—we will stand before this temple and in Your presence (for Your name is in this temple), and cry out to You in our affliction, and You will hear and save." (2 Chron. 20:6–9)

God's deeply reassuring response came through a priest named Jahaziel:

And he said, "Listen, all you of Judah and you inhabitants of Jerusalem, and you, King Jehoshaphat! Thus says the Lord to you: 'Do not be afraid nor dismayed because of this great multitude, for the battle is not yours, but God's. Tomorrow go down against them. They will surely come up by the Ascent of Ziz, and you will find them at the end of the brook before the Wilderness of Jeruel. You will not need to fight in this battle. Position yourselves, stand still and see the salvation of the LORD, who is with you, O Judah and Jerusalem!' Do not fear or be dismayed; tomorrow go out against them, for the LORD is with you." (vv. 15–17)

With that promise in mind, the next day Jehoshaphat encouraged the people to "believe in the LORD your God, and you shall be established; believe His prophets, and you shall prosper" (v. 20). Then, as was common military practice for God's chosen people, he gathered a choir together and had them march in front of his troops, singing their "fight song." His instructions focused on the most important thing the people could do in that situation:

And when he had consulted with the people, he appointed those who should sing to the Lord, and who should praise the beauty of holiness, as they went out before the army and were saying:

> "Praise the Lord,
> For His mercy endures forever."

> Now when they began to sing and to praise, the Lord set ambushes against the people of Ammon, Moab, and Mount Seir, who had come against Judah; and they were defeated. (vv. 21–22)

That is how we are to respond to life's difficulties and disappointments and the suffering that can—and most likely will—come to us. If we get ourselves out of the way, and focus our attention upon the God of our sufficiency, then we, too, can be singing songs of victory. With full-throated confidence, we can shout out with Paul:

> What then shall we say to these things? If God is for us, who can be against us? . . . Who shall separate us from the love of Christ? Shall tribulation, or distress, or persecution, or famine, or nakedness, or peril, or sword? . . .
> Yet in all these things we are more than conquerors through Him who loved us. For I am persuaded that neither death nor life, nor angels nor principalities nor powers, nor things present nor things to come, nor height nor depth, nor any other created thing, shall be able to separate us from the love of God which is in Christ Jesus our Lord. (Rom. 8:31, 35, 37–39)

Death to Self as Reality and Appearance

As I mentioned earlier, we must not confuse death to self with the psychological dynamics of self-hatred that may lead a person to take his own life. When Jesus said, "He who loves his life will lose it, and he who hates his life in this world will keep it for eternal life" (John 12:25), he was talking about *how it will appear* to the world when we do not live a life centered around our own desires.

When you become a Psalm 23 person, people will notice. Imagine the unimaginable: a person who works for a large corporation, but who is not trying to advance himself. The people who are watching that person will immediately decide there is something wrong with this individual; he must either be independently wealthy or hate his career. Similarly, if you knew that Jesus could have avoided his crucifixion, but then saw him let it happen, you might conclude that he hated his own life and wanted it to be over.

Death to self may appear to others as if we hate ourselves, but a great part of our growth includes disengaging from the expectations of others. As we do, it will not be long before people begin to identify us as joyful, peaceful, composed people, free from anxiety and animosity and in the grip of a deep happiness that comes to the person who has been liberated from the domination of desire. What may appear to others to be self-hatred is, in fact, the only way to become our true selves.

Don't Mistake Me for a Doormat

I spoke earlier about people who struggle with dying to self because they do not want to become doormats for Jesus. Death to self is not like that at all; it will turn you into a rock! Take Moses, for example. He was said to be the humblest man on earth (Num. 12:3), but he was hardly a doormat to Pharaoh or to the people of Israel. He was dead to himself, which meant that he was completely dead to other people's efforts to act from self. It will be the same for us. When we see people dominated by their lust for glory or insisting that their will be done, we will be in a position where we can be very firm in not cooperating with them, even if they're our loved ones. When we live in the Shepherd's sufficiency and die to our selves, we become the most firmly established people in this world.

Here, as always, Jesus is our example. Returning to the story of his crucifixion, think about how Jesus stood silent, like a rock, before Pilate. Pilate thought that he was in charge, that Jesus' fate was in his hands. Jesus knew differently and told him so: "You could have no power at all against Me unless it had been given you from above" (John 19:11).

When he was arrested in the Garden of Gethsemane and Peter lashed out with his sword, Jesus rebuked him with these words: "Put your sword in its place . . . do you think that I cannot now pray to My Father, and He will provide Me with more than twelve legions of angels?" (Matt. 26:52–53). He had already told them he was going to lay down his life, spoken in the very context in which he claimed to be Shepherd of the sheep:

> I am the good shepherd. The good shepherd gives His life for the sheep. . . .
>
> Therefore My Father loves Me, because I lay down My life that I may take it again. No one takes it from Me, but I lay it down of Myself. I have power to lay it down, and I have power to take it again. This command I have received from My Father. (John 10:11, 17–18)

It could not be clearer who was in control of Jesus' fate. At any moment, he could have put a stop to the madness and injustice of his arrest and trial. All he had to do was speak the words, and his Father would have ended it all. He made it work just like he wanted it to—not according to his own desires, but according to the will of God. "Not My will, but Yours, be done" (Luke 22:42).

Jesus was no doormat; he was simply dead to self, and fully alive to God. Dignity—*real dignity*—comes to the person who, by the grace of God, has embraced death to self. Such people are the only ones who can stand up to other selves, which, of course, includes serving them in ways that are good and right. Death to self gives us the place to stand in real dignity, in the yoke of Jesus, and not cooperate with the efforts of other people to live out their fleshly fantasies, whatever they may be.

Whatever Happened to Self-Worth?

Dying to self does not exclude having a proper sense of self-worth, including the need to feel recognized and valued. Recognition from others is a good and proper thing. But it must not be what controls our lives. It must not become *the* goal of our existence. If we find that our need for recognition is consuming our thoughts and determining our behavior, then we need to move to a higher source for our sense of our personal worth. That source is, of course, God's love for us. Apart from that, nothing fills the void that is left in our hearts. The knowledge that Jesus Christ died for us is the foundation of our self-worth.

That is probably not news to you; we hear this often in our churches, and we say it to each other repeatedly, which is precisely why we may need to work on personalizing it. We may need to say to ourselves, "Jesus died *for me!*" and ask God to bring this truth home to our hearts. We must take time with this in prayer and meditate on passages about God's love for us. Set aside days to spend alone with God to seek his face and to imagine that face shining with joy as it looks at you. As the ancient Jewish benediction puts it:

> *The Lord bless you and keep you;*
> *The Lord make His face shine upon you,*
> *And be gracious to you;*
> *The Lord lift up His countenance upon you* [look right at you]
> *And give you peace.*

(Num. 6:24–26)

It is the experience of having God look you right in the eye and saying, "I love *you*! I approve of *you*!" that is the unshakable ground of our self-worth. Our ultimate approval is from God, not from other human beings.

Yet we must beware of misunderstanding or misapplying this truth. Recognition by others is important, and, in fact, it is a good check on our pride, for one sign of pride is to disregard entirely what others say about us. Many people are puffed up in their pride and disregard what everyone else says, thinking, "Who are you? God alone is my judge." No. There is a very real sense in which others are my judges. I am supposed to listen to you. I need to know what you think about what I am doing. That is a part of what it means to be a member of the church and at peace with others (Heb. 12:14).

This is certainly true for those in professional ministry. In humility, every Christian leader is subject to the people to whom he or she ministers. This is, after all, what ministry is, professional or not—being subject to the needs of other people. That involves listening to them, being attentive to them. But if we become dependent on their opinions, we have ruined any chance of truly helping them, because now our primary concern is to gain their approval.

To keep a right heart we must remember that the face of God shining upon us in gracious approval is the basis of our value. We see this exemplified within the family. The child who lives under the shining face of a mother and father has no problem of self-worth. But when the faces of the parents turn away and withdraw, they become troubled. God does not withdraw his affection and approval from us; indeed, as Paul reminded us when he declared that nothing is able to separate us from the love of God that is in Christ Jesus our Lord (Rom. 8:38–39), therein lies the true and sure basis of self-worth.

Following Jesus on the Path to Death to Self

Humility is the beautiful condition of people who have learned to surrender their desires, their glory, and their power. Such people are in the process of becoming who they were meant to be in God's kingdom by giving up the life of the self. It is an essential quality for anyone who desires to live a life without lack as Jesus himself did. As Andrew Murray wrote:

> Humility is the path to death, because in death it gives the highest proof of its perfection. Humility is the blossom of which death to self is the perfect fruit. Jesus humbled Himself unto death, and opened the path in which we too must walk.*

According to the account in the gospel of Matthew that most of us are familiar with, Jesus concluded his teaching of how to pray with a statement of surrender to God: "Yours is the kingdom. Yours is the power. Yours is the glory" (6:13 PAR). When we pray this we are saying, "Lord, I give it up. It's all yours." We are then able to walk in humility as Jesus himself walked. This models the words King David, Jesus' great-, great-, great-, great- . . . grandfather, used many years before in his prayer dedicating the building materials that would be used in the construction of the temple in Jerusalem:

> Blessed are You, LORD God of Israel, our Father, forever
> and ever.
> Yours, O LORD, is the greatness,
> The power and the glory,
> The victory and the majesty;
> For all that is in heaven and in earth is Yours;

---

* Andrew Murray, *Humility* (New York: Anson D. F. Randolph & Co., 1895). The complete text of *Humility* is included in Appendix B of this book.

Yours is the kingdom, O Lord,
And You are exalted as head over all.

(1 Chron. 29:10–11)

When we walk in this way, we begin to know what Jesus was inviting us to when he said,

> "Come to me, all you who labor and are heavy laden, and I will give you rest. Take my yoke upon you and learn from Me, for I am gentle and lowly in heart, and you will find rest for your souls." (Matt. 11:28–29)

Yokes are used to "break in" a horse or an ox, to train them. When you harness a trained horse with one that is not trained, they don't need to pull the plow around the field very many times before the untrained horse has learned what to do. It is the same with us. When we put ourselves in the yoke with Jesus, we are learning that posture of a life beyond death that brings forth much fruit.

It is not unusual to find ourselves slipping out from under the yoke, with the self clamoring for us to do this or have that. We may have thought we were fine with surrendering our selves completely, but then realize this is not the case. We should not be taken aback by this; such experiences can give us important insight into how the process of dying to our selves works. We come up against a desire and discover that we are not as willing to give it up as we imagined. This becomes an opportunity to repent and receive further instruction in humility, through the realization that we are more in the habit of getting what we want than we were previously willing to admit.

I Surrender All

I was once asked if the death-to-self experience is a "once and for all" matter. We must certainly start with a "once," when we give ourselves up to God, saying, "Lord, by your grace now I am going to surrender what I want to you. I am going to surrender my glory and my recognition and my power to you. Help me!" While the practical working out of this will be progressive, there must be a point in time when we give up our desires to God, and we say, "Lord, you can have anything." One old hymn puts it well:

Here I give my all to Thee:
Friends and time and earthly store;
Soul and body Thine to be,
Wholly Thine forevermore.[3]

There must be a time when, in our own words and in our own way, we say to God, "Do with me what you will." Until we experience an abandonment of this kind, faith simply cannot be given to us safely. One of the main reasons we have such little faith is that we have not lived through the process of abandonment and come to the place where God can trust us with great faith. Once we have abandoned our lives to God, we are ready to receive the gift of faith that will enable us to love others well. Love with patience. Love without conditions. Love without irritation or anger. The kind of love we receive when we walk in the humility that comes from having died to our selves. As we shall see in the next chapter, that will be the fulfillment of love in the life without lack in the kingdom of God.

I will close this chapter with the famous prayer of the French martyr, Charles de Foucauld, as it so beautifully captures the spirit of the death-to-self life:

Father, I abandon myself
into your hands.
Do with me what you will.
Whatever you may do, I thank you,
I am ready for all, I accept all.

Let only your will be done in me
and in all your creatures.
I wish no more than this, O Lord.
Into your hands I commend my soul.
I offer it to you with all the love of my heart,
for I love you, Lord,
and so need to give myself,
to surrender myself into your hands
without reserve
and with boundless confidence,
for you are my Father.[4]

—Charles de Foucauld

CHAPTER 7

Sufficiency Completed in Love

Love seeks one thing only: the good of the one loved.

—THOMAS MERTON

Faith (trust), death to self, and agape love support our Psalm 23 life as a triangle of sufficiency. Each is a precious gift of God, who, in his graciousness, gives them to us and enables us to receive them in ever increasing abundance. He gives them to the willing, seeking heart through a process in which that willing and seeking is consistent, and even that is a gift.

God loves us, and because he loves us he delights in us, focuses upon us, relates to us, and serves us. So when we hear that a person is seeking God, it is evidence that God first loved him and has already "found" him. John 15:16 says, "You did not choose Me, but I chose you." It's as if there were a sign on the door that leads to eternal life that said, "Whosoever will may come." So you chose to walk through that door, and when you turned around to look back, you saw a sign above the door that said, "You did not choose Me, but I chose you."[1]

God's gracious gifts of faith, death to self, and agape love empower and enable our journey of growth into their fullness and into the abundance of eternal life we have in Jesus our Shepherd. John 3:16 beautifully captures the essence of this new life from above: "For God so loved the world that He gave His only begotten Son, that whoever believes in Him should not perish but have everlasting life."

From Faith to Death to Love

Trust in God and death to self open the floodgates for God's agape love to flow into us. God supplies the faith you need for this to happen, and your job is to position yourself so you can receive it. We are often troubled about our faith because we are trying to have faith for a particular thing, like patience. But the faith God wants to give us is not for that thing, but for trusting him.

Remember, faith has two parts: will and vision. We must be willing to see God as he is before God can further reveal himself to us and give us more faith. This requires us to live in such a way that we are consistently seeking him and growing in our faith, and this attitude of life requires more and more death to self as we go along.

Death to self is submitting all your desires to God. This abandonment of the self to God is the way to experience abundance in God. It means that, in God's hands, we are content for him to take charge of outcomes. And in that posture we make way for him to live in us and be with us, in order to achieve what is best for us and for others far beyond anything we can even imagine.

The more faith we have in God, the more death to self becomes the natural daily way for us. Jesus' suffering and physical death on the cross became the extreme expression of death to self as well as the ultimate symbol of our new life. He so graced the ugly instrument on which he died that the cross has become the most widely exhibited and recognized symbol on earth. But it is more than a symbol for us; it is a new way of living in confident fullness in God and his goodness.

It is essential to remember that Jesus did not give himself up to God in death with an attitude of resignation. He gave himself up *in faith*, certain that he would rise again and that the kernel of wheat that fell to the ground would bring forth abundant fruit. Death to self is abandonment to God *in faith*. It is laying down the satisfaction of my desires *with confidence* in the greatness and plenitude of God.

We can practice this through spiritual disciplines such as fasting, which can help us stay sweet and strong when we do not get what we want. If we can cheerily give up Twinkies, and peanuts, and steak, and things of that sort for a while, this will bring us to the place where we can say, "Lord, you're quite sufficient for me. If you want to take it away forever, that would be fine." This is how we do our part to practice surrendering to God. This is very serious business. Serious enough to be included in the Sermon on the Mount, where Jesus teaches about surrendering our own desires and laying down our efforts to secure ourselves by storing up treasures on earth (Matt. 6). He didn't say, "Don't have treasures." He didn't say, "Don't own things," or, "Don't eat steak." He didn't say any of that. He said, "Don't make this your god."

Then Comes Love

Faith has drawn us nearer to God and positioned us to receive his blessings. Death to self has made our life a willing receptacle for him, and now agape love flows into us like a river and out into a desperately thirsty world, completing the triangle to fulfill all that is needed for a life without lack.

To aid your understanding about the nature of love as it is alive in the life of a disciple, I want simply to present several passages of Scripture. Please take time to read these slowly, asking God to open your mind to receive these words as a gift that God is ready to give you. Let them be a vision of what your life is becoming as you journey in the light and easy yoke of Jesus Christ. Because, after all, God is love—and that is not an explanation of who God is; that's an explanation of what love is. He wants to give himself to you so you can more joyfully and freely give yourself and his love to others.*

---

* I am using the New Living Translation in these readings. I think it will help us see some of the things we need to appreciate, perhaps in a deeper way, as we come to think about love.

Luke 6:27–38 NLT

But to you who are willing to listen, I say, love your enemies! Do good to those who hate you. Bless those who curse you. Pray for those who hurt you. If someone slaps you on one cheek, offer the other cheek also. If someone demands your coat, offer your shirt also. Give to anyone who asks; and when things are taken away from you, don't try to get them back. Do to others as you would like them to do to you.

If you love only those who love you, why should you get credit for that? Even sinners love those who love them! And if you do good only to those who do good to you, why should you get credit? Even sinners do that much! And if you lend money only to those who can repay you, why should you get credit? Even sinners will lend to other sinners for a full return.

Love your enemies! Do good to them. Lend to them without expecting to be repaid. Then your reward from heaven will be very great, and you will truly be acting as children of the Most High, for he is kind to those who are unthankful and wicked. You must be compassionate, just as your Father is compassionate.

Do not judge others, and you will not be judged. Do not condemn others, or it will all come back against you. Forgive others, and you will be forgiven. Give, and you will receive. Your gift will return to you in full—pressed down, shaken together to make room for more, running over, and poured into your lap. The amount you give will determine the amount you get back.

John 13:31–35 NLT

As soon as Judas left the room, Jesus said, "The time has come for the Son of Man to enter into his glory, and God will be glorified because of him. And since God receives glory because of the Son, he will give his own glory to the Son, and he will do so at once. Dear children, I will be with you only a little longer. And as I told the Jewish leaders, you will search for me, but you can't come where I am going. So now I am giving you a new commandment: Love each other. Just as I have loved you, you should love each other. Your love for one another will prove to the world that you are my disciples."

Romans 12:9–10 NLT

Don't just pretend to love others. Really love them. Hate what is wrong. Hold tightly to what is good. Love each other with genuine affection, and take delight in honoring each other.

Romans 13:8–10 NLT

Owe nothing to anyone—except for your obligation to love one another. If you love your neighbor, you will fulfill the requirements of God's law. For the commandments say, "You must not commit adultery. You must not murder. You must not steal. You must not covet." These—and other such commandments—are summed up in this one commandment: "Love your neighbor as yourself." Love does no wrong to others, so love fulfills the requirements of God's law.

1 John 4:11–21 NLT

Dear friends, since God loved us that much, we surely ought to love each other. No one has ever seen God. But if we love each other, God lives in us, and his love is brought to full expression in us.

And God has given us his Spirit as proof that we live in him and he in us. Furthermore, we have seen with our own eyes and now testify that the Father sent his Son to be the Savior of the world. All who declare that Jesus is the Son of God have God living in them, and they live in God. We know how much God loves us, and we have put our trust in his love.

God is love, and all who live in love live in God, and God lives in them. And as we live in God, our love grows more perfect. So we will not be afraid on the day of judgment, but we can face him with confidence because we live like Jesus here in this world.

Such love has no fear, because perfect love expels all fear. If we are afraid, it is for fear of punishment, and this shows that we have not fully experienced his perfect love. We love each other because he loved us first.

If someone says, "I love God," but hates a fellow believer, that person is a liar; for if we don't love people we can see, how can we love God, whom we cannot see? And he has given us this command: Those who love God must also love their fellow believers.

1 Corinthians 13:4–7 NLT

Love is patient and kind. Love is not jealous or boastful or proud or rude. It does not demand its own way. It is not irritable, and it keeps no record of being wronged. It does not rejoice about injustice but rejoices whenever the truth wins out. Love never gives up, never loses faith, is always hopeful, and endures through every circumstance.

All You Need Is Love

While sitting in church one morning, I noticed a woman holding a little baby in her lap. The baby was looking into the woman's face. As I watched, I could almost see the substance of love moving from the one to the other. The little child, who was only a few months old, would look for a moment and then its face would spread out in a great big grin. Of course, the woman was looking back into the eyes of the child. A little child can look endlessly into your eyes without any self-consciousness or uneasiness. The adult in that situation can do the same. As a mother or father, or a grandparent with a grandchild, we are able simply to pour ourselves into that child in love.

When people love one another like this it creates a self-contained circle within which there is complete sufficiency in human terms. Children who are deeply loved and raised within such a circle can endure almost anything. I believe there is something about little children before the world has rubbed off on them that comes from being freshly knitted together by God in the womb (Ps. 139:13). They have a glow, an innocence, and a purity of trust. I think this is why Jesus used children to illustrate so many truths, such as, "Assuredly, I say to you, unless you are converted and become as little children, you will by no means enter the kingdom of heaven" (Matt. 18:3).

The pure, unfiltered love of children is why they have such a redeeming effect on people, and why in Isaiah's vision of the kingdom of God on earth he tells us that "a little child shall lead them" (Isa. 11:6). Little children have a way of somehow readjusting the adult world. They are not always able to do this, and many times they suffer because of that world, but in the love between a small child and a parent, we come the closest to seeing and experiencing love in its purest form.

We speak of falling or jumping headlong into love with someone. This can be harmful if understood as the source of our ultimate happiness, yet this is an expression of the unique character of love: it has within it something of that self-sufficiency and completeness of God himself. That is one reason love is such a powerful force. People who have grown up in an environment of love, even if it is only human love without a consciousness of God, will always have a tremendous resource that can never be taken away from them. If they have been loved rightly by their family, they have a treasure. Unfortunately, many people who were not loved rightly in their families enter marriage thinking, *Now, at last, I am really going to be loved*, but they soon find out that both they and their spouse are hampered in loving each other.

All these things direct us to the truth that perfect love is only found in God. Love is a gift from God, who is love. We can seek a gift and we can receive a gift, but we do not perform for a gift. So, when we read passages of Scripture like those above, we must remember that the call to us is not to *do* as much as it is to *receive*. We love him *because he first loved us*. This is why the preaching of the gospel is essential, and why there is nothing more important on the face of the earth than ministers and teachers of the gospel teaching plainly—*plainly!*—the love of God toward every person. That is why John 3:16 is so vital: "For God so *loved* the world . . ."

He First Loved Us

I love old hymns. They have a beautiful way of expressing truth, and the lyrics are often taken directly from the Scripture. These two stanzas from an eighteenth-century German hymn based on Luke 15:2 plainly illustrate the wide embrace of God's great love:

> Christ receiveth sinful men,
> spread this word of grace to all
> who the heavenly pathway leave,
> all who linger, all who fall.
> Sing it o'er and o'er again;
> Christ receiveth sinful men.
> Make the message clear and plain:
> Christ receiveth sinful men.[2]

One of the accusations the Pharisees made against Jesus was that he received sinners. This is very important for us to know. Jesus is the expression of the love of God for us, and in him we see the many ways God deals with people in mercy and grace. Jesus delighted in every individual; so, too, with us. He focused on what was of value in them; so, too, with us. He related to them, he associated with them, he got right down where they were and served them. So, too, with us; he meets us where we are, wherever we are. The darkest valley doesn't frighten him away. In the gospel of Mark we find a beautiful description of his affection for his disciples:

And He went up on the mountain and called to Him those He Himself wanted. And they came to Him. Then He appointed twelve, that they might be with Him and that He might send them out to preach, and to have power to heal sicknesses and to cast out demons. (Mark 3:13–15)

Notice the love of God in action: Jesus called "those *He Himself wanted.*" He wanted them. Why? First and foremost, so "that they might be with him." Yes, he had a mission for them, and that mission was to carry the love of God out into the world. But first he wanted them to be with him. He delighted in them.

The relational nature of Christ reflects the love of God, showing us what it is like and that it is *for us.* As we read in Romans 5:8, "God demonstrates His own love toward us, in that while we were still sinners, Christ died for us." Do not miss that phrase, "*while we were still sinners.*" That is what God is like: "He is kind to the unthankful and evil" (Luke 6:35). That is the gift we are seeking from the God who is love.

Acting in Love, or Just Acting?

Most people know that love is not just about the things we do. Love is an attitude of the heart. We know we can *act* in a loving way without really loving. (Obligation, obedience, reputation, or personal benefit may be our motive.) We sense and appreciate when things are done for us because someone truly loves us.

When pastors and therapists are helping someone, they often have to overcome the individual's attitude that says, "Well, you're just acting in a loving way toward me because it's your job." Attempts to assure them that they are truly cared for are necessary, but it usually takes time for them to believe that. And during that time, the counselors naturally tend to care more and more for those they are helping.

Service to others is one of the easiest ways to begin loving someone. Helping people is something we all can do, and it allows us to grow in our ability to relate to others. There are many levels in relating to people, including choosing to be with them, being present and engaged with them, and experiencing the *gift* of love as we move into delighting in them. But there is also a way of *not* being with people when we are with them. You have probably had the experience of someone being both present and absent at the same time.

It is not easy to consistently love our families and friends at the heart level, much less our enemies. We may be able to focus on what is good and valuable in them, but delighting in them as God delights in us is a more difficult matter. Delight in those who have just cursed us or who have hurt us, who have taken something we value and scorned us and looked down upon us? It is hard to do—very hard. This is where we often give up on love.

Paul knew that when we think like this we are working at the wrong level. We should not try to love that person; we should train to become the kind of person who would love them. Only then can the ideal of love pass into a real possibility and practice. Our aim under love is not to be loving to this or that person, or in this or that kind of situation, but to be a person possessed by love as an overall character of life. Our responses to the specific occasions when we are to act flow out of our overall character. I do not come to my enemies and then try to love them; I come to them as a loving person. The good tree bearing good fruit.

What Is Love?

As you can imagine, there have been many attempts to gain a clear and precise understanding of the "many splendored thing" we call love. The primary word for love found in the New Testament is *agape*. One of the better efforts at describing agape love is that of Thomas Oord in his book, *The Science of Love.* Oord precisely defines love as "acting intentionally, in sympathetic response to others (including God), to promote overall well-being."[3] Importantly, this definition distinguishes love from desire and locates it in the will, leaving room for desire and feeling to play an appropriate role in love without making them the heart of the matter.[4]

In our cultural context, it is necessary to emphasize that love and emotion are not identical. We can act in loving ways even when we do not "feel loving." It cannot be said too often that agape love is not the same as desire or delight, although these might accompany agape love. Desire and feelings generally have a different nature than love. To be confused about this is to remain helpless to enter into love and to receive it into ourselves.

Desire and feelings are more matters of impulse than of considering and choosing the best alternative. They are concerned with their own satisfaction, not with what is better and possibly best. If a choice is made with a vision broad enough and clarified by love, it will find what is good and right. If choice is surrendered to God, united with his will, it will be able to do what is best.

Nonetheless, I believe that Oord's definition fails to capture central features of love, especially those presented by Jesus and Paul. For them, love is something that has three essential characteristics:

1. Love arises in people whose lives are already marked by certain qualities of the whole self, chief of which are faith in our all-sufficient God and joyful embracing of death to self.
2. Love involves an orientation of the whole self toward what is good and right.
3. Love has amazing, supernatural power for good as it indwells the individual.

These are essential characteristics of agape love as Paul and the New Testament present it. Notice here that *love is not action*; it is *a source of action.* Love is a condition out of which actions of a certain type emerge. It is a condition that explains how the three marks of love could be true and must be true.

Love is not an abstract ideal impossible to realize in our day-to-day lives. It is an overall condition of real people, living in the real world, who are poised to promote the well-being of those within their range of influence. Such people are ready to act in ways that bring about good. But again, love is not an action or a feeling or an emotion or an intention, even though it gives rise to intentions and to actions and is associated with some "feelings" and resistant to others. Only such an understanding of agape love as an overall disposition does justice to the New Testament teachings about love and gives us a coherent idea of love that can be aimed at in practice and implemented. After all, love is meant to be lived.

Such love is holistic, not something one turns on or off for this or that person or thing. Its orientation is toward life as a whole. It dwells on good wherever it may be found and supports it in action. Love is nourished by the good and the right and the beautiful. That is why Paul wrote to his Philippian friends:

> Finally, brethren, whatever things are true, whatever things are noble, whatever things are just, whatever things are pure, whatever things are lovely, whatever things are of good report, if there is any virtue and if there is anything praiseworthy—meditate on these things." (Phil. 4:8)

Remember, deeper than the fact that God loves us is this: he *is* love. He wills nothing but what is good. That is his identity, and it explains why he loves individuals even when he is not pleased with them or loved by them in return. When Paul directed us to "be imitators of God, as beloved children, and live in love, as Christ loved us and gave himself up for us," this is what he was talking about

(Eph. 5:1–2 NRSV). We are called and enabled to love as God loves by becoming like God as loving persons.

An Anatomy of Love

When we understand that love is an overall disposition to bring about good, we can better understand some of Paul's statements such as, "Now the purpose of the commandment is love from a pure heart, from a good conscience, and from sincere faith" (1 Tim. 1:5). Notice that the aim of Christian instruction (that is, what "commandment" refers to) is love. This love arises "*from* a pure heart"—one that is not wallowing in fantasies of sensual gratification or malice—and "*from* a good conscience"—one unburdened with guilt from the failure to do the good and the right—and "*from* sincere faith"—genuine confidence in God's goodness and care for us, a love from which nothing can separate us.* We do not achieve the disposition of agape love *by direct effort*, but by training: attending to and putting into place the conditions out of which it arises. This is where the regular practice of the spiritual disciplines comes strongly into play.[5] Once again, the goal is not to be people who do loving things but to become the kind of people who naturally, joyfully, and easily love.

The law is not the source of righteousness, but it is always the way of the righteous. It guides people into actions that conform to what is good and right. Love seeks the same result but from the innermost place from which our actions come (John 7:38; Luke 6:45). This is in keeping with Jeremiah's vision of the time when God will write his law on the hearts of his people (Jer. 31:33). If we take care of the source of our action—the heart—action will take care of itself.** Then we won't be constantly hindered or defeated by

---

* Romans 8:37–39.
** This was certainly Jesus' understanding of the nature of acts such as murder and adultery. See Matt. 5:21–30.

our conflicted self, which winds up doing what it "intends" not to do or not doing what it "intends" to do.*

When we read 1 Corinthians 13, it is important to understand that Paul is not issuing commands; he is not saying that *we* ought to be patient, kind, humble, and so forth. He is describing love itself as having these characteristics. That, after all, is what the passage actually says. So we "pursue love" by advancing our faith and dying to self through appropriate training and practice, and the love we receive from God takes care of the rest. These virtues arise from the overall disposition of love, because love, by its very nature, seeks what is good and right before God.

Love enables a person to not only refrain from hating his enemies but to instead seek what is good for them along with all others involved. This does not mean always giving in to what the enemies (or friends) want or letting them have their way. That might be the worst thing you could do to them and, therefore, cannot be the loving thing.

Love, then, is a condition of the will, embodied in the fundamental dimensions of the human personality, guiding them for the purpose of serving the good. In the deepest sense, love is not something you choose to *do*; it is what you become—a loving person. Your will is your capacity to bring things and events and processes into existence. It is the control center of the self: the "heart" or the human spirit. It is meant to direct all aspects of the self. When love pervades your will, all these other dimensions—your mind (with its thoughts, images and feelings, desires and emotions), your body, your social relationships, indeed your whole soul**—work in

---

* As examples of a conflicted self, see Peter's three denials of Christ (Matt. 26:34, 69-75) or Paul's experience described in Romans 7:14-24.
** "Soul" is here defined as the hidden or "spiritual" side of the person. It includes an individual's thoughts and feelings, along with heart or will, with its intents and choices. It also includes an individual's bodily life and social relations, which, in their inner meaning and nature, are just as "hidden" as the thoughts and feelings.

harmony with and in service to the kingdom of God, and your life becomes a testimony to the God who meets your every need.[6]

The Heart of a Servant

One of the hallmarks of those who live a life without lack is the freedom to serve others. From Jesus' perspective, there is no greater calling than to be a servant.* And whatever our place in life, as love fills and flows through us we will be engaged in caring for the welfare of others. The Shepherd Psalm portrays this as it poetically describes the abundance of God's provision in the language of a feast at which the psalmist is an honored guest.

Speaking to God, he says, "You prepare a table before me" (v. 5). On this table is a full banquet, including a cup that is overflowing. But that's not all. Surprise guests are in the room—the psalmist's enemies! The Lord has prepared this meal "in the presence of my enemies" (v. 5). We do not know if they are sitting at the table with him, but they are in his presence. I imagine that David, lacking nothing, and realizing that he certainly does not deserve this kind of divine accommodation, stops and serves his enemies, offering them food and drink and inviting them into the fellowship of the Shepherd's sufficiency. Having *been* served, he is free *to* serve.

Jesus, of course, is our master and model in this regard. Next to the passion events that led up to and included his crucifixion, there may be no clearer and more powerful expression of Jesus' servant heart than what took place at another feast, in an Upper Room hours before his passion began.

The scene is described in the thirteenth chapter of the gospel of John, which begins with these words: "Now before the Feast of the Passover, when Jesus knew that His hour had come that He should depart from this world to the Father, having loved His own

---

* Matthew 23:11: "The greatest among you will be your servant."

who were in the world, He loved them to the end" (v. 1). Clearly, John is preparing his readers for a lesson in how Jesus "loved them to the end."

For Jesus, this meal was the beginning of that end. He recognized that the hour had come in which he was going to be killed. He knew that in just a few hours he would be taken by the Roman soldiers and the priests who were guiding them, and he would lay down his life. A normal person would be preoccupied with this knowledge. But when Jesus came to this moment he was thinking, *What would be the most important lesson for me to leave my friends?* John's narrative continues:

> Jesus, knowing that the Father had given all things into His hands, and that He had come from God and was going to God, rose from supper and laid aside His garments, took a towel and girded Himself. After that, He poured water into a basin and began to wash the disciples' feet, and to wipe them with the towel with which He was girded. (John 13:3–5)

This is faith. Everything was in his hands. Everything! Yet he was free to give it up, for he was secure in his knowledge that "he had come from God and was going to God." It was in that confidence that he was prepared to do what he did—in the Upper Room with his disciples, then later in the garden, in Pilate's hall, and on the cross.

As he was washing the disciples' feet he came to Peter who, obviously troubled by what Jesus was doing, exclaimed, "Master, you shouldn't be washing our feet like this." Jesus was not surprised at this response. He had observed the dynamics of this little group and had chosen to answer the question on everyone's mind: "Who is going to wash our feet?" Their unspoken answer had unanimously been, "Not me! I'm not going to wash any feet." We can be sure this question had been on their minds because at this particular meal there was no host. The host normally would arrange for the foot washing.

All having answered the question by their silence; they were ready for an essential lesson about love. So Jesus engaged in serving them by meeting their needs. First, the need for clean feet. In those days feet really needed to be washed. It should have been done before the meal, because in that time they ate lying down, so noses and feet were not all that far apart. It would have been nice if the feet had been washed and anointed before the meal. But the disciples were unwilling to stoop (literally) to do that, which proved they had a far deeper need than dirty feet; they needed to learn about the servant heart of love. Apparently even after Jesus showed them, they still did not understand. So he made sure they got the point:

> So when He had washed their feet, taken His garments, and sat down again, He said to them, "Do you know what I have done to you? You call Me Teacher and Lord, and you say well, for so I am. If I then, your Lord and Teacher, have washed your feet, you also ought to wash one another's feet. For I have given you an example, that you should do as I have done to you. Most assuredly, I say to you, a servant is not greater than his master; nor is he who is sent greater than he who sent him. If you know these things, blessed are you if you do them. (vv. 12–17)

One way we have responded to this story is to have foot-washing ceremonies, often on Maundy Thursday of Holy Week.* While these services can be meaningful, often the main benefit is bestowed upon the person who is doing the washing, rather than on the one receiving it. This is because there is no unmet need being addressed;

---

* *Maundy* is derived from the Latin *mandatum* for "mandate," because Jesus gives us a mandate, a new commandment, to love one another as he has loved us.

the recipient's feet are not in need of cleaning. Foot washing is symbolic of a duty to be humble, which, while certainly a praiseworthy virtue, is not the only point Jesus was making. He was actually helping people, delighting in them, relating to them in meaningful ways to meet a need and promote their well-being. In this sense we should hear him say, "A new commandment I give to you, that you love one another; as I have loved you, that you also love one another. By this all will know that you are My disciples, if you have love for one another" (John 13:34–35).

The Brand-New Old Commandment

What was "new" about this commandment? Certainly it was not new in the sense that it had never been heard before. John used similar language in his first epistle when he wrote, "An old commandment I give to you," and then he said, "No, it's a new commandment" (1 John 2:7–8 PAR). So which is it, old or new? Jesus was essentially saying, "Listen, you have heard about love ever since Moses told you to love your neighbor as yourself. I am showing you what that really means. You are to love one another with the same concern with which I have loved you. Do that and it will be obvious that you are my disciples." The newness of the commandment lies in the kind of love Jesus was demonstrating, a love flowing freely and easily from his God-rooted resources. When we love like this it is not the result of human effort, but of the radical with-God-ness we have in him. It is a gift of God.

If you look at Mohammed, or Buddha, or Confucius, or any other leaders, you will never find anyone who loved his disciples the way Jesus did. Not one of them. Some people, in an attempt to prove the superiority of Christ, focus on the fact that only he rose from the dead. That is true. But deeper still, the very character of Jesus stands out in how he related to his followers. None of these other leaders were willing to die for their disciples. And when you read their teachings, you can clearly see that Jesus was the only one living in the realm of agape love.

Within the academic world there are those, like the late John Hick, who seek to grade world religions by comparing their power to transform and fulfill human personality.[7] On this basis, every religion in the world flunks except Christianity. Only Jesus passes that test. Only Jesus enables his followers to live a life of selfless, joyful, anxiety-free, loving service on behalf of others. Having said that, the sad truth is that our churches today do not preach this as *the* message of the gospel. They have not offered this matchless life to people. They have not asked, "Would you actually like to live like this? Would you like to be possessed by this kind of love?"

You can be. God will give it to you, and when he does, these things that Jesus and Paul say about love will be realized in your life, not because you did it, but because you welcomed love in and let it take possession of you. You will be able to say with the old hymn, "I was sinking deep in sin, far from the peaceful shore . . ." but "Love lifted me."[8]

While it is good to remember that love saves us, it is equally true that love is meant to enter our lives, our bodies, and our hearts. We are to be temples of the Holy Spirit, sacred spaces in which God dwells. He is the Spirit of Love who desires to reside within us and empower us to love as he loves. When the gospel of Jesus Christ is fully proclaimed, it includes offering this kind of life to people. The opportunity to be able to love people—*all people*—like Jesus does must be clearly presented, and then we must decide if that is something we want. If we truly want love like that, God will give it to us. But if we do not choose to become as loving as Jesus, we will never know a life without lack. For such a life is realized through love filling our lives. Faith is only completed in love, because our faith is in a God of love—no other. The more this faith grows in us, the more we will experience the carefree joy of Christ's love.

How to Love Somebody (But Not Everybody)

You might be saying, "Well, you don't know the people in my life. If you did, you'd realize how hard it is to love them. I've tried, and it just doesn't work!" Without denying that it can be tough, the reality is that these are just the kind of people we need to love, and whom God can enable us to love. Of course, we must *want* to love people, and we need to be willing to think about it in practical ways. More precisely, we need to decide who we are going to love and how we are going to do it. This is something the Lord must lead us into, and there are some simple steps we can take as we seek to enter a life of love.

First, we must realize that we are not called to love everybody. We are called to love people, but "everybody" is not a living, flesh-and-blood person (which is one of the things that makes the thought of loving "everybody" so delightful!). If you are going to love at all, you are going to love "somebody," not "everybody." To be sure, love is inclusive. God's embrace is meant for all people. God loves everybody, but God has bigger arms and a bigger heart than we do. You are not infinite, and you cannot pick up the slack for other people who are not fulfilling their obligations to love those around them.

We are called to love our neighbor. *Neighbor* is an old English word that means, literally, "the boor who is neigh thee," that is, nearby. Not the *bore* who is nearby! A boor is a farmer, and a neighboor is the farmer nearby. You are called to love those who are neigh thee—your family, your friends, your coworkers, the folks in your neighborhood, and, yes, even the "enemies" in your life, the ones who irritate, demean, frustrate, and mistreat you.

I have neighbors who come to my door and want to borrow my tools. That's where the rubber meets the road for me. I like my tools. You may know what that's like. You like your tools, and you like to have them there when you need them; they are a part of your power to cope with life! So here comes my neighbor who says, "I want to borrow your crescent wrench." And I pull it out of the toolbox—kiss it!—and hand it to him. That is loving my neighbor, dying to self, and trusting in God (for the return of my wrench)—all wrapped up in one simple act of obedience.

Finding That Special Somebody to Love

It is important for us to get away from the idea of loving everyone. We cannot love everyone; it is not physically possible. When I was a child, my dear father would tip his hat to every car he met as we drove down the road. Imagine tipping your hat to all the cars you meet today. You would wear out your hat, and your head! You cannot love *every*-body. Only *some*-body.

The question is then, "which somebody?" Who are you going to choose for your experiment in love? You will likely do better if you begin with people who are not your closest friends and family. Of course, God may have gifted you such that you truly do love those who are close to you. But perhaps these are the relationships you find the most difficult, and you need to start elsewhere. There could be someone at the office or someone at work whom it will be easier to love. Eventually you will be ready to focus on the more difficult, and probably more important, relationships. God desires to heal our souls, and then we are better able to love the people he brings into our lives.

Jesus said, "Love your enemies" (Matt. 5:44), and I take that to include a promise. It is a promise that the burden of hatred and enmity can be lifted from me toward that person. He also said, "Forgive" (Mark 11:25). That, too, is a promise that I can escape the burden of unforgiveness. He will help me do that. But it will take time, training, and grace, and it is a good expression of proper humility that we not begin with the hard cases. Everyone has heard, "Love your enemies," but usually when we try to do that we fail because it does not work the way we thought it would. So select someone with whom you have a fairly good relationship, and practice loving that person.

Next, set a time frame. Focus on that one person for one week. Remember, this does not mean you try to have pleasant feelings about them. It is fine to have such feelings, but that is not the goal of loving them, nor are these feelings necessary in order to love. Loving them means caring for them, and it starts with your decision to love them. You will not drift into love; you must decide to love. And then ask God to help you, because you will only be able to love as God assists you in the realities of that concrete relationship. Ask God to show you something in this person that is good and for which you can be thankful. Let the Lord show you a good thing about them, and then love them *by being thankful for them.*

It is likely that you will want to *do something* for the person for whom you are thankful. Gratitude calls forth a response. Since love involves service, you will want to think about ways you can help your chosen someone. Is there a need you can supply? Is there a hardship you can help relieve? Is there a load you can lighten? Think of things *you* can actually do to help them. Love always involves the use of your own resources and abilities—the gifts God has given you—for the purpose of serving his kingdom by serving others. If a friend needs legal help, and you are a computer engineer, you may not be able to help her *in that particular need.* But you may be able to refer her to an honest and experienced lawyer whom you know. Or you may be able to offer financial assistance. You certainly can pray for her. Indeed, prayer should always be involved. The point is that love is expressed in service that truly helps someone by the use of our abilities and resources.

Because love seeks to be helpful in practical ways, you may have to be secretive in your plan. If your friend finds out you are doing this, she may become very uneasy about it, and the result might be that you are unable to improve her life in any way. While you do not want to lie about it, neither do you just walk up to someone and announce, "I'm going to love you by doing this helpful thing for you." Just begin to work toward her good. The aim is *to be* a loving person, not just to be *seen as* a loving person. We are not trying to prove anything to anyone. Love does not force itself upon others. If a neighbor asks to borrow your lawnmower because his is broken, do not tell him, "Yes, you can borrow my lawnmower, and you must also borrow all my other tools, since I am supposed to go the extra mile, like Jesus said." If you do this, you are serving yourself, not your neighbor.

Love Means Being Able to Say No

One more practical matter: because love seeks the well-being of the beloved, at times saying no may be the loving thing to do. When such an occasion arises, it is best to prayerfully sit and talk with the person, explaining the reasons for your noncooperation. A child, for example, might ask his parents to lie for him for a "good" reason. That is something you just cannot do in love. You serve a child in that circumstance by explaining to him that truth is extremely important. If he has been led into fellowship with Jesus and has understood some truths from the Bible, you might even teach him how the foundation of the kingdom of evil is based upon lies, as we discussed in chapter 3. You could ask him how he would like being lied to and say, "If I lie to them for you, how will you ever trust me, since you know I lie for people?" Of course, you would have to be prepared for the child—and for adults as well—to be very unhappy with you. You need to receive that response patiently and lovingly and be firm without irritation. With children that is often the primary challenge.

If you need to resist a neighbor's request for his own good—or yours—remember this important truth from the last chapter: true death to self means we do not allow others to exalt their desires to the ultimate place and then expect us to conform to those desires. This is very important, and it may cause them to say, "Well, you don't really love me." We, in turn, must be prepared to respond,

"No, I really do love you, and that is why I cannot do as you ask." We must be very firm on this, again trusting God to be at work in the neighbor's life and having a firm place to stand in the midst of his upset response.

In all this we must be careful not to get our egos involved. We are not serving people to prove something about ourselves. If you find yourself in that position, just lay it down before God.* It is a spiritual problem that you and God need to work out together. Since this is an internal issue of the heart, not visible to others, you may be able to continue to help them, but you will need to address it.

Another reason we must keep our egos in check is that some people, especially those with severe emotional problems, will make us a god in their lives. This is a situation where the church or our fellowship can be of tremendous help when great demands are being placed upon us. We should come to our brothers and sisters and talk to them about such a situation, asking for guidance and prayer and possibly for others to share the load. Helping people can include a lot of traps for you and for those being helped.

As you see, effective, loving service requires deep maturity. The only thing that can guide us well is faith in God, a genuine concern for the well-being of others, and an unwillingness to do or cooperate with what is wrong. Some things can be quite complex, such as addictions or marriage problems or involvement in illegal activities. You need to know your own limitations in helping directly and when it is best to connect someone with organizations qualified to deal with the more significant issues. You must be careful.

The Joy of Loving

As you grow in your capacity to love, something is going to happen to you: you will find that you have great joy. One of the greatest

---

* This may be your motivation if you become irritable with the people involved when they do not respond as you desire.

things in the world is to love people. It is so much better than hatred or indifference. We were created for love. This is the source of the attractive power of the great prayer called "The Sower" or "The Peace Prayer," often attributed to Saint Francis of Assisi.*

> Lord, make me an instrument of thy peace.
> Where there is hatred, let me sow love.
> Where there is injury, pardon.
> Where there is doubt, faith.
> Where there is despair, hope.
> Where there is darkness, light.
> Where there is sadness, joy.
> Oh, Divine Master, grant that I may not so much seek
> to be consoled, as to console.
> To be understood as to understand.
> To be loved as to love.
> For it is in giving that we receive.
> It is in pardoning that we are pardoned.
> It is in dying that we are born to eternal life.

"It is in giving that we receive." Jesus taught what we may call the reciprocity of goodness:

> Judge not, and you shall not be judged. Condemn not, and you shall not be condemned. Forgive, and you will be forgiven. Give, and it will be given to you: good measure, pressed down, shaken together, and running over will be put into your bosom. For with the same measure that you use, it will be measured back to you. (Luke 6:37–38)

---

* Editor's Note: There is good reason to believe that Saint Francis is not the author of the prayer, which did not appear in public until 1915. See "The Story Behind the Peace Prayer of St. Francis," Franciscan Archive, https://franciscan-archive.org/patriarcha/peace.html.

As you give love, you receive love and experience joy. Joy in turn will increase your capacity to love, and you will become capable of being kind to the "hard-to-loves" in your life.

They may be those in your family. Parents often have hard times with their children because, if mine are anything representative, they do not always do what we believe they should do. We are wounded by this and tend to feel that they are walking evidence that we have been wrong, that we are not good people. Or the reverse may be true for a child having to deal with a difficult parent.

In either case we begin by asking God to help us delight in them, focus on what is good for them, and celebrate what is valuable within them. This may involve going back in our memories, and saying, "Lord, help me to remember the good." Because it may be that things have been so bad that you are unable to see anything good or valuable. No one is only an unvarnished lump of bad. We must seek to see them, to relate to them, to be with them as it is appropriate and good. Set your mind to be with them, and pay attention to them. Do what is good for them. Look into their eyes, and talk to them and listen to them; serve them, help them, give to them. Enjoy them. Praise God for them.

Love Means Getting to Say, "I Forgive You"

This kind of response has all the power of God in it for dealing with other people. If there is any hope for people, it is that they can be redeemed through love. As Peter learned firsthand, "love will cover a multitude of sins" (1 Peter 4:8). Love can redeem. While we must not assume the responsibility of redeeming our enemies—that is God's business—we can be set free from bondage to our enemies. The person who has the most power over your life is the person you have not forgiven. That person holds a part of you in bondage. To forgive is to regain your self.

Forgiveness is a special kind of relationship, which, if you do not dwell in it fully, you cannot dwell in it at all. This is why Jesus said that unless you forgive, you will not be forgiven. You cannot receive forgiveness if you do not give forgiveness, because you will never understand the heart of God unless you see that mercy should govern all our relationships to one another. Forgiveness is not like a spigot you can turn on for one person and turn off for another. It is much deeper than that.

When you set out to forgive someone, it will help you greatly if you can set aside three common errors that have been attached to forgiveness in our society. First, forgiveness does not require reconciliation with your enemy. Reconciliation is two-sided, and both sides must be willing participants. Even God himself will not steamroll over the will of another person. If a person is sufficiently resolute in his heart and resistant to the Spirit of God, there can be no reconciliation.

Second, forgiveness does not require you to forget what happened. It is simply wrong to say to another person, "Oh, come on, if you really forgave me, you would have forgotten it." You may never forget what a person did, and you may find that you treat them differently because you have learned something about their character that you didn't know before, but you can choose to love them for who you now know them to be and support their efforts to grow. Forgiveness lets people off the hook and frees us to love them.

Third, forgiveness does not mean you stop hurting. This is a common issue between a husband and wife when one has been unfaithful. The offending party may ask forgiveness, and the wounded one says, "Yes, I'll forgive you," but remains deeply wounded. The guilty one, who becomes offended and hurt because the other person is still in pain, says in effect, "Stop hurting so I can stop hurting! If you don't stop hurting, that means you haven't forgiven me!" Forgiveness is the choice not to punish or seek revenge. It is not—*it cannot be*—the choice to stop hurting. Forgiveness can come long before the healing is complete.

Once we make that choice to forgive we will need God's help. Like love and faith and death to self, we cannot fully forgive without God's supply of forgiveness (Col. 3:13). We can, however, choose not to punish the one who has hurt us, and we can ask God to help us be aware when we start to entertain the idea of possible punishment or revenge. Those ideas are often coming down the track long before they go into play, and we can see them growing larger in the corner of our mental eye. That's the way temptation works. Temptation never hits you without announcing itself beforehand and giving you a choice. You must be prepared to call out for God's help to find the way of escape (1 Cor. 10:13). It also helps to remember this: to forgive is to love is to be set free . . . and to know deep joy.

A Dynamic Life Without Lack

Faith. Death to self. Agape love. I have described these as the three points of the triangle of sufficiency at the heart of the life without lack. They are not in a static, but a dynamic relationship to each other. There is a divine synergism between them, as each one nourishes the other. Faith feeds death to self, death to self feeds love, love feeds faith, and on it gloriously goes.

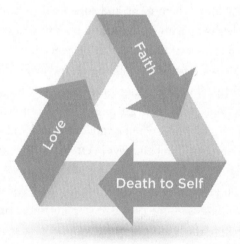

When these are fundamental realities in your life, you are exactly where David was when he said, "The Lord is my shepherd, I shall not want." You will find yourself saying, "What about that thing I was wishing for? I thought I needed it. But now, I find that I am just fine without it!" When you get to that point, your life is so full of good that you are prepared to take the absence of something from your life as sufficient proof that you do not need it. Not because you are trying to make it happen, but because it simply happens to those who know the all-sufficiency of God. This is not something you can make happen, but God can . . . and will. The ultimate freedom that comes to the one whose life is characterized by faith, death to self, and love is the assurance that you have everything you need in God.

CHAPTER 8

All the Days of My Life

God, I want to give You every minute of this year.
I shall try to keep You in mind every moment of my
waking hours. . . .
I shall try to let You be the speaker and direct
every word.
I shall try to let You direct my acts.
I shall try to learn Your language.

—FRANK LAUBACH

The closing verse of Psalm 23 says, "Surely goodness and mercy shall follow me all the days of my life; and I will dwell in the house of the LORD forever" (v. 6). How does this come to be? What is our part in dwelling with the Lord and living our days in such a way that goodness and mercy follow us in our wake? We move now from knowing to doing, from the idea of a life without lack into its reality. It is time to apply what we've been studying, and make plans to spend a day with Jesus. This will not be a day where you go away alone with him on a retreat; this will be a day when you invite him to stay with you throughout a normal "day in the life of [insert your name here]."

The emphasis throughout the Shepherd's Psalm is the fact that God is with us. The life without lack flows out of our relationship with him. Our challenge is to stay with him in the increasing belief that God truly desires to be with us. God wants to be with *me*. He wants to be with *you*. It is true. I assure you it is true. It is the testimony of the biblical writers from beginning to end.[1] In particular, it is the clear promise of a favorite passage of mine—Hebrews 13:5–6:

> Let your conduct be without covetousness; be content with such things as you have. For He Himself has said, "I will never leave you nor forsake you." So we may boldly say: "The LORD is my helper; I will not fear. What can man do to me?"

Don't covet; be content with what you have. The freedom from the frantic desire to *have* is grounded in God's promise to *never leave us*. Whatever we have or do not have makes no difference because we are with the one who will provide everything we need, and this allows us to be content.

The only caveat is that God's promise is made to those who trust him; who desire to be with him and to be about his business. It is important for us to understand what his business is, and especially to understand that it is not some exclusive category of "ministry" that only a select group of seminary graduates can engage in. Of course, it does not exclude seminary graduates either, but their "religious" training can tend to crowd out the things a person really needs to know in order to live before God and help others do the same.[2]

Shortly before he departed earth, Jesus gave his "great commission" to his disciples, saying,

> Go therefore and make disciples of all the nations, baptizing them in the name of the Father and of the Son and of the Holy Spirit, teaching them to observe all things that I have commanded you; and lo, I am with you always, even to the end of the age. (Matt. 28:19–20)

We are given a clue here that Jesus' promises to us are for the road. They are given to those walking the road with him, those who are going about their lives intent on doing what he says to do. This is what we must always keep in mind: nobody is excluded; everyone is included. Every person—and that includes *you*—is invited *by* Jesus to be *with* Jesus. If we are with him, everything is taken care of.

Section 1: Preliminaries for Going on the Road with Jesus

All journeys require preparation. We make our plans, deciding where we will go and when we will leave. We make sure we have the right clothes, enough money, and sufficient snacks to get us from point A to point B. We want our journey to be both pleasant and successful, so we do our best to be prepared ahead of time. It is the same with spending a day with Jesus. We need to prepare for it beforehand. We have three essential preliminaries to attend to.

Preliminary 1: Determining Your Desire

The pressing question for each of us is this: "How can I be with him as I go?" What is it we can *do* in the ordinary days of our lives so we might experience the Twenty-Third Psalm presence of the Shepherd throughout the day? Since this is a practical question about how we are going to spend our time, we must first answer another practical question: "Do I really want this?" This question needs answering for the simple reason that *if God is going to be with us, we should expect that our lives will be extremely different from ordinary human life.*[3] That is, our ordinary lives, our day-to-day-at-home-at-work-at-play-maybe-even-at-church lives will be *extra-ordinary*. We should expect nothing less. Of course, the reality is that most of religion is organized around keeping God at a distance, allowing us to "go see him" when we want. We say things such as, "Lord, this morning we come into thy presence," to which God might be saying, "Really? Where have you been?" For God has always been present. As the psalmist rhetorically asked,

> Where can I go from Your Spirit?
> Or where can I flee from Your presence?
> If I ascend into heaven, You are there;
> If I make my bed in hell, behold, You are there.
> If I take the wings of the morning,
> And dwell in the uttermost parts of the sea,
> Even there Your hand shall lead me,
> And Your right hand shall hold me.
>
> (Ps. 139:7–10)

Here the inescapability of God is experienced as a good thing, but many people are not so sure about this. God reveals himself, but in a way that allows him to be hidden to all but those who resolutely seek him (Jer. 29:13). One can deny God. That is a choice. But it is a choice that he has made possible. We are the ones who wander, who flee, who often would rather be anywhere but in the presence of God. But if we believe—truly believe—that God is like Jesus, and that Jesus is the Good Shepherd under whose care we are provided with all we need, then the opportunity to spend our days with him should be, as we say, a no-brainer.

But still the question remains for you to answer: do you really want to experience extraordinary days in the presence of Jesus? You need to be honest with yourself about this. Many regard Jesus as necessary, but not desirable; necessary for salvation, but not desirable as a friend and teacher. You should ask yourself, "Am I really enthralled with Jesus or only prepared to put up with him?" Your answer may not be as holy as you would like it to be, but you must not attempt to fake it. God already knows your answer, and the level of your desire for Jesus to be with you has no bearing on how much he loves you. Depending on your answer, you can decide either to close this book now, or keep reading.

Preliminary 2: In a Mirror, Dimly

As President John Adams famously put it, facts are stubborn things. They are also immensely practical things. This is as true in the spiritual realm as it is in the physical. As we prepare to spend a day with Jesus, we need to start with two facts.

Fact 1: It is okay to be who you are wherever you are. We must begin with the fact that God accepts us as we are wherever we are, so that we can then accept ourselves. It is important for each of us to honestly be who we are, no matter what has happened to us, what we've done, or any of our other inner qualities. It's okay to be who we are. God isn't afraid to meet us where we are, even to the very depths of Sheol (Ps. 86:13).

We don't have to try to be someone we are not. Indeed, we cannot be someone we are not, and we won't find God's blessing there anyway because God has yet to bless anyone except where they actually are. We can *become* someone we are not, but we must begin with who we are now. You—the right-now you—are the person Jesus desires to be with. If you doubt this, ask God to give you the faith to believe it.

Jesus illustrates his Father's unconditional acceptance and blessing in his Sermon on the Mount (Matt. 5–7). The opening, often called the Beatitudes, targets the lie that we must be other than who we are if God is going to be with us and bless us. All the types of people that he mentions as being blessed—the poor in spirit, the mournful, the meek, the oppressed, the tenderhearted, and so on—are those the world considers to be the not-okay ones. Clearly Jesus has a different opinion about their standing with God. From his perspective, such people—indeed, all people—are able to receive God's favor and companionship, just as they are. The secret to this blessed life is God being with them in the here-and-now of their real lives. Spending a day with Jesus is an opportunity to live in acknowledgement that this is so.[4]

Fact 2: What is true about you as a person is also true

about your work. Unless you are engaged in activities that are harmful to people, your work is valuable. It is good. God put us here to work, and all the fundamental occupations of humanity are good. If you drive a truck, or deliver the mail, or teach, or sell insurance, or manage investments, or mend broken bones—whatever you do, it is good in God's kingdom. The main thing that will ruin any possibility of staying with Jesus throughout one full day is the feeling that it is not okay to be who you are or to do the work you are doing. If that is your view of life, the opportunity to be with Jesus will be cut off before it starts.

So, it is critical that you realize and trust that your "okay-ness" comes from the heart of Jesus' message. You can—no, you *must*—do your work with the words of Jesus echoing in your mind, "As the Father has sent Me, I also send you" (John 20:21). Every follower of Christ is sent by God to be Christ to the world in the concrete circumstances of their life. On the basis of hearing this message *and trusting it to be true*, you come to understand that it is good that you are alive: your life is good, it is good that you are who you are, and it is good that you do the work you do.

Preliminary 3: Deciding to Do It

You cannot drift into a life of constant companionship with Jesus any more than you can drift into marriage. You must make the decision to have Jesus with you. A decision is an inward resolve to do whatever is necessary to bring something to pass. If you want to go to Hawaii for a vacation, you will need to decide to do many things, like buying your airline tickets, arranging for a place to stay, choosing what clothes to bring, and so forth. It will come down to doing those things at specific times. If you do not do them, you will not find yourself relaxing on the beach. It is the same with spending time with Jesus; you must decide to do it.

Of course, if you make this decision to invite Jesus to be with you always and do all the necessary things to make it happen, you may find yourself feeling a little claustrophobic. It may feel like someone has invaded your space. That is only because he has; that is what happens when you ask him to join you. At times you may feel the need to ask Jesus to give you a little more room to "be yourself" and to live on your own. You may want to reserve the option of taking a few little "vacations" from God so you can do a few things that might be embarrassing if Jesus were sitting beside you. If you are used to living your life on your own, this is understandable. Jesus understands too. The question is, are you willing to work this out with him, to be honest with him, and let him be honest with you?

Section 2: Preview of Things to Come

In making such a decision it helps to have some idea of what it would be like to go through a day with Jesus. Some may imagine that it is simply sitting with your eyes closed, hands folded, meditating all day. While you might want to spend some time like that, this is not how the day will be. Remember, being with Jesus is a matter of being on the road with him. You are to go about your day in the same way he would go about it if he were you. You need to imagine what your day would look like with Jesus at your side—*as he will be*. What would characterize such a day?

Strength to Please

If we were to go through a day with Jesus, we would find the strength to do the things that would please him. We would be in places where he would be, interacting with people as he would, responding to situations as he would. We would find ourselves being kind, being helpful, being present, being pleasant, being patient, and being thankful.

Be careful, however, how you think about this. You may imagine that being with Jesus means that you would never do anything wrong. That would be nice, but it is not required. You especially do not want to set yourself up to come to the end of the day believing you were unsuccessful in making it through a full day with Jesus because you did something wrong. This would depend on how we experienced our connection with Jesus in the moment when we did the wrong thing—what our thoughts and intentions were at the time.

Suppose you come to a point in the day when you find yourself desiring to do something you are nearly certain Jesus would never do. In such a situation, you might decide to say, "Now, Lord, I would very much appreciate it if you would just look the other way now so I can do this." He would probably do as you asked. He is not going to hang around where he is not wanted. On the other hand, it is quite possible to become the kind of person who goes through a day without doing anything wrong while never specifically thinking of Jesus. Spending a day with Jesus is not the same thing as never making a mistake.

You will learn a great deal about yourself during your day with Jesus by paying attention to what happens if you are faced with a temptation to do something you believe is wrong, and you decide to do it. How will you handle that? Imagine what it would be like to ask Jesus not to leave, but to stay with you while you go ahead with your little plan. My point is that spending a day with Jesus is not merely a matter of never doing anything that would disappoint him. If we want him to stay with us, he will stay with us, even if we choose to do something displeasing to him. Remember, *Christ receiveth sinful men.*[5] He receives sinful men and women and boys and girls.

Jesus was repeatedly criticized because of the kind of folks he associated with—tax collectors, prostitutes, and other various and sundry sinners. That is a great encouragement for us. He receives us and is glad to spend a day with us—all our days, in fact. Of course, when he receives us, it puts tension on us because we want to do what pleases him. We must learn how to deal with this tension by applying his grace when we fail. But in a day spent with him, we can expect to be receiving his strength to do those things that will please him, and avoid those things that bring him pain.

As we grow, we can look forward to some days in which we don't do anything that displeases God. I realize that the very suggestion that it may be possible to go through a day without sinning by either omission or commission may sound like heresy, but I need to be sure you understand that this is possible for us. It is within God's ability to keep us from stumbling (2 Peter 1:10), and Jesus would not be displeased with us if we did not displease him "in thought, word, and deed" throughout an entire day. We really can become people who naturally obey his commandments (1 John 3:22), and we wouldn't even have to be especially perfect to do that. We are his children, and in his goodness he receives us as a child and helps us just as we are.

Joy and Confidence

The strength you experience in this day with Jesus will be followed by a deep sense of joy and confidence. You can count on that. Jesus was full of joy, and he means for us to be full as well. The New Testament is full of joy:

> These things I have spoken to you, that My joy may remain in you, and that your joy may be full. (John 15:11)

> Until now you have asked nothing in My name. Ask, and you will receive, that your joy may be full. (John 16:24)

> But now I come to You, and these things I speak in the world, that they may have My joy fulfilled in themselves. (John 17:13, Jesus praying for his followers)

When we are with Jesus, the resources available to us are in such overflowing abundance that Paul is emphatic about what our general response should be: "Rejoice in the Lord always. Again I will say, rejoice!" (Phil. 4:4). Joy brings with it confidence. It is, in fact, mainly a matter of confidence. It is not some kind of superecstatic state. Joy is a pervasive sense of well-being that claims your entire body and soul, both the physical and the nonphysical side of the human self. Joy comes naturally when we are confident (*con-fide*, literally acting "with faith") about who we are and what we are doing. To be with Jesus is to have both.

Loving Thy Neighbor

To be with Jesus is also to be with others—being fully present to them, caring for them, using what God has given us to help them. If you go through a day with Jesus, you will discover a fresh awareness of those around you. I am especially conscious of this because there was a time when I became quite burdened about my own lack of awareness of others.

I was zooming on down the track of my life, focused on whatever it was I was doing, oblivious to the people around me. I was deeply burdened when I realized that I had been living this way. How could I love my neighbors if I wasn't even aware of them? This conviction came as a result of my being with Jesus. It may be that this has not been a problem for you. Even so, being with Jesus will bring a new quality to your awareness of yourself and others; you will begin to see people with new eyes, with new appreciation and love, even though they have not changed.

Tag—He's It!

When you were young you probably played a game called tag. This was not my game of choice when I was a very small child. The big kids always made sure the little kids were "it." Once a smaller child was tagged, just about all hope was lost. The big kids could run so much faster that it felt like the little one would be "it" forever. I did all I could to avoid being "it."

A day with Jesus is just the opposite. Jesus is "it," and you are "not it," as we all declared at the start of a game. It's not up to you to make everything happen now. Yoked to Jesus, allow him to carry most of the load as you go about your day in his uplifting presence. This is a great relief. As you work better and accomplish good things, your mind will be clearer; you will be working with strength and peace in your heart.

Not so when you are "it." When everything depends on you, it can feel like your feet are bolted to the floor, everything becomes a burden, you become irritated, even hopeless and despairing, fretting your day away. So if you find yourself lapsing back into the role of being "it," simply reach out and say to Jesus, "Tag—you're it!" He's much better at being "it" than any of us are, anyway.

Your Own Personal Super-Assistant

One of the marks of the Spirit-assisted, with-God life is that things happen that you cannot explain in terms of your own natural ability. During your day with Jesus you will see him engaging in the things that concern you and working with you to accomplish far more than you could have on your own. In some measure this is going to be a matter of how much faith you have. Generally speaking, if we are not "it," then we are going to be asking and trusting him to do things, and I believe that every day we will see him answering us in concrete ways.

Of course, it is assumed here that the things you are concerned to accomplish are in keeping with the kingdom of God—that they are in harmony with and aid in the promotion of human well-being. We need to ask God to help us see our work in this way, and to guide us back into such activities if we stray. As we do, we will see Jesus multiplying our efforts like he multiplied the loaves and fishes.

Speaking and Hearing

One final and wonderful experience you can expect during your time with Jesus is that there will be a lot of communication between you and him. Whenever two people share life together, there is communication. Life with someone who chooses not to communicate with you is almost unbearable. It simply would not be a shared life. A day shared with Jesus is a day of continuous conversation. We will learn to hear his voice. I mean this in ways other than how we can hear his speaking to us in the Scriptures and elsewhere. Jesus will speak to us individually.[6]

A day with Jesus is a day worth planning for.

Section 3: The Plan

You cannot spend a day with Jesus unless you intend to do so, and if you truly intend to do something, you will make the necessary plans to accomplish it. This will not happen merely through a happy accident. Jesus has his part to play, and we have ours. Our part includes planning, just like we would plan an outing with the family, or a wedding day, or any other occasion we truly cared about. I do not mean that God's hands are tied without us or that the relationship is a quid pro quo, where God only responds in measure to our efforts. He might just make it happen, and I suspect there are many occasions when he does.

I often hear people talk about how God is constantly speaking to them, and how they could see his hand at work from the moment they gave their life to Christ. They regularly have a sense of having gone through the whole day with him. Generally speaking, that experience does not last long, because we are called to make intentional decisions in taking steps that will move us into a place of greater interaction with God. So we must create and execute a plan, and make the necessary arrangements to accomplish this goal. When we make plans for an upcoming event, we always start before the day of the occasion, not moment by moment as the event moves along. It is the same when we decide to spend a day with Jesus.

Ask the other members of your household for any help you may need with your planning and preparations. Spouses may need to arrange to take turns caring for the children. You may be able to plan a prayer time with your spouse or family, or it may be a great accomplishment just to get everyone to agree to leave you alone with your coffee in the morning.

The Day Begins . . . at Sundown

Since this is going to be a special day, you may begin by thinking about it in a special way, a biblical way. The biblical day begins at sundown—the early evening, we might call it. It is the end that is also the beginning. God appoints an end to man's labors with darkness, as is beautifully described by the psalmist:

> He appointed the moon for seasons;
> The sun knows its going down.
> You make darkness, and it is night,
> In which all the beasts of the forest creep about.
> The young lions roar after their prey,
> And seek their food from God.
> When the sun rises, they gather together
> And lie down in their dens.
> Man goes out to his work
> And to his labor until the evening.
>
> O LORD, how manifold are Your works!
> In wisdom You have made them all.
>
> (Ps. 104:19–24)

That is the ancient rhythm of God for us, and Mr. Edison's invention of the lightbulb has not made that rhythm obsolete. Electric lights disturb the natural units of time, and this is significant for our practice of spirituality because we are not built for that. We have a deep biological connection to light and darkness.

Therefore, at the end of the day, you gather together as humankind has done for centuries; you recollect, praise, dream, confess, and prepare for tomorrow, all in the security of God's love. So clear your calendar ahead of time, making sure to leave the evening free as the start of your time with Jesus.

If there is conflict within your family or between you and another person, this is the time to resolve it. There should be nothing between us and the other members of our household ("Nothing between my soul and my Savior," as the old song says).[7] If you are not in harmony with your loved ones, this will follow you through the night and be with you when you wake up in the morning. It is also likely to affect your dreams, which can then set the tone of your day. We need to take these measures to calm our souls so we can arise with praise to God.

Rest in Faith

Above all, you must also arrange to rest. Rest is an act of faith, especially today. Few people get the rest God intends for their well-being. Remember that the Sabbath is one of the Ten Commandments, an entire day to be set aside for rest. But how often do you keep the Sabbath? Spiritual practices such as Sabbath, rest, solitude, and silence are essentially "casting all your care upon Him" (1 Peter 5:7). When you've done this enough to convince yourself that the world will be able to function without you, you will find true rest. This is fundamental to our lives, yet because of the way this world is set up, one of our primary temptations is to not get enough rest.

This is one reason we have so much addiction and abuse. People can be very hard on one another because they are tired and frantic. They unintentionally hurt the people they love—usually their own family members. Don't let your life be like this. Make rest a priority in your life and in the lives of those you love. *Plan* for it!

You are not meant to live in a constant state of fatigue. Tiredness is a spiritual problem, not because it is a sin, but because being tired creates difficulties for your spiritual life, robbing you of the energy needed to pursue God. You may not be getting enough restful and refreshing sleep. You might even empathize with David when he wasn't sleeping because he had people chasing after him in an effort to kill him. In Psalm 3, David declared that his situation was so bad that people were saying that even God couldn't help him. But he cried out to God and was heard (v. 4), and then he could sleep. In verse 5 we read, "I lay down and slept; I awoke, for the LORD sustained me." David went on to say that he would not be afraid; salvation belongs to the Lord. As you see here, our ability to sleep is a sign of our faith.

Our confidence in God can lead us to "lie down in green pastures" and rest in God, putting our minds at ease because our hearts are at peace, so that we wake the next morning refreshed and thankful. If this is a problem for you, make it a spiritual priority to find out why you are not sleeping and how to solve it. This may involve not watching late-night television (something I personally find to be quite soporific), or maybe you are overeating or doing something else that keeps you from getting to sleep. Whatever it may be, it must be identified and dealt with, because you need to rest.

So make the necessary arrangements to get the rest you need, planning to begin your morning with Jesus on the foundation of a quiet evening and a good night's sleep. Then, as you retire to bed, commit to meet with God first thing when you wake, and go over in your mind how that will be. This is a wonderful way to fall asleep in prayer. You can also use the simple prayers of childhood, the Lord's Prayer, or Psalm 23 to lead you into restful sleep. Whatever you choose, let it include this simple prayer of faith: "I will both lie down in peace, and sleep; for You alone, O LORD, make me dwell in safety" (Ps. 4:8). If you approach the evening in this way, you will awaken with great anticipation of your day with Jesus.

The Day Dawns: Rising with Praise, Petition, and Planning

Praise

The morning was made for the praises of God's people:

> Light is sown for the righteous,
> And gladness for the upright in heart.
> Rejoice in the LORD, you righteous,
> And give thanks at the remembrance of His holy name.
>
> (Ps. 97:11–12)

It is fitting that we arise with thankfulness and praise to God. This is fundamental and will be a natural (and supernatural!) beginning to your day after having retired in faith and prayer. The supposition is that when you wake rested you are apt to find the morning beautiful. If you are not rested, you are likely to find it less pleasant; the light will be an insult to your eyes! Assuming you are rested, you are able to get up in time to enjoy the freshness of the new day. You may walk out in your backyard or on your veranda where you can look upon the goodness and greatness of this world. Try to find a place where you can listen to the birds, or the soft breeze, or the patter of the rain. Drink it in for a moment, and just say, "Thank you, God, for this new day. Thank you for this new beginning."

Seek seclusion, and if you are able, kneel for five or ten minutes and welcome the presence of Jesus. You may not think it will make any difference to kneel when you pray, but try it anyway. Then consider the difference it may have made. As you pray, give the day up to God, renewing your invitation to him to be with you each moment.

You may wish to use the following Celtic prayer to help you focus and personalize this time with Jesus as you greet him and invite him to spend the day with you. The prayer in its entirety was written to be used at the beginning of a new year, but the portion below is fitting for the beginning of any new day.

The Opening Door

Enter, Lord Christ—
I have joy in Your coming.
You have given me life;
and I welcome Your coming.
I turn now to face You,
I lift up my eyes.
Be blessing my face, Lord;
be blessing my eyes.
May all my eye looks on
be blessed and be bright,
my neighbors, my loved ones
be blessed in Your sight.
You have given me life
and I welcome Your coming.
Be with me, Lord,
I have joy, I have joy.*

Petition: Casting Your Cares on Him

Having risen in praise and thankfulness, then you pray for yourself, for the people in your life, and for the things you are facing that day. Declare your dependence upon God, asking him to remove all fear and to fill you with his love for your life and all that enters it. This is where you move from praise to genuine love for the life God has given you. Do you love your life? Does the love of God

---

* Editor's Note: We included this prayer as a means of helping you joyfully embrace your new day with Jesus. From Northumbria Community Trust Ltd., *Celtic Daily Prayer* (New York: HarperOne, 2002), 238. Wording adapted.

come through you to everything you deal with in your life? This is how you will carry Christ through the day. So if you have specific concerns, call them out, lay them before the Lord, and submit them to his care.

Normally our days include some regular things that throw us off track, like things you might worry about during a day not spent with Jesus, the things you must get done, the people you're going to meet. Prayer is not the same thing as worrying. This is a time to again follow the advice of Peter and cast "all your care upon Him, for He cares for you" (1 Peter 5:7). Address God, tell him what you're hoping for, and then watch for how the hand of God works through the day.

This can also be a time of confession, in which you ask for the strength to deal with the failures you experience day by day. Ask in particular for the faith, death to self, and love that make the Shepherd's sufficiency your own. Remember, these are the marks of Jesus himself. To be with him is to become like him. His life is contagious among those who are susceptible to it, who desire it. Let him know that you want to be infected! Pray, "Lord, make me an instrument of thy peace!" It is truly an expression of the heart of Jesus.

As you are developing this holy habit of beginning your day with Jesus, you will find it requires effort, and you may encounter resistance from older, more established habits. It may be your usual practice to get up, fix your coffee, and spend some time reading the newspaper. You might simply invite Jesus to read the paper with you, making comments to him about the news of the day. Repeatedly turn your attention to him, praising him for being in control of the world, asking him to intervene in matters on your heart, thanking him for the promise of his presence throughout the day to come. Transform your normal activities into opportunities for communion with your Lord. Once you have gotten into this mode, you will not find it a problem to begin your day consciously in his presence. This is not more work; this is joy.

Planning: When Will I See You Again?

Since you have decided to spend the entire day with Jesus, it is fitting that, before heading into your day, you make plans to have another session with your Lord. I suggest that you have it soon, maybe right after breakfast, before you dive into your first project of the day. Maybe it will be in the car as you drive to work. By that time you have (hopefully) pulled everything together, and now you are on your way into your day. This could be a good time to meet Jesus expressly.

In Psalm 119:164 we find a hint of how the psalmist spent his day: "Seven times a day I praise You, because of Your righteous judgments." Seven is often used to indicate completeness or fullness, as in "I praise you *all the time*" or the apostle Paul's admonition to "pray *without ceasing*" (1 Thess. 5:17). It certainly points to a life in which constant communion with God was a regular part of every day. Imagine what it would be like if you met with Jesus seven times through the day, and seven days through the week; you would likely grow quite accustomed to his company. And his sufficiency! In the New Testament, we see that there were, in fact, three times each day when faithful Jews would stop and pray: 9:00 a.m., noon, and 3:00 p.m.*

In the monastic period of Christianity, monks divided the day according to seven appointed hours. I share these not to burden you with the suggestion that you should do this, but simply to give you an example of what seriously planning your day can be like. The seven basic hours of prayer were as follows:

- Lauds: Dawn (6:00 a.m.)
- Terce: Third Hour (9:00 a.m.)
- Sext: Sixth Hour (Noon)
- None: Ninth Hour (3:00 p.m.)

---

* Examples: Daniel 6:10–13; Acts 3:1; 10:2–9, 30.

- Vespers or Evensong (6:00 p.m.)
- Compline (9:00 p.m.)
- Vigils: At various hours during the middle of the night

These folks were serious about meeting with Jesus, and the purposeful arrangement of their days reflected that commitment. Your day will need to be purposefully arranged as well. While I do not think following the "divine hours" would be totally unsuitable for you, I am not explicitly suggesting it. You should schedule your day in keeping with your occupation and your family responsibilities. What is important is to understand that *you must plan those times to turn your mind to God.*

Remember the principle I laid down in the first chapter: the most important thing about you is your mind, and the most important thing about your mind is what it is fixed upon. So the object is to have your mind always fixed on the Lord. This is only possible through constantly renewed effort, choosing to "retain God in [your] knowledge" (Rom. 1:28) and to "set your mind on things above, not on things on the earth" (Col. 3:2). Frank Laubach, that wonderful Presbyterian missionary to the Maoris in the Philippines, experimented with turning his mind constantly back toward God. A brilliant and highly educated man, he was not only a profound Christian and an influential leader in worldwide literacy education but an insightful psychologist of the religious life.* He was so impressed with the Muslims in the Philippines and how they wanted to live every moment in submission to God, that he could not understand how, as a Christian, he could do anything less than give himself to the practice of turning his mind constantly to God.

The question before him was a simple one, though stated in

---

* His undergraduate degree is from Princeton University, along with a master's and doctorate from Columbia University, and a divinity degree from Union Theological Seminary.

somewhat philosophical language: "Can I bring God back in my mind-flow every few seconds so that God will always be in my mind as an after-image, shall always be an element in every concept and precept? I choose to make the rest of my life an experiment in answering this question."[8] From that experiment he learned how to walk moment by moment with Jesus, by redirecting his mind toward God once a minute throughout the day.[9] You may want to try something like this, but only if it seems inviting, not burdensome. This is to be *your* day with Jesus, not Frank Laubach's or Dallas Willard's.

Whatever you decide to try, your day should involve scheduled times of meeting with Jesus. I would suggest planning to take ten minutes or so every two to three hours during the day to lift your heart and mind to God in praise, thanksgiving, and sharing the concerns on your heart. Do this alone if possible. Sometimes you may do this by going outside and looking at the beauty of a flower or the magnificence of the sky, or maybe by listening to beautiful music. Frank Laubach did this by bringing to mind the Lord's Prayer, an image of the cross, or simply a thought of the Father who is over all.

Honing Holy Habits

In these brief intervals of praise and prayer and in the longer planned sessions, you will be establishing habits of turning your mind to God. This is the practice that establishes the habits. Thus, when you plan them, you must do them by the clock. Do not wait until you feel especially spiritual. Set specific times during the day, and then keep to your schedule. You can trust God to take care of them if you do them by the clock. Trust him to help you deal with the little voice that whispers, "No, you don't want to do this now" or "You don't really have time for this."

Of course, emergencies may arise, and you will need to use your good judgment about what is necessary. God is not going to judge you as guilty of sin if the plan needs to change. He understands. Yet emergencies are always temptations to not trust God and to lapse back into the mode of "I'm in control." An emergency is like getting tagged, "You're *it!*" You are instantly on the spot. But the time you spend off the spot, practicing God's presence, will allow you to discern whether to refuse to be "it" and then act with trust in God. Emergencies are opportunities to bring God into the realities of your life.

In all of this—the praise, the petitions, and the planning—you are expressing your dependence upon God, but you may want to make this explicit, telling him out loud or silently that you are going to rely upon him to realize his presence with you as the day proceeds. Thank him in advance for what will come. Then move out into your day in confidence, joy, and expectation, turning to the things you need to accomplish.

The Day Unfolds

As you move through the day, invite Jesus into each new situation or interaction. Watch for him to accomplish God's loving purposes in these occasions, and give thanks. Develop the habit of seeing the world through God's eyes. You can use passages like Psalm 33:13–22 to give you images of how the world looks to God. Keep those in your mind to help you gain a "God's-eye view" of your world and what is transpiring around you.

As you engage with others, ask Jesus to bless them. You can consciously *will* the peace, joy, and confidence that you are experiencing to pass from you, like "living waters," to those with whom you are interacting. They are flowing from Jesus into you, and you can will them to enter others. Sometimes it occurs by benediction (literally, "good speaking") and sometimes in complete silence, spirit to spirit. Watch it happen. Trust that God can work in and through you in these ways.

Everything that comes into your day—every person, every activity, and even (or especially!) every interruption—is an opportunity for you and Jesus to bless. If you're going to make biscuits, bless them. They will taste better. No matter what you are doing, try to remember to bless it. Whatever it is, say, "The Lord bless you. The Lord cause his face to shine on you. The Lord make you to be the best you that you can be!" See this as resting under the government of God, under his loving gaze and care. Lift everything up to him in that way.

Train yourself to use each change of person or event to remind you to pray and to bless, so that mere change becomes a signal to turn your mind back to God. Do this and you will shortly master the secrets of praying without ceasing. Such interactions with Jesus will be brief moments before diving back into your day. As you do, ask him to dive back in with you. Invite him to be a part of your work and interactions with others. I guarantee that as you do, you and those around you will notice differences of a very positive nature.

With your heart and mind centered on God, you turn to the things that need to be done. The specific activities that will make up your day with Jesus will differ from those of others. What you do, the challenges you will encounter, the distractions that arise, and the temptations you will meet—all of which will touch upon your faith, death to self, and love—these will be uniquely yours, for the simple reason that no one is living your life but you.

During the day you may find that you become weary. One thing that will help you spiritually is arranging to have a nice nap. Remember, resting is a primary test of our faith. Can we rest? All these little things like food and sleep are fundamental ways in which we learn to submit ourselves to God through our bodily nature. We rest in the Lord and wait patiently on him. So, if you are weary, and if you can, take a nap. Rest. Then thank God for that and return to your day's activities.

The Day Concludes . . . with Grace-Drenched Reflection

At some point in the late afternoon, preferably before dinner, while you are still experiencing the strength and rest of God, take fifteen minutes in quiet solitude to review and examine the day. This time of reflection is not the same as your later evening exercises, which are a part of the new day that begins at sunset. Rather, this is a time to be with Jesus so the two of you can look back over your day to see what happened, to give thanks for the successes, and to try to understand any failures that may have occurred.

Ask Jesus for guidance in continuing the project. If you find you failed on some point, don't give up. Think about what went wrong, and ask the Lord to help you understand and do better tomorrow. He is more interested in this project than you are, because he has a clearer vision of what is good for you. If you honestly desire to understand what went wrong, and how you can do things differently in the future, he will give you insight. At this point it is essential that you are well grounded in the grace-drenched message of God's acceptance of us. There is no room for—because there is no possibility of—self-righteousness here. God in love accepts us as we are, because he cannot accept us the way we aren't. The only way you and I can come to God is, as the old hymn puts it, "just as I am."[10] There is great freedom in this—the freedom to become God's vision of you.

All of us, if we are honest, know we have done or said or thought things for which we are ashamed. When I look back and remember the things I stole and the lies I told when I was a kid—when I was more than a kid!—I am bitterly ashamed. I am grieved by the unloving and unkind ways I hurt my friends and my relatives. But that is who I am. I am the person who did that. You are the person who has done the things you have done. It is a great help if we can accept that and just be honest about who we are. This is not a matter of being held responsible and having to pay for what we have done. God forgives us.

Nonetheless, we still need to understand how we are the kind of people who can do those things that are wrong. We have to accept that, and when we do we can be honest before the Lord and say, "Lord, I need help with this. Please forgive me. I wasn't patient. I didn't listen. I was vain. I was thinking about myself, and I was wondering if they understood how good I was." Of course, we are not only asking to be forgiven, we are asking for guidance and wisdom and strength to respond differently tomorrow. And if lapses occurred from how we had planned to take special times with Jesus during the day, we do not berate ourselves or fuss over our failures. Jesus doesn't. We have better things to do, like thanking him for being such a good friend, and making plans to resume our course with him tomorrow.

Such planning should include identifying the things in your life that you believe trouble Jesus—impatience, overeating, lying, or whatever it may be for you. A good way to do that is simply to sit down and make a list, looking back over your day and asking where you have failed to walk in the presence of Jesus. Then, as incidents come to mind, just lift them up to the Lord and say, "Jesus, I need your help with these things. I confess that I have been troubled with things that I believe trouble you, like when I wondered if people were noticing how good I was today." (You may not think of wanting people to notice how good you are as a significant sin. But pride and managing our outward image is the basic stuff of which many of our problems consist.) As we are honest in our confession to the Lord, we can trust that he will give us the help we seek.

This time of reflection should also include thanksgiving for all the ways the day went well. God is not in our life merely to deal with our sin. He would have a place in our life if we had never sinned. The abundant life that Jesus promises us in John 10:10 is far more than the forgiveness of sin. As Paul put it, life in the kingdom of

God is marked by "righteousness and peace and joy in the Holy Spirit" (Rom. 14:17).

So ends your day with Jesus. Now what?

A New Day Begins, and a New Life

If after your day you decide to carry on with your experiment in living moment by moment with Jesus, this familiar instruction applies: "Repeat the above." Make your plans and do it again. And then again. I assure you that not many days will pass before you begin to understand the sweetness of walking with Jesus in the sufficiency of the Good Shepherd. Remember that these are ordinary days we've been describing. There are other holy days throughout the year that call for different activities that serve specific purposes. You should also have full days set aside at regular intervals for the practice of solitude, silence, service, and other spiritual disciplines. These are all good and healthy ways for us to spend all the days of our lives with Jesus.

A beautiful poem by the Baptist pastor and theologian Walter Rauschenbusch expresses his experience of coming into the presence of God using the image of walking through a small gate into the presence of God and into an Edenic peace that transforms his world. It's a rather long poem, so I will just share a taste of his moving words:

A Little Gate to God

In the castle of my soul
Is a little postern gate,*
Whereat, when I enter,

---

* *Postern* is a diminutive term that refers to a little back gate. "I slip out to that little back gate."

I am in the presence of God.
In a moment, in the turning of a thought,
I am where God is.
This is a fact.

The world of men is made of jangling noises.
With God it is a great silence.
But that silence is a melody
Sweet as the contentment of love,
Thrilling as a touch of flame.

When I enter into God,
All life has a meaning.
Without asking, I know;
My desires are even now fulfilled,
My fever is gone
In the great quiet of God.
My troubles are but pebbles on the road,
My joys are like the everlasting hills,
So it is when I step through the gate of prayer
From time into eternity.

When I am in the consciousness of God
my fellow men are not far off and forgotten,
but close and strangely near.
Those whom I love
Have a mystic value.
They shine, as if a light were glowing within them.

So it is when my soul steps through the postern gate
Into the presence of God.
Big things become small, and small things become great.
The near becomes far, and the future is near.

The lowly and despised is shot through with glory . . .
God is the substance of all revolutions;
When I am in him, I am in the Kingdom of God
And the Fatherland of my Soul.[11]

What Rauschenbusch describes here is nothing other than life in the presence of the all-sufficient Shepherd whose voice calls us to walk often through the gate into God's presence. It is the life for which you were created. As you practice living your days in the sufficiency of the Good Shepherd, you will make tremendous progress in experiencing the Psalm 23 life that Christ came to provide. You will see remarkable growth, and all the good things Jesus desires to give us—a rich life of joy and power, abundant in supernatural results, with a constant, clear vision of your never-ending life in God's world and an abiding sense of your work day by day—will become the common, yet extraordinary, realities in your life.

To that end, I pray for you in the words of Saint Paul:

That you may be filled with the knowledge of His will in all wisdom and spiritual understanding; that you may walk worthy of the Lord, fully pleasing Him, being fruitful in every good work and increasing in the knowledge of God; strengthened with all might, according to His glorious power, for all patience and longsuffering with joy; giving thanks to the Father who has qualified us to be partakers of the inheritance of the saints in the light. (Col. 1:9–12)

In other words, may you know increasingly, *by joyful experience,* a life abundant in rest, provision, and blessing—a life without lack.

Closing Prayer

Gracious Lord,

Help us to see and understand—with the eyes of faith and the mind you have given us—your magnificent, glorious, self-sufficient being, and the greatness of your kingdom into which we are invited. May we grasp the deep significance of the words, "in Him we live and move and have our being,"* and know that in that safest of places—in you—there simply is no lack.

Open our eyes to the high privilege of being created in your image. Convince us that nothing makes you happier than seeing those redeemed by your grace devoting their days to the good of other people and your creation. Win over our timid and doubting hearts with the conviction that we are your greatest treasure in all creation.

Give us sober yet fearless awareness of Satan's ploys and deceits. Strengthen our hearts in the knowledge that we have nothing to fear, for you have defeated him. We are so glad to know that greater are you who are in us than he that is in the world.** May our hearts carry that message as we contemplate the awesome reality of the spiritual battle around us.

Tender Father, you have taught us so clearly that faith—trust—is essential to a life without lack. We confess that while we believe in you, we need to believe more fully, more deeply, more constantly. In his life, death, and resurrection Jesus showed us that you are completely and utterly trustworthy, and even in the shadow of death there is nothing to fear, for you are with us.

---

* Acts 17:28.
** 1 John 4:4.

Bring us to the place of peace where we no longer feel a need to defend ourselves, or to worry about who's going to take care of us, or to be recognized, or to get our way, or to make sure things turn out right. Lord, free us through the knowledge that because you are with us, working in our lives, we have everything we need.

And now, with the truth of who you are deeply engraved in our hearts, give us the confidence and power to love all who are in our lives just as we are being loved by you—freely, fully, joyfully. Let your Spirit move in our minds and hearts so we believe ever more fully that because you are our all-sufficient Shepherd, we shall never want.

We ask all this because we would have it no other way.

Amen.

APPENDIX A

Passages Testifying to the Abundant Provision of God

The following passages from the Bible bear witness to God's loving care for those who love and trust him and the sufficiency of his provisions to meet our every need, including our need of forgiveness and restoration. Reading through these verses slowly and thoughtfully is another way you can conform your mind to the truth about God, which is the primary secret to a life without lack. In some cases you will want to read the entire context of the quoted passage to give you a better understanding of the nature of God's provision.

Genesis 3:21

Also for Adam and his wife the LORD God made tunics of skin, and clothed them.

Genesis 8:20–22

Then Noah built an altar to the LORD, and took of every clean animal and of every clean bird, and offered burnt offerings on the altar. And the LORD smelled a soothing aroma. Then the LORD said in His heart, "I will never again curse the ground for man's sake, although the imagination of man's heart is evil from his youth; nor will I again destroy every living thing as I have done.

"While the earth remains,
Seedtime and harvest,
Cold and heat,
Winter and summer,
And day and night
Shall not cease."

Genesis 9:3

Every moving thing that lives shall be food for you. I have given you all things, even as the green herbs.

Genesis 13:14–17

And the Lord said to Abram, after Lot had separated from him: "Lift your eyes now and look from the place where you are—northward, southward, eastward, and westward; for all the land which you see I give to you and your descendants forever. And I will make your descendants as the dust of the earth; so that if a man could number the dust of the earth, then your descendants also could be numbered. Arise, walk in the land through its length and its width, for I give it to you."

Genesis 22:13–14

Then Abraham lifted his eyes and looked, and there behind him was a ram caught in a thicket by its horns. So Abraham went and took the ram, and offered it up for a burnt offering instead of his son. And Abraham called the name of the place, The-Lord-Will-Provide; as it is said to this day, "In the Mount of the Lord it shall be provided."

Exodus 14:21–22

Then Moses stretched out his hand over the sea; and the Lord caused the sea to go back by a strong east wind all that night, and made the sea into dry land, and the waters were divided. So the children of Israel went into the midst of the sea on the dry ground, and the waters were a wall to them on their right hand and on their left.

Deuteronomy 2:7

For the LORD your God has blessed you in all the work of your hand. He knows your trudging through this great wilderness. These forty years the LORD your God has been with you; you have lacked nothing.

Deuteronomy 29:5

And I have led you forty years in the wilderness. Your clothes have not worn out on you, and your sandals have not worn out on your feet.

Psalm 34:10

The young lions lack and suffer hunger;
But those who seek the LORD shall not lack any good thing.

Psalm 36:7–8

How precious is Your lovingkindness, O God!
Therefore the children of men put their trust under the
shadow of Your wings.
They are abundantly satisfied with the fullness of Your house,
And You give them drink from the river of Your pleasures.

Psalm 37:25

I have been young, and now am old;
Yet I have not seen the righteous forsaken,
Nor his descendants begging bread.

Psalm 78:21–25

Therefore the LORD heard this and was furious;
So a fire was kindled against Jacob,
And anger also came up against Israel,
Because they did not believe in God,
And did not trust in His salvation.
Yet He had commanded the clouds above,
And opened the doors of heaven,
Had rained down manna on them to eat,
And given them of the bread of heaven.

Men ate angels' food;
He sent them food to the full.

Psalm 81:10

I am the LORD your God,
Who brought you out of the land of Egypt;
Open your mouth wide, and I will fill it.

Proverbs 3:5–6

Trust in the LORD with all your heart,
And lean not on your own understanding;
In all your ways acknowledge Him,
And He shall direct your paths.

Isaiah 55:7

Let the wicked forsake his way,
And the unrighteous man his thoughts;
Let him return to the LORD,
And He will have mercy on him;
And to our God,
For He will abundantly pardon.

Jeremiah 29:11–13

For I know the thoughts that I think toward you, says the LORD,
thoughts of peace and not of evil, to give you a future and a hope.
Then you will call upon Me and go and pray to Me, and I will listen
to you. And you will seek Me and find Me, when you search for Me
with all your heart.

Malachi 3:10

"Bring all the tithes into the storehouse,
That there may be food in My house,
And try Me now in this,"
Says the LORD of hosts,
"If I will not open for you the windows of heaven

And pour out for you such blessing
That there will not be room enough to receive it.

Matthew 6:26–33 (Luke 12:22–34)

Look at the birds of the air, for they neither sow nor reap nor gather into barns; yet your heavenly Father feeds them. Are you not of more value than they? Which of you by worrying can add one cubit to his stature?

So why do you worry about clothing? Consider the lilies of the field, how they grow: they neither toil nor spin; and yet I say to you that even Solomon in all his glory was not arrayed like one of these. Now if God so clothes the grass of the field, which today is, and tomorrow is thrown into the oven, will He not much more clothe you, O you of little faith?

Therefore do not worry, saying, "What shall we eat?" or "What shall we drink?" or "What shall we wear?" For after all these things the Gentiles seek. For your heavenly Father knows that you need all these things. But seek first the kingdom of God and His righteousness, and all these things shall be added to you.

Matthew 7:7–11 (Luke 11:9–13)

Ask, and it will be given to you; seek, and you will find; knock, and it will be opened to you. For everyone who asks receives, and he who seeks finds, and to him who knocks it will be opened. Or what man is there among you who, if his son asks for bread, will give him a stone? Or if he asks for a fish, will he give him a serpent? If you then, being evil, know how to give good gifts to your children, how much more will your Father who is in heaven give good things to those who ask Him!

Matthew 11:28–29

Come to Me, all you who labor and are heavy laden, and I will give you rest. Take My yoke upon you and learn from Me, for I am gentle and lowly in heart, and you will find rest for your souls.

John 10:10

The thief does not come except to steal, and to kill, and to destroy. I have come that they may have life, and that they may have it more abundantly.

John 16:23–24

Most assuredly, I say to you, whatever you ask the Father in My name He will give you. Until now you have asked nothing in My name. Ask, and you will receive, that your joy may be full.

Romans 8:31–35, 37–39

What then shall we say to these things? If God is for us, who can be against us? He who did not spare His own Son, but delivered Him up for us all, how shall He not with Him also freely give us all things? Who shall bring a charge against God's elect? It is God who justifies. Who is he who condemns? It is Christ who died, and furthermore is also risen, who is even at the right hand of God, who also makes intercession for us. Who shall separate us from the love of Christ? Shall tribulation, or distress, or persecution, or famine, or nakedness, or peril, or sword? . . . Yet in all these things we are more than conquerors through Him who loved us. For I am persuaded that neither death nor life, nor angels nor principalities nor powers, nor things present nor things to come, nor height nor depth, nor any other created thing, shall be able to separate us from the love of God which is in Christ Jesus our Lord.

2 Corinthians 9:8–11, 15

And God is able to make all grace abound toward you, that you, always having all sufficiency in all things, may have an abundance for every good work. As it is written:

> "He has dispersed abroad,
> He has given to the poor;
> His righteousness endures forever."

Now may He who supplies seed to the sower, and bread for food, supply and multiply the seed you have sown and increase the fruits of your righteousness, while you are enriched in everything for all liberality, which causes thanksgiving through us to God. . . . Thanks be to God for His indescribable gift!

Ephesians 3:20–21

Now to Him who is able to do exceedingly abundantly above all that we ask or think, according to the power that works in us, to Him be glory in the church by Christ Jesus to all generations, forever and ever. Amen.

Philippians 4:19

And my God shall supply all your need according to His riches in glory by Christ Jesus.

Hebrews 11:6

But without faith it is impossible to please Him, for he who comes to God must believe that He is, and that He is a rewarder of those who diligently seek Him.

Hebrews 13:5

Let your conduct be without covetousness; be content with such things as you have. For He Himself has said, "I will never leave you nor forsake you."

2 Peter 1:2–4

Grace and peace be multiplied to you in the knowledge of God and of Jesus our Lord, as His divine power has given to us all things that pertain to life and godliness, through the knowledge of Him who called us by glory and virtue, by which have been given to us exceedingly great and precious promises, that through these you may be partakers of the divine nature, having escaped the corruption that is in the world through lust.

1 John 3:22

And whatever we ask we receive from Him, because we keep His commandments and do those things that are pleasing in His sight.

APPENDIX B

Humility and Death to Self

ANDREW MURRAY

He humbled Himself and became
obedient to the point of death.

—PHILIPPIANS 2:8

Humility is the path to death, because in death it gives the highest proof of its perfection. Humility is the blossom of which death to self, is the perfect fruit. Jesus humbled Himself unto death, and opened the path in which we too must walk. As there was no way for Him to prove His surrender to God to the very uttermost, or to give up and rise out of our human nature to the glory of the Father but through death, so with us too. Humility must lead us to die to self: so we prove how wholly we have given ourselves up to it and to God; so alone we are freed from fallen nature, and find the path that leads to life in God, to that full birth of the new nature, of which humility is the breath and the joy.[1]

We have spoken of what Jesus did for His disciples when He communicated His resurrection life to them, when in the descent of the Holy Spirit He, the glorified and enthroned Meekness, actually came from heaven Himself to dwell in them. He won the power to do this through death: in its inmost nature the life He imparted was a life out of death, a life that had been surrendered to death, and been won through death. He who came to dwell in them, was Himself One who had been dead and now lives for evermore. His life, His person, His presence, bears the marks of death, of being a life begotten out of death. That life in His disciples ever bears the death marks too; it is only as the Spirit of the death, of the dying One, dwells and works in the soul, that the power of His life can be known. The first and chief of the marks of the dying of the Lord Jesus, of the death-marks that show the true follower of Jesus, is humility. For these two reasons: only humility leads to perfect death; only death perfects humility. Humility and death are in their very nature one: humility is the bud; in death the fruit is ripened to perfection.

Humility leads to perfect death. Humility means the giving up of self and the taking of the place of perfect nothingness before God. Jesus humbled Himself, and became obedient unto death. In death He gave the highest, the perfect proof of having given up His will to the will of God. In death He gave up His self, with its natural reluctance to drink the cup; He gave up the life He had in union with our human nature; He died to self, and the sin that tempted Him; so, as man, He entered into the perfect life of God. If it had not been for His boundless humility, counting Himself as nothing except as a servant to do and suffer the will of God, He never would have died.

This gives us the answer to the question so often asked, and of which the meaning is so seldom clearly apprehended: How can I die to self? The death to self is not your work, it is God's work. In Christ you are dead to sin, the life that is in you has gone through the process of death and resurrection; you may be sure you are indeed dead to sin. But the full manifestation of the power of this death in your disposition and conduct depends upon the measure in which the Holy Spirit imparts the power of the death of Christ. And here it is that the teaching is needed: if you would enter into full fellowship with Christ in His death, and know the full deliverance from self, humble yourself. This is your one duty. Place yourself before God in your utter helplessness; consent heartily to the fact of your impotence to slay or make alive yourself; sink down into your own nothingness, in the spirit of meek and patient and trustful surrender to God. Accept every humiliation, look upon every fellow-man who tries or vexes you, as a means of grace to humble you. Use every opportunity of humbling yourself before your fellow-men as a help to abide humble before God. God will accept such humbling of yourself as the proof that your whole heart desires it, as the very best prayer for it, as your preparation for His mighty work of grace, when, by the mighty strengthening of His Holy Spirit, He reveals Christ fully in you, so that He, in His form of a servant, is truly formed in you, and dwells in your heart. It is the path of humility which leads to perfect death, the full and perfect experience that we are dead in Christ.

Then follows: Only this death leads to perfect humility. O, beware of the mistake so many make, who would fain be humble, but are afraid to be too humble. They have so many qualifications and limitations, so many reasonings and questionings, as to what true humility is to be and to do, that they never unreservedly yield themselves to it. Beware of this. Humble yourself unto death. It is in the death to self that humility is perfected. Be sure that at the root of all real experience of more grace, of all true advance in consecration, of all actually increasing conformity to the likeness of Jesus, there must be a deadness to self that proves itself to God and men in our dispositions and habits. It is sadly possible to speak of the death-life and the Spirit-walk, while even the tenderest love cannot but see how much there is of self. The death to self has no surer deathmark than a humility which makes itself of no reputation, which empties out itself, and takes the form of a servant. It is possible to speak much and honestly of fellowship with a despised and rejected Jesus, and of bearing His cross, while the meek and lowly, the kind and gentle humility of the Lamb of God is not seen, is scarcely sought. The Lamb of God means two things—meekness and death. Let us seek to receive Him in both forms. In Him they are inseparable: they must be in us too.

What a hopeless task if we had to do the work! Nature never can overcome nature, not even with the help of grace. Self can never cast out self, even in the regenerate man. Praise God! the work has been done, and finished and perfected forever. The death of Jesus, once and forever, is our death to self. And the ascension of Jesus, His entering once and for ever into the Holiest, has given us the Holy Spirit to communicate to us in power, and make our very own, the power of the death-life. As the soul, in the pursuit and practice of humility, follows in the steps of Jesus, its consciousness of the need of something more is awakened, its desire and hope is quickened, its faith is strengthened, and it learns to look up and claim and receive that true fullness of the Spirit of Jesus, which can daily maintain His death to self and sin in its full power, and make humility the all pervading spirit of our life.

"Are you ignorant that all we who were baptized into Jesus Christ were baptized into His death? Reckon yourselves to be dead unto sin, but alive unto God in Christ Jesus. Present yourself unto God, as alive from the dead." The whole self-consciousness of the Christian is to be imbued and characterized by the spirit that animated the death of Christ. He has ever to present himself to God as one who has died in Christ, and in Christ is alive from the dead, bearing about in his body the dying of the Lord Jesus. His life ever bears the two-fold mark: its roots striking in true humility deep into the grave of Jesus, the death to sin and self; its head lifted up in resurrection power to the heaven where Jesus is.

Believer, claim in faith the death and the life of Jesus as yours. Enter in His grave into the rest from self and its work—the rest of God. With Christ, who committed His spirit into the Father's hands, humble yourself and descend each day into that perfect, helpless dependence upon God. God will raise you up and exalt you. Sink every morning in deep, deep nothingness into the grave of Jesus; every day the life of Jesus will be manifest in you. Let a willing, loving, restful, happy humility be the mark that you have indeed claimed your birthright—the baptism into the death of Christ. "By one offering He has perfected forever them that are sanctified." The souls that enter into His humiliation will find in Him the power to see and count self-dead, and, as those who have learned and received of Him, to walk with all lowliness and meekness, forbearing one another in love. The death-life is seen in a meekness and lowliness like that of Christ.

Acknowledgments

Larry Burtoft:

Because it took me twenty-six years to bring Dallas's teaching on Psalm 23 into print, there are many who have given me input, feedback, and encouragement along the way. Rather than include some and risk omitting others, I will count on the fact that you know who you are. I deeply appreciate what your support has meant. May this book be the blessing you assured me it would be.

The first step in transforming Dallas's spoken words into written form was that of transcription; warm thanks for this essential work goes to Janet Perreault. For freely offering the wisdom gleaned from her deep experience in helping others grasp the transformative power of Dallas's insights, a special word of gratitude goes also to Jan Johnson.

More than a decade ago, my pastor, Steve Brooks, with his wife, Linda, greatly encouraged and materially supported my desire to put into writing the truths of the Psalm 23 life as so richly presented in Dallas's sessions. While this is a different version than we envisioned at that time, and although Steve has since moved into the fullness of that life, my heartfelt gratitude goes out to both of them.

As I mention in the preface, the editing journey that eventuated in this book was one on which I was accompanied by Dallas's daughter, Rebecca Willard Heatley. To her name must also be added that of her husband, Bill Heatley, whose broad knowledge of the Willardian corpus helped fill out the meaning and substance of some of the off-hand comments and underdeveloped points Dallas made during the course of the original talks. This is particularly true in the discussion on work in chapter 3.

I'm deeply grateful for the vision of Steve Hanselman of LevelFive Media, and Webb Younce, Executive Editor at Nelson Books. A mere "thank you" is far from adequate; it is nonetheless sincere. For her keen editorial skills that smoothed out the rough and fuzzy spots, high kudos go to Jennifer McNeil, as they do to Janene MacIvor, Aryn VanDyke, Jessalyn Foggy, and Sara Broun for their efforts in guiding the production and marketing process.

Finally, I must mention the members of Valley Vista Christian Community who gathered to hear Dallas's messages of buoyant hope and empowering comfort, echoing Jesus' words to all who will follow him: "Fear not little flock, for it is your Father's good pleasure to give you the kingdom" (Luke 12:32).

Rebecca Willard Heatley:

The book in your hands would not exist were it not for Larry Burtoft. In 1991, while my parents were part of his church, he arranged for my father to teach this series on Psalm 23. Larry ensured that the classes would be recorded, he participated in every session, asked penetrating questions, and took extensive notes. Larry recognized the life-changing and eternal value of this material at the time the words were spoken, and never let go of his agreement with my father that it should be published.

In my very first reading of the initial draft of *Life Without Lack*, Larry drew me into that Upper Room where I could sense the love and fellowship my parents shared with their "fellow pilgrims" at Valley Vista Community Church. The text beautifully maintains my father's voice while clearly displaying his love for Jesus, his gentle ways, and his profound wisdom and humor. It has been an honor and a joy for me to partner with Larry in bringing you this teaching about the fullness of life that is available to us in the care of our Good Shepherd.

So, along with a hearty "Amen" to all those Larry has mentioned above, my family and I want to extend our heartfelt thank you and many blessings to Larry Burtoft for a job well done.

Notes

Introduction

1. See Dallas Willard, *The Divine Conspiracy: Rediscovering Our Hidden Life in God* (San Francisco: HarperSanFrancisco, 1998), 105.
2. Editor's Note: Except for passages where Dallas's comments depend upon a different translation, all Scripture quotations are taken from the New King James Version.
3. Matthew 1:22–23; see Isaiah 7:14. Editor's Note: This idea of the essential relationship between our experience of sufficiency and living in the presence of God developed into the concept of the "with-God life" that is a central emphasis in the Renovaré Movement and the *Renovaré Spiritual Formation Bible* (San Francisco: HarperSanFrancisco, 2005).

Chapter 1: God in Himself, Part 1

1. We emphasize here the importance of the mind because of its centrality in the process of restoration and renewal in Christ (Rom. 12:2). This does not, however, exclude or diminish the value of the soul or the whole person. For a more elaborate understanding about the role of the mind (thoughts and feelings) in the life of a believer, see Dallas Willard, *Renovation of the Heart* (Colorado Springs: NavPress, 2002), chapters 6 and 7.
2. C. S. Lewis, *The Four Loves* (New York: Harcourt Brace & Co., 1960), 126.
3. Adam Clarke, as quoted in John McClintock and James Strong, eds., *Cyclopaedia of Biblical, Theological, and Ecclesiastical Literature,* vol. 3, s.v. (New York: Harper & Brothers, 1894), 903, http://www.biblicalcyclopedia .com/G/god.html.
4. Adam Clarke, *Christian Theology* (London: Thomas Tegg & Son, 1835), 66.

Chapter 2: God in Himself, Part 2

1. For a further explanation of the mind-brain relationship, see Dallas Willard, "Gray Matter and the Soul" in *Renewing the Christian Mind* (New York: HarperOne, 2016), 158–160.
2. Editor's Note: This quotation is best credited to Josh Billings, "It ain't so much the things we don't know that gets us into trouble. It's the things we know that just ain't so." Ralph Keyes, *The Quote Verifier: Who Said What, Where, and When* (New York: St. Martin's Griffin, 2006), 3.

3. Editor's Note: This is Dallas's distillation of Peale's counsel found in Norman Vincent Peale, *Overcoming Anxiety and Fear* (Pawling, NY: 1966, 1994).

4. George Townsend, *The Acts and Monuments of John Foxe: a New and Complete Edition: with a Preliminary Dissertation* (London: R. B. Sweeley and W. Burnside, 1837), 693–694.

5. For an in-depth discussion of the meaning of Jesus' teachings on blessedness, see Willard, *The Divine Conspiracy*, especially chapter 4.

Chapter 3: Why There Are People on Earth

1. Editor's Note: This section includes ideas Dallas developed in his preface to Bill Heatley, *The Gift of Work: Spiritual Disciplines for the Workplace* (Colorado Springs, CO: NavPress, 2008), as well as in appendix A of that book, pages 147–148.

2. Phillips Brooks, *Best Methods for Promoting Spiritual Life* (London: Service & Paton, 1897), 12–13.

3. Ibid., 35.

4. Corrie ten Boom, *In My Father's House* (Grand Rapids: Fleming H. Revell, 1976), 167.

Chapter 4: Why Such Lack and Evil?

1. For more on the various heavens, see Willard, *The Divine Conspiracy*, 73–74, and McClintock and Strong's *Cyclopaedia of Biblical, Theological, and Ecclesiastical Literature*, vol. 4, s.v. "heaven," 122–127.

2. Editor's Note: This section includes ideas further explored by Dallas in his "The Craftiness of Christ," from Jorge Gracia, ed., *Mel Gibson's "Passion" and Philosophy: The Cross, the Questions, the Controversy* (Chicago: Open Court Publishers, 2004).

3. This phenomenon is discussed extensively in Dallas's article "Living in the Vision of God," © Church of the Savior, Washington, DC, July 2002, http://www.dwillard.org/articles/artview.asp?artID=96.

Chapter 5: Trust in God: The Key to Life

1. For a more in-depth exploration of this topic see Dallas Willard, *The Allure of Gentleness* (San Francisco: HarperOne, 2015), chapter 6, "The Problem of Pain and Evil."

Chapter 6: Trust Completed in Death to Self

1. "I Want What I Want," from the operetta *Mlle. Modiste* by Victor Herbert, lyrics by Henry Blossom (New York: M. Witmark & Sons, 1905).

2. See the discussion of the discipline of celebration in Dallas Willard, *The Spirit of the Disciplines: Understanding How God Changes Lives* (San Francisco: Harper and Row, 1988).

3. William McDonald, "I Am Coming to the Cross," in *The American Baptist Praise Book* (1871), http://www.hymntime.com/tch/htm/i/m/c /imcoming.htm.

4. While this prayer can be found in many online resources, this version is taken from *Jesus Caritas,* an archive dedicated to Foucauld, at http://www .jesuscaritas.info/jcd/fr/school-life-prayer-abandon-charles-de-foucauld.

Chapter 7: Sufficiency Completed in Love

1. Attributed to Donald Gray Barnhouse.

2. Erdmann Neumeister, "Jesus nimmt die Sünder an!" *Evangelischer Nachklang* (Hamburg, Germany, 1718). "Christ Receiveth Sinful Men," translated from the German by Emma F. Bevan, in *Songs of Eternal Life* (London, 1858), http://cyberhymnal.org/htm/c/h/chrisrec.htm.

3. Thomas Jay Oord, *Science of Love: The Wisdom of Well-Being* (West Conshohocken, PA: Templeton Foundation Press, 2004), 31.

4. Editor's Note: This section includes ideas developed by Dallas for "Getting Love Right," a paper presented at the American Association of Christian Counselors conference in Nashville, Tennessee, in 2007. It is available in a Kindle edition on Amazon, https://www.amazon.com /Getting-Love-Right-ebook/dp/B0071I65D0.

5. For additional details on the role and practice of spiritual disciplines in the disciple's life, read Richard Foster, *Celebration of Discipline*, 25th anniversary edition, written with Mike Yaconelli (San Francisco: HarperSanFrancisco, 2009), Willard, *The Spirit of the Disciplines* and Willard, *Renovation of the Heart.*

6. Editor's Note: See Dallas Willard's discussion of "Personal Soul Care" in Neil B. Wiseman, *The Pastor's Guide to Effective Ministry* (Kansas City, MO: Beacon Hill Press, 2003), and in Dallas Willard, *The Great Omission* (San Francisco: HarperSanFrancisco, 2006).

7. See for example John Hick and H. G. Wood, "On Grading Religions," *Religious Studies* 17, no. 04 (1981), 451–467.

8. James Rowe and Howard E. Smith, "Love Lifted Me," 1912.

Chapter 8: All the Days of My Life

1. Genesis 5:22; 21:14–22; 28:11–21; 39:3, 21–23; Exodus 4:1–15; 1 Samuel 18:12–16; 2 Chronicles 15:2, 15; Ezra 8:22, 31; Psalm 23, 37, 121; Matthew 28:20; John 14:16–17; Hebrews 13:5–6; Revelation 21:3.

2. Editor's Note: For further insight into the problematic aspects of seminary

education, see Dallas's article, "Spirituality Made Hard," *The Door*, May/June 1993, no. 129; 14–17, http://www.dwillard.org/articles/artview.asp?artID=175: "Seminary traumatizes people. Most ministers and leaders rarely get free from the voices that still ring in their head from that period."

3. Editor's Note: Dallas acknowledged in a talk given in 2001 that it is now statistically and anecdotally common to find that Christians generally do not differ significantly from non-Christians in our culture. But he also stated that "if you survey correctly you will find that there is a group of Christians that do differ radically from non-Christians; but that kind of commitment is, even among Christians themselves, understood to be a kind of spiritual option or luxury." The talk was later published as "Spiritual Formation in Christ is for the Whole Life and the Whole Person," in Dallas Willard, *The Great Omission*. This quote is on page 54.

4. For a fuller discussion of the Beatitudes, and the entire Sermon on the Mount, see Willard, *The Divine Conspiracy*.

5. Eerdmann Neumeister, "Christ Receiveth Sinful Men," originally published as *Evangelischer Nachlang*.

6. For a fuller treatment of what is involved in having a conversational relationship with God, see Dallas Willard, *Hearing God,* updated and expanded ed. (Downers Grove: IVP Books, 2012), especially chapter 8, "Recognizing the Voice of God."

7. Charles A. Tindley, "Nothing Between My Soul and the Savior," 1905.

8. Frank Laubach, *Letters by a Modern Mystic,* 3rd ed. (Colorado Springs: Purposeful Design Publications, 2007), 20.

9. To read the details of his experiment and its deeply transforming effects on his life, see Frank C. Laubach, *The Game with Minutes* (Eastford, CT: Martino Fine Books, 2012) and Laubach, *Letters by a Modern Mystic*. See also "Frank Laubach's *Letters by a Modern Mystic*," http://www.dwillard.org/articles/artview.asp?artID=43.

10. Charlotte Elliott, "Just As I Am, Without One Plea," 1836.

11. Walter Rauschenbusch, *Selected Writings,* Winthrop S. Hudson, ed. (San Francisco: HarperOne, 2008), xv–xvii. It is also found in Dores Robinson Sharpe, *Walter Rauschenbusch* (New York: The MacMillan Company, 1942).

Appendix B

1. This appendix is taken from Andrew Murray, *Humility*, chapter 10. Originally published in New York: Anson D. F. Randolph & Co. 1895. Currently in the public domain. Original language updated by Ted Hildebrandt. Accessed at https://faculty.gordon.edu/hu/bi/ted_hildebrandt/spiritualformation/texts/murray_humility/murray_humility.pdf on December 5, 2016.

About the Author

Dallas Willard (1935–2013) was a professor at the University of Southern California's School of Philosophy from 1965 until his retirement in 2012. His groundbreaking books *The Divine Conspiracy, The Great Omission, Knowing Christ Today, The Spirit of the Disciplines, Renovation of the Heart,* and *Hearing God* forever changed the way thousands of Christians experience their faith.